Becoming Bilingual

BILINGUAL EDUCATION AND BILINGUALISM

Series Editors
Professor Colin Baker, *University of Wales, Bangor, Wales, Great Britain*
and Professor Nancy H. Hornberger, *University of Pennsylvania, Philadelphia, USA*

Other Books in the Series
Building Bridges: Multilingual Resources for Children
  MULTILINGUAL RESOURCES FOR CHILDREN PROJECT
Curriculum Related Assessment, Cummins and Bilingual Children
  TONY CLINE and NORAH FREDERICKSON (eds)
Foundations of Bilingual Education and Bilingualism
  COLIN BAKER
Language Minority Students in the Mainstream Classroom
  ANGELA L. CARRASQUILLO and VIVIAN RODRIGUEZ
A Parents' and Teachers' Guide to Bilingualism
  COLIN BAKER
Policy and Practice in Bilingual Education
  O. GARCIA and C. BAKER (eds)
Multicultural Child Care
  P. VEDDER, E. BOUWER and T. PELS
Teaching Science to Language Minority Students
  JUDITH W. ROSENTHAL
Working with Bilingual Children
  M.K. VERMA, K.P. CORRIGAN and S. FIRTH (eds)

Other Books of Interest
The Age Factor in Second Language Acquistion
  D. SINGLETON and Z. LENGYEL (eds)
Child Language
  MICHELLE ALDRIDGE (ed.)
Language Policies in English-Dominant Countries
  MICHAEL HERRIMAN and BARBARA BURNABY (eds)
Making Multicultural Education Work
  STEPHEN MAY
Three Generations – Two Languages – One Family
  LI WEI

Please contact us for the latest book information:
Multilingual Matters Ltd, Frankfurt Lodge, Clevedon Hall,
Victoria Road, Clevedon BS21 7SJ, UK

BILINGUAL EDUCATION AND BILINGUALISM 11
Series Editors: Colin Baker and Nancy Hornberger

Becoming Bilingual

Language Acquisition
in a Bilingual Community

Jean Lyon

MULTILINGUAL MATTERS LTD
Clevedon • Philadelphia • Toronto • Adelaide • Johannesburg

LB
1139
.L3
L96
1996
mar 2004

Library of Congress Cataloging in Publication Data

Lyon, Jean
Becoming Bilingual: Language Acquisition in a Bilingual Community/Jean Lyon
Bilingual Education and Bilingualism: 11
Includes bibliographical references and index
1. Children–Language. 2. Bilingualism in children. 3. Language acquisition.
4. Education, Bilingual. I. Title. II. Series.
LB1139.L3L96   1996
401'.93–dc20   96-15893

British Library Cataloguing in Publication Data

A CIP catalogue record for this book is available from the British Library.

ISBN 1-85359-318-4 (hbk)
ISBN 1-85359-317-6 (pbk)

Multilingual Matters Ltd

UK: Frankfurt Lodge, Clevedon Hall, Victoria Road, Clevedon BS21 7SJ.
USA: 1900 Frost Road, Suite 101, Bristol, PA 19007, USA.
Canada: OISE, 712 Gordon Baker Road, Toronto, Ontario, Canada M2H 3R7.
Australia: P.O. Box 6025, 95 Gilles Street, Adelaide, SA 5000, Australia.
South Africa: PO Box 1080, Northcliffe 2115, Johannesburg, South Africa.

Typeset by Bookcraft, Stroud, Glos.
Printed and bound in Great Britain by the Cromwell Press.

Contents

Acknowledgements

As I was completing this book, I heard that Derrick Sharp had died. It was he who first suggested that I write it, and gently reminded me when a script was not forthcoming. For that I am extremely grateful to him. I am glad he knew that his encouragement had borne fruit, but sad that he will not see the book in print. I will miss his kindness and his courtesy.

The research project upon which this book rests was inspired by long arguments and discussions with Dr Nick Ellis, a psychologist and researcher of immense stature. The questions raised in these conversations shaped the Anglesey Project, and he guided me through the intricacies of measuring and making sense of interactive processes. I greatly appreciate the precision and clarity of his thinking and I have tried to emulate them. I am very much in his debt.

Then I met the children I was to study in depth. They were each so different: Becky who loved an audience; David who wanted to play outside; Emyr who knew all about lorries; Gareth who used two languages so fluently before he was three; Iwan who made a bridge from a broken table; Llywela who told wonderful stories; Nerys who was too shy to speak to me at first; Nia who didn't like donkeys; Mathew who wanted me to read to him; and Michael who created an imaginary pond full of wildlife. That part of it was fun and they and their families have my heartfelt thanks for welcoming me into their homes.

The hard work came later, and that was where I appreciated the support, tolerance and interest of my non-bilingual husband, Jim. He was my sounding board. He didn't check the spelling or review chapters for me. He just asked lots of deceptively simple questions that kept me on target throughout the research and the writing of this book.

During the research stage I received financial support from the Research Committee of Gwynedd Health Authority (before Health Authorities went out of fashion), I also received a great deal of help from many supportive colleagues, both clinical and academic. I'd like to thank them all for their advice and for their critical enouragement.

Finally, and most importantly of all, I am deeply indebted to Professor Colin Baker. He taught me how to write a book and not a research report. He gave generously of his time at all stages of the writing, making thoughtful and sensible suggestions for its improvement. He has the rare ability of combining sharp, pertinent criticism with flattering appreciation. He remained consistently supportive throughout. If I became blocked, I only had to ring Colin and his enthusiasm rekindled mine. I have been fortunate indeed in my friends and colleagues, and I am extremely grateful. Dioch am galon i bawb.

Jean Lyon
August 1995

Introduction

Background

Language is one of humanity's greatest achievements, and yet one which virtually all children achieve remarkably quickly. How much more remarkable then when children learn to use not one but two languages?

This book grew from the questions of a worried parent. Her son John, who was about 30 months old, was slow to develop language, although his general development seemed fine. Professionals usually recommend that such children obtain as much experience of playing with and talking to a peer group as possible. However, John's parents were English speaking and they lived in a mainly Welsh-speaking part of Anglesey in North Wales. Should John be sent to the local Welsh-speaking playgroup, or would it only confuse him to be confronted with a second language before his first was established?

The Speech and Language Therapist was not sure and, as a Clinical Psychologist, I was asked for an opinion. I turned to the literature but this was not very helpful. Most research described the planned bilingual language acquisition of the children of linguists. Nothing was directly relevant to John's situation, and there was little to indicate how ordinary children cope with a bilingual environment. After discussions about the variety of ways in which small children learn to communicate, the family were encouraged to send John to the Welsh-speaking playgroup. His language skills began to improve, and he could use both languages in primary school.

His predicament set in motion an investigation of the process whereby children born into a bilingual community (in this case Anglesey in North Wales) learn to use one or two languages. Although it might be predicted that children from Welsh-speaking families will speak Welsh and children from English-speaking families will speak English, there are no certainties about who will be bilingual. Parents who really want their children to acquire two languages can adopt strategies to maximise the chances that

1

their children will become bilingual, but for ordinary families, with parents speaking a mixture of Welsh and English, there is no way of telling which children will become bilingual before school entry, or what can be done to influence the outcome. After school entry, the language policy of the local Education Department becomes a strong influence on the child's language, either by encouraging bilingual development, or by default. Therefore, the aims of this book are twofold;

(1) To examine how very young children become bilingual.
(2) To discover what features in the infant's background predict early childhood bilingualism.

Questions and More Questions

Curiosity about the experience of learning to communicate in a bilingual environment and the difficulty of knowing which children would become bilingual leads to a large number of questions, such as:

- What language is a bilingual child learning?
- Is the early language acquisition sequence the same for all children, bilingual as well as monolingual?
- How do mother/child dyads differ linguistically?
- Do mothers play similar communication games?
- Do fathers have an identifiable influence?
- What are the advantages of learning two languages?
- What are the problems in learning two languages?
- What beliefs/opinions do mothers hold about the language of children?
- Is it still possible for a child in Wales to learn only Welsh before age three?
- What do bilingual children learn to do with language before age three?
- What sorts of bilingual family are there?
- What does it mean when you say a child is bilingual?

There are many further questions, and not many of them have been addressed previously. What follows is an attempt to look more closely at a few clearly articulated questions. This can be no more than a beginning, and readers with an interest in research will not lack fresh corners to explore.

The first broad questions are normative ones. The knowledge base available for language acquisition relates to monolingual children. Are there notable differences in that process for bilingual children? It seems probable that the stages of development will be similarly invariate, and that acquisition of, for instance, Brown's (1973) first 14 morphemes will be reflected in the growing language of bilingual children, but will the acquisition of these stages be slower?

This leads to the second kind of broad question, which is of a more theoretical nature. How can one account for the bilingual acquisition of language? Are the two languages processed simultaneously, in which case one might expect a slow but smooth progress through the sequence? Or are the two languages processed sequentially, possibly resulting in a more erratic pace? In either case, as more work is needed to acquire two systems, do the stages each take longer to achieve? Or can two or more languages be acquired as one, and separated only much later?

The third type of question is comparative. If children grow up in different language backgrounds, does their language development differ in ways that can be ascribed to their language background? If differences can be so ascribed, what are those differences? A wide net of investigation would be needed to find all possible differences, but perhaps there are obvious ones.

Broad questions in the last set are descriptive. These concern the ways in which individual children make use of their emerging skills with language, whether monolingual or bilingual. This set of questions is fraught with danger as the richness and variety of early communicative strategies merit study on their own. Questions here relate to the development of pragmatic understanding and of metalinguistic awareness, and to the possibility of differing dyadic styles.

Research Fields

One of the reasons for the paucity of research into bilingual language acquisition so far is that there is no single body of work that encompasses the field. Much of the work on monolingual language acquisition is directly relevant; however, understanding of the social, bilingual context is also essential if only to monitor the language input to the child. Furthermore, issues relating to bilingualism at large are often relevant to bilingual language acquisition; monolingualism is unremarkable in England, but exceptional in most of the world. It is therefore necessary to see what can be gathered from the fields of language acquisition and general bilingualism as well as childhood bilingualism.

Over the last few decades there has been a great deal of interest in children's acquisition of language and communication skills (Bullowa,

1979; Anisfeld, 1984; Slobin, 1985; Wanner & Gleitman, 1986). Particular attention has focused on the very early days, the beginning of dialogue and the development of a competent language user. By three years of age, virtually all children learn to communicate, usually through whatever language they have heard. There is good agreement on the importance of the communicative environment of the infant and on the speech addressed to her or him for the acquisition of language and communicative competence. Many setting features in the environment have been described and analysed. In the bulk of this work the assumption is that the child is being exposed to one language, and that language can therefore be a stable factor in the investigation.

In the field of bilingualism, it cannot be assumed that language is a stable factor. In a culture where more than one language is common currency, children grow up listening to more than just language variations. They need to accommodate two or more language systems, even if they eventually ignore one of them. It is not a simple matter to describe how much exposure any one child has to each language. Monolingual families using the dominant language may use no more than occasional borrowed words, whereas families who would prefer to use only the non-dominant language may be obliged to use a second (or even third) language for practical reasons, and there will be a range of differences between. It is therefore necessary to find a way of describing relevant features in the language background.

This book deals only with the language development of pre-school children, that is before they are routinely exposed to language influences in school. However, this includes children who are exposed to a range of monolingual and bilingual experiences both within the home and, as they get more independent, with peers and adults outside of the home. Some will be bilingual, and some will become bilingual and some will remain monolingual.

The most frequent reports of bilingual language acquisition come from researchers such as linguists who report on the development of two languages in their own offspring. These children are in a different situation from most children. They have parents with a special interest in language who are willing and able to foster the bilingualism of their children. However, many of the phenomena they report have been observed in the commonplace world, and their comments may well have wider application.

Plan of the Book

Chapter 1   How do children acquire language?

The first chapter looks at children's monolingual language acquisition, from the earliest attempts to communicate to the richness of language used by three-year-olds. The early attempt at communication with another person is the beginning of language, and so it is arguable that an understanding of language development is best approached through the early interactions between infant and caregiver, usually, but not necessarily, the mother. Although this is generally accepted, there is still room for dispute about the role played by the child's social environment in his or her acquisition of language. As in all research, underlying theories of language acquisition, and theories of the nature of language itself, direct investigation of the phenomena and colour interpretation of the results.

The significance of 'motherese' and the role of maternal–child dialogue are examined prior to following the child's communication skills through the one-word stage to the production of simple and then more complex utterances. This book explores the language of children up to the age of three, by which time most children are competent communicators, able to hold their own in dialogue with strangers as well as within the family. To assist description of the emerging language of the child, there follows a brief explanation of key linguistic terms and of the key terms used by psychologists. The stages often used to mark a child's language development are also described.

The next issue to be explored is the relationship between language and thinking; is language necessary for thought, or is thought a prerequisite for language? And what is happening when the child becomes aware of language? Is that a cognitive process? The argument remains unresolved. It does seem, however, that the social context of both thought and language plays an important part in the development of both. Lastly, the way children learn to use language pragmatically, the constraints a society places on language use and the effects of paternal language on the child, are all discussed.

Chapter 2   Where do you find bilingual children?

In the search for bilingual children, the second chapter gives an overview of some of the broader issues within bilingualism including national policies towards languages. If children are to acquire language bilingually, the language environment is crucial, both within the family and within the neighbourhood. Therefore, bilingual communities are described, as are the attitudes that people hold about languages. An attempt is then made to describe kinds of bilingual family, and to look at some of the case studies by linguists of their children's bilingual language acquisition (Ronjat, 1913; Leopold, 1949ab, 1954). A more recent case study (DeHouwer, 1990), illustrates many of the issues that recur throughout the literature, including different kinds of bilingual language acquisition, the bilingual child's environment and the issue of code switching. Second language learning and types of bilingual education are discussed only briefly.

Chapter 3   What is meant by childhood bilingualism?

The chapter starts with an examination of definitions of bilingualism, its measurement and the difference between language performance and language competence. This is a version of the traditional distinction between what people do and what they say they can do. Concepts commonly used in connections with childhood bilingualism are then discussed, along with the idea of multilingualism. Theories of bilingual language acquisition are at an early stage of development. Pertinent theories which explain language acquisition or development *per se*, second language learning, and bilingualism in general are explored for what they might have to contribute to such a theory. Three theories of bilingual language acquisition are then described: the Gradual Differentiation Theory, the Separate Development Theory, and finally, the Threshold Theory. This last theory became of special interest and it is suggested that it might lend itself to extension.

Concepts such as language switching, language mixing, word borrowing and language awareness have all been involved in explanations of the process of bilingual language acquisition. Unfortunately, there remains a lack of clarity about what these concepts mean. Finally, language awareness and metalingual awareness have been subsumed under the general heading of cognitive abilities, or higher mental functioning, the last section of this chapter. This links in with the seminal work of Vygotsky (1986, originally published in 1962) who suggested that cognitively, bilinguals had an advantage over monolinguals.

Chapter 4   How can child language be studied?

This chapter looks first at some of the approaches that can be made to the study of the language of young children, and in particular to case study and questionnaire approaches. The advantages and disadvantages of these approaches are discussed. It then describes the methods employed by the author and the reasons for their choice.

For the Anglesey Project, all families on Anglesey in North Wales into which a baby was born in course of a full year received a questionnaire, hereafter called QI. This asked for details of the past and present language use of both parents. On the basis of these answers couples were divided into language background groups. Once the groups were defined, representative families were chosen from each group for study in depth, using recordings of their conversations with their parents (mostly mothers) from age 15 months to 37 months. The focus was on pre-school children before they were routinely exposed to language influences outside of the home. The results were analysed quantitatively and qualitatively and the children were also assessed psychometrically and descriptively.

About three years later, a second questionnaire (hereafter called QII) was sent to those families who replied to QI, asking about current language use, and about the language development of their children. These data were used as the normative sample against which those from the small group could be compared. They were also used with data from QI to identify factors predicting language use.

Chapter 5   What language backgrounds are there?

This chapter looks at attempts to describe kinds of bilingual family in more detail. Most useful has been the work of Schmidt-Mackey (1971) and Romaine (1995) who have both described families in terms of the language strategy used by parents .

It then describes the five language backgrounds used in the Anglesey Project which were defined on the basis of a parental language use questionnaire. From the results of QI, families were defined as mostly Welsh speaking (WW), mostly English speaking (EE), having a Welsh speaking mother and non Welsh speaking father (WM), having a Welsh speaking father and a non Welsh speaking mother (WF), or having both parents with both languages in their background (MM). MM, the least cohesive group, was not used in all analyses. These are the backgrounds against which children acquire language/s. Differences and similarities between these backgrounds are then examined.

Chapter 6   What opinions do parents hold about language?

The Language Background Questionnaire (QI), (and a subsequent Language Development Questionnaire (QII)) provide the foundation for this chapter, which looks at the attitudes that parents in Wales hold about the Welsh language. In particular, it focuses on their opinions and wishes regarding the learning of Welsh by their children. The reasons for wanting (or not wanting) children to learn Welsh are analysed. In general these reasons fit the division suggested by Gardner and Lambert (1972), namely instrumental and integrative reasons.

Comparisons are made between these parental opinions (and the reasons given for them) when their children were born, and three years later when those children were about to start nursery school.

Chapter 7   A close look at the language of young children

The next two chapters focus mainly on the ten individual children, and the development of their communicative skills. Looking closely at samples of their conversation with their mothers, it is possible to explore what languages they are learning and what percentage of each language they are using. To facilitate this close examination, a dictionary of Common words has been created, words that are common to Welsh and English.

The population sample is then used for comparison. There is little evidence that parents use a one person-one language strategy to facilitate bilingual development.

Chapter 8   How do children in a bilingual community learn language?

This is an exploration of the process of language acquisition, and in particular of the mechanisms that lead to bilingualism. The main measures used are mean length of utterance (MLU) and Stages of Language Development. These are used to follow the progress of both English and Welsh in the small sample.

Although the bulk of this chapter explores the development of ten individual children, the population sample provides a good comparison group. By age three, it was possible to estimate which children are monolingual (Welsh or English) and which are becoming bilingual.

Chapter 9   How do young children use language and do they know what they are doing?

This chapter looks at the ways in which children use language, and become aware of language as a tool. Language is used to achieve a multitude of differing ends, from establishing that you are present in a situation, to making it clear through judicial silence that there is more to be said on a subject! Children learn the functions of language as they learn language, and this chapter will illustrate the ways in which they do this.

Using language is not necessarily a conscious process. However, once awareness of language is there, language can be used even more effectively for achieving one's aims. It has been suggested that such awareness is closely associated with the development of bilingualism. The children who notice that there are two equivalent words for the same thing notice something about language itself as well as about their own bilingual environment. It is not simple to decide when children first become aware of language without contaminating the evidence, but this chapter presents examples which indicate that children below the age of three years *can* become aware of language itself. It then explores the relationship between bilingualism and language awareness.

Chapter 10   Which parent has more influence on the language of the home?

Using data from the first questionnaire, this chapter explores the differences between parents in the manner in which they use two languages in the home. Firstly this is examined in general terms, and then in the more specific one-to-one situation. Differences in language use when talking to one another are particularly evident in cross-language partnerships.

After a discussion of parental roles and the influence of cross-language marriages, gender differences remain important. Although the language itself has some influence on language choice here, gender plays a powerful role.

Chapter 11   What predicts a child's language?

The chapter starts with a reprise of how bilingual and monolingual children were identified at age three. Then, using data provided by parents when their children were born, the chapter goes on to look for factors which are associated with the language/s these children were using when they were three years old.

It was thought that the family background itself would be the best predictor, and this and a number of other possibilities are explored. However, in a series of multiple regression analyses, it is shown that maternal language when the child is born is the best predictor of a child's language at age three.

Chapter 12   How do young children become bilingual?

Major issues remain regarding the methodology adopted when studying bilingual language acquisition. Perhaps the most important are which
children you choose to study, and how you define bilingualism. Theories
and theoretical issues are also revisited, in particular the question of the
phenomenon of 'language mixing'. Common language does seem to be a
helpful way of making sense of the evidence, although the concept still
needs clarifying.

A third theory, the sequential model of bilingual language acquisition,
is suggested; namely that children learn first one language to a certain stage
and then the next to that stage, in a stepwise fashion. The relationship
between this theory and an extended version of the Threshold Model is
explored. Finally, this chapter attempts to draw together the evidence and
to reach some conclusions about the present state of research in this area.

Although the research reported here is rooted in the bilingual situation
in North Wales, the questions it asks and the answers it suggests have a
wider application. Many small countries are facing similar pressures on
their language from a more international language. Many families are
facing similar choices about their children's language development. There
are still many gaps in our understanding of the bilingual development of
children at around school entry. However, it is hoped that some of the
general conclusions and suggestions outlined here might have been of
practical assistance to John and his family.

1 How do Children Acquire Language?

Introduction

Theories

This chapter begins by broadly describing when children learn language, and continues with a discussion of theories of language acquisition. People have speculated about the origins of language since biblical times, but this discussion will begin with the ideas of this century, starting with those of Piaget, Vygotsky, Skinner, Chomsky and Bruner.

Communication

These thinkers have been influential and lead to an examination of early language users and their carers. Adult–child dyads begin to communicate before language can be said to exist in the infant. These interactions, usually between mother and child, teach sharing before infants have words to exchange, and turn-taking before they have questions to ask. The language used with small children differs from its adult form. This language code, called 'motherese' or 'babytalk', has been observed widely, but its significance is disputed.

The development of words will follow. Many interpretations have been made of the meaning of these first single words, including the suggestion that they can stand for a sentence. Eventually children learn to join words together, and to take part in conversations not just with parents but with many different people.

Descriptions

The chapter then provides an outline of how language is described by linguists and by psychologists. Commonly occurring linguistic terms are

11

explained, although to provide definitive descriptions would go beyond the scope of the present work. The stages of language acquisition outlined by Brown (1973) and Crystal (1976) are then described. Brown recorded the language progress of three small children, and in order to make sense of his data he counted the average length of the children's comments. This concept he called the mean length of utterance (MLU), and he used MLU and analysis of language function to define stages (Brown, 1973). Others have described pragmatic and semantic scales, and the functions of early dialogue.

Cognition

In any examination of the communication and language development mention of cognition is unavoidable. Thus, theories of cognitive development and the relationship between language and cognition follow.

Society

Finally, the wider context of language acquisition is highlighted. Cultural differences are examined, there is a brief description of pragmatics or language use in context, and differences are examined in how parents use language with young children. Children need to learn to use language in context if they are to become competent language users.

Theories of Language Development

Learning to talk

Children can only make sounds when they are born, and yet by the time they are about a year old they can usually produce a small number of intelligible single words. By about two years old they can put two words together to make a range of simple utterances. By age three years they can hold conversations, changing the form of words to suit the context, asking questions, referring to the past, and stringing together a comprehensible narrative. A three-year-old child is a competent language user and the years that follow see a broadening and a refinement of that basic skill. The complexity of this commonplace achievement is rarely considered unless something goes wrong, but it is an extraordinary achievement none the less, and one that has caught the imagination of psychologists, linguists and educationalists alike, especially in the last 30 years.

Theories

Researchers from these disciplines have added a wealth of detail to the rudimentary description above, but have done so from their own standpoint. Linguistic accounts have been able to elucidate the growth of phonology, morphology and syntax, (e.g. Leopold, 1949ab; Crystal, 1976; Menn, 1982; Bowerman, 1985). Educationalists have looked back to early childhood and developed assessment techniques to identify the difficulties experienced by some nursery and school children (e.g. Crystal *et al*, 1976). They have clarified many of the features in the home and school environment that encourage language (Stubbs, 1981; Wells, 1981). Finally, psychologists have tried to understand and explain the development of language, partly for its own sake, but partly as a way of understanding cognition, cognitive processes and social relationships.

Piaget (1952, 1959) explored the development of children's language primarily for the insights it could give into how children learn to think. For him, language was a reflection of thought and not a shaper of thoughts. He saw children as learning by interacting with the world and using classification (and language) to understand their experience (Piaget, 1926). Research with deaf children had indicated that the social transmission of spoken language was not essential for classification (and thus for cognition). His investigations of children's early verbalisations led him to believe that, 'Although language is an important factor in building logical structures, it is not the essential factor, even for children with normal hearing.' (Inhelder & Piaget, 1964:4). Language is a series of assimilations which accelerates the process of cognitive development.

Piaget's (1936) theory of stages of development has also been important in the field of language acquisition, and particularly in relation to Brown (1973), whose work is central to the present investigation. Piaget postulated the existence of stages of intellectual development, rather than a steady developmental progression, with children as active participants in their own development. They act, assimilate their actions and the effects of their actions within the framework of their current world view, their current 'theory' of how things work. When new experience can no longer be accommodated within that theory, they extend and adapt the theory to fit their increased understanding. They move on to the next stage.

A number of key features identify Piagetian stages. Firstly, stages of development are universal and invariate. Secondly, each stage is necessarily assimilated before the next is attained, and therefore stage achievement is not automatic. Thirdly, stages are not age governed, although they are age related. Finally, only one stage ahead of the child's present stage is in part comprehensible, and as such it is attractive to the child, providing the spur to further development.

Piaget (1936) saw his stage theory as having wider application than to intellectual development alone, and other stages theories have been developed following his seminal work. Examples include Kohlberg's (1976) theory of moral development and Selman's (1980) theory of the development of social perspective-taking. Brown (1973) uses a stage model of language development which has some of the features of Piagetian stageness (such as their age relatedness rather than age governedness), but does not follow his ideas of accommodation and assimilation so closely.

Vygotsky (1962) is usually contrasted with Piaget, the one from a socialist the other from a capitalist country, and it is widely suggested that the ideological debate can be traced through their work (e.g. Elliot, 1981). Whereas Piaget saw the child as an egocentric explorer, Vygotsky (1962) saw children as social explorers. For him language makes thought possible. To begin with, the child learns names, then how to name, and finally speech turns inwards. It should be noted that both Vygotsky and Piaget saw speech and thought as developing separately, but as becoming intimately related as the child progresses. Vygotsky emphasised the importance of the environment, the socialising context, and Piaget emphasised the natural egocentrism of the child.

With the advent of powerful behavioural techniques for examining human learning, it was initially assumed that acquiring language could be explained by conditioning theories. Early language was seen as a learned process, with children improving their grasp of language through imitation, encouraged by parental praise and rewarded by the results they achieved. Skinner (1959) maintained that even complex language learning could be explained within the stimulus–response paradigm. His book, *Verbal Behavior*, provoked a strongly critical review from Chomsky (1959), who subsequently developed his own theory, of 'Generative Transformational Grammar', to explain how language is acquired (1965, 1968). He suggested that children had an innate Language Acquisition Device (LAD), which pre-programmed them to acquire language. They did not learn sentences by rote but, after exposure to language, could create new sentences as they needed them. 'In short, the language is 'reinvented every time it is learned' (Chomsky, 1968:75).

Chomsky's ideas were almost entirely theoretical. He was not interested in the details of children's language, but in describing the syntactic structure that underpinned all language. He called this a 'Generative Grammar', and suggested that the surface form of language is built upon deep structures which native speakers know but never need to learn. Thus, you may never have read, for example, the sentence 'multi-coloured apples hummed silently falling behind the toe house', but not only can you make some sense of it, but you can probably make up the next sentence and continue it as a story to a child. The sentence, though unusual, has a surface structure which conforms to rules of grammar at a deep structure level, unlike, for instance 'apples the falling silently house hummed'.

Chomsky made no attempt to explain how children went about using their LAD, or how, given the rich and inaccurate plethora of language they were exposed to, they managed to sort out where to begin. Bruner (1978ab) addressed the question to some extent when he highlighted the role of dialogue in language acquisition. He described three possible models: an Input Model, much like Skinner's (1959) idea of the environment shaping the child's language; an Output Model, with the child actively generating language; and a Transactional Model, wherein the child and the social environment interact. The emergence of language he described as an interactive process, recognising the vital role played by social factors in enabling children to make use of their latent abilities. Partners (and usually parents) are essential for the normal emergence of language in a child. They highlight salient features of the world, encourage and model language, and create play routines. Later Bruner called this a Language Acquisition Support System (LASS), a language framework involving familiar, routine transactional formats. Included in this framework are feedback which makes communicative intentions plain, and play 'events' which can be recreated by language and enable the generalisation of linguistic and psychological processes (Bruner, 1983). This model has been described by other workers (such as Halliday, 1975; Bever, 1982) and it is that adopted throughout this book.

Communication

Pre-verbal communication

Long before there is language there is communication. Babies respond to sound and touch from a few days old. They start to imitate and learn to smile within a few weeks of birth and look at faces in preference to anything else (Fantz, 1961; Kaye, 1977; Higgins, 1988). This is no one-sided relationship. Caregivers spend a lot of their time talking to babies, looking at them and touching them. It was Trevarthen's pioneering work in the 1970s which showed that babies can do more than had been imagined. By videotaping mothers and babies in parallel when at play, he was able to show that babies from as young as three weeks old can respond to their mothers in a reliable fashion. From six weeks old, a baby can respond to the facial expression of the mother, who in turn has generated her expression from that of her baby (Trevarthen, 1979). Later he and Murray were able to show how important the baby was in this partnership by manipulating the videoed feedback to the mother (Murray & Trevarthen, 1986).

The features of this early exchange have been studied extensively in recent years (for example, Snow, 1977ab; Schaffer, 1977; Bullowa, 1979). Bateson (1979) lists features of this interaction as alternating, overlapping vocalisations, of regular pattern, with pauses, and involving sustained attention and mutual gaze. One of the basic characteristics of interactional behaviour, according to Condon (1979), is synchrony in speech and body movements. He has shown that babies and mothers mirror one another's head, hand and arm movements and vocalisations. It is important for both partners to get this rhythm right from early on. Many researchers have linked this to an innate mechanism, namely sucking. This synchronised interpersonal exchange sets the pattern for later interactive games (Kaye, 1977).

Newson (1974, 1977) also describes this relationship in terms of shared context, shared history and shared game-like rituals. Each is continually aware of the other and, as with all rituals, each knows what to expect of the other. The baby thus learns one of the basic features of dialogue, turn-taking, within the first few months of life. As Schaffer has stated 'mother and infant come to share a code of conduct long before they share a linguistic code' (Schaffer, 1977:15). The importance of this can best be seen on the rare occasions when it does not occur. Autistic children do not recognise the mother's bid for a response, and even when they do attend to faces, they do not imitate expressions (Christie & Wimpory 1986).

External factors can interfere with the development of this smooth, rich interaction. An impoverished environment can limit the social intercourse available to a baby; there may be no mother figure consistently to hand (see Clarke & Clarke, 1976). Alternatively, the baby may have difficulty responding to/initiating interactions. Deaf children have been found to develop language in stages similar to hearing children, but more slowly (Mogford & Gregory, 1980) and Down's Syndrome children, who also go through a similar but slower developmental process, tend to have problems with articulation (Mittler, 1974). Many children with a mental handicap have difficulty acquiring language, and research has highlighted a number of ways in which this can be facilitated. Of most interest to the present discussion is evidence that adults try too hard with these children, and so spoil the natural dialogue (McConkey & O'Connor, 1981).

Dialogue

It is difficult to decide what constitutes the social/behavioural interaction between mother and infant and what constitutes the beginnings of dialogue. Is the early rhythm of sucking, pausing, jiggling, smiling and sucking the social context of language or the earliest dialogue? Are later cooing games that mothers and babies play the beginning of communication, or of socialisation? To some extent the answer to this lies in the theoretical stance of the writer. As the two aspects are not easily separable, this chapter will only look at those aspects of early interaction which seem to echo the way that later dialogue works – what Brown has called 'the management of shared attention' (Brown, 1973).

Snow (1977a) describes early conversation as the result of the mother's intuitive belief that babies are capable of reciprocating. They talk to babies and take the response they get as a speech turn, whether it is a movement, an expression or a vocalisation. Maternal speech changes in response to the infant's growing ability to respond, rather than in response to their comprehension. Most of these changes begin to occur at about seven months.

On the other hand, Trevarthen (1979), rejected the idea that it is the mother who fabricates the structure of dialogue. He talks of the growth of a mutual understanding in two to three month old babies. This he calls 'primary intersubjectivity' wherein there is innovation of meaning by the infant and by the mother. He suggests that the baby 'invites her to share a dance of expressions and excitements. The infant needs a partner but knows the principle of the dance well enough, and is not just a puppet to be animated by a miming mother who "pretends" her baby knows better', (Trevarthen, 1979:347).

Bruner (1977, 1978b) believes that children learn about communication before they learn about language, and that this enables them to learn about language: 'Mother and child develop a variety of procedures for operating jointly and in support of each other.' (Bruner, 1977:274). It seems clear that mother–child communication is a joint enterprise, with both partners having an essential contribution to make.

Newson (1977, 1979) and the Nottingham group make a clear distinction between studying infant behaviour and studying the emergence of cognitive and linguistic understanding in children. They lay greater emphasis on the mother's role, and view this early dialogue as:

an attempt by the mother to enter into a meaningful set of exchanges with her infant, despite the fact that she herself will often be aware that the semantic element in any resulting communication lies more in her own imagination than in the mental experience of her baby. (Newson, 1977:47).

However, they too emphasise the interactive nature of this process, seeing both partners as able to generate activity directed towards the other. They describe this as a chain of communication gestures, where most links serve a dual function; they answer the preceding signal and they invite the next signal. Clearly, the two partners are operating at differing levels of competence, but the mother's role decreases as the baby develops. Primarily, they see mothers as providing an elaborate framework for keeping the dialogue going.

Motherese

In the work described above, the primary caretaker, usually the mother, is universally recognised as playing an important role. However, researchers have been divided into those who thought her role was facilitative, that she provided the LASS (Language Acquisition Support System) (Bruner, 1977, 1978b) for her child, and those who thought her role was essential, the necessary model and teacher for the young language learner. This last is clearly a more behavioural position.

Motherese is the description given to the special way in which most caregivers talk to babies. Such speech is clearly enunciated, frequently repeated and refers to concrete objects in the immediate environment (e.g. Snow, 1977ab). It tends to clarify and simplify meaning, and is more expressive than in normal adult speech. There is general agreement that motherese – or babytalk (BT) as it is sometimes termed – is a valuable concept. What is disputed is the influence that motherese has on the child's acquisition of language. Furrow and colleagues, (Furrow et al., 1979), suggested that in some ways motherese is responsible for the acquisition of language. They describe it as a teaching language, using language in a context that makes it highly interpretable. Others have studied the characteristics of motherese, but found that 'many properties of motherese have no effect on language growth at all' (Newport et al., 1977:136). They suggest that children learn language almost despite motherese. According to Gleitman and colleagues, the range of adult speech heard is too limited to account for the language children actually use (Gleitman et al., 1984).

As with many disputes, the extreme positions are no longer held. Furrow and Nelson (1986), showed that although mothers structure situations to encourage learning, and rephrase to facilitate understanding, 'the child brings certain ... biases ... to the learning process,' (1986:176). Gleitman and colleagues (1984), have acknowledged that the effects of maternal characteristics vary with the language stage of younger children. Neither innate abilities nor environmental influences alone can account for the acquisition of language.

The first words and beyond

Children spend a long time at the single-word stage. At one time it was suggested that these single words stood for complete utterances, holophrases, as the memory or the physiology of the child was too immature to make full expression possible, (Menyuk, 1969, for example). The variations in stress, intonation, and gesturing which accompanies much early word use, were cited as evidence for this position.

Bloom (1973) was opposed to this notion, seeing single-word usage as a simple, single phenomenon. She felt that most investigators had credited children with more knowledge about syntax than could legitimately be imputed; children were naming. However Dore (1974, 1979), felt that there was more to single words than merely labelling. He suggested that the single word represents an intention and involves a relation to a concept or participant or other aspect of the conversation. He gives the example of a child pointing to an empty space and saying 'pot' to a nurse who replies 'Yes, I'm gonna bring the pot out', (Dore, 1979:349). Asking about an absent coffee pot does not seem like a single simple phenomenon. A wider understanding than simple naming is needed.

This was Kamhi's (1986) position. He published an account of the development of single words by his daughter in which he argues strongly for the necessity of understanding. Once his daughter seemed to understand the meaning of a childish naming game she had played rather passively with him, she took the lead and pestered her parents for the names of things. Naming insight is the important factor in the development of referential speech.

A model for the development of word use was suggested by Barrett (1985, 1987). Initially words are extremely context or event bound. He gives the example of his son, Adam, who said 'duck' only when knocking the toy duck off the side of the bath, not even when playing with the toy ducks elsewhere or differently. He suggests that to call this naming is to overinterpret what is happening. The child is engaged in a ritualised response in a particular context. Later the use of the word becomes decontextualised. Adam began to name his ducks when not knocking them off the side of the bath. It is postulated that at this stage, words are mental representations or prototypes. Next the principal features of the prototype are identified. Adam began to use 'duck' to refer to real ducks, and pictures of ducks and duck-like birds. Lastly the word is assigned to a semantic field, (Adam knew that a duck went with a swan and geese) and contrastive features are identified (Adam stopped using the word 'duck' to name swans). Adam's understanding of the concept had increased, and by this time, he was putting two words together (Barrett, 1985).

Bloom's (1973) position was similar. She suggested that children can only put words together when they have a prior concept, some understanding of what they say. Thus cognition is a prerequisite for sentences. The growth of language and the growth of cognition are intimately related, and their relationship warrants consideration in its own right.

Describing Language

Linguistic terms

The terminology of linguists is often precise, but quite difficult to follow in its pursuit of nice and accurate descriptions of parts of language. This section includes simple straightforward definitions for some areas of enquiry within linguistics which facilitate discussion of the communication process.

Syntax deals with the rules by which words combine to form sentences (loosely referred to as 'grammar').

Phonology describes the sounds of a given language, and their function, (phonetics refers to how a word is pronounced).

Morphology deals with the internal structure of words (a morpheme is the smallest unit of meaning).

Semantics is the study of the meaning or content of words and of the units they comprise.

The above definitions are adapted from John Lyons' standard work, *Introduction to Theoretical Linguistics* (1968) (with some parenthetical additions).

Surprisingly, the following are not included (except that prosody is defined as an aspect of phonology). All of these words, while retaining traditional meanings, have been used in a new way of late. Consequently, the definitions given are somewhat hesitant.

Pragmatics: the study of language use in context; what can be said in what situation; the features of an event which predict the type of communicative transaction.

Prosody: the study of the melody of spoken language. More than just intonation, it includes the alteration in meaning that can be understood from differing pronunciations and emphasis.

Discourse analysis: analysis of the set of shared assumptions that underlie a communication and the features which indicate the relationship between the speakers.

Psychologists

Over the past two decades interest has shifted from the syntactic, phonological and morphological aspects of language acquisition to semantics, pragmatics and, more recently, to discourse analysis. Some of this interest has been sparked by the artificial intelligence field. Computers can be taught to simulate syntactically accurate speech (which is rule bound), but that highlights the subtler features of language which they cannot copy. This has alerted people to the multi-level nature of even the simplest discourse between human speakers who, for instance, know what shared knowledge can be taken for granted in any conversation.

This leads into the field of pragmatics, the use of language in context. For psychologists especially, the fascination is with the social context of communication. People know what can be said to whom and how. They adopt roles and styles of speech appropriate to the circumstances (code-switching) and much comedy is based on the breaking of these unwritten rules. Children learn this language use early. At as young as 24 months old they have been recorded varying the intonation of their voices when talking to a puppet or a doll (Andersen, 1990). Words and speech (or silence and omissions) can be used to achieve a whole variety of ends and to communicate a vast range of messages, frequently apart from their surface meanings (Halliday, 1975).

Mean length of utterance

At its simplest, mean length of utterance (MLU) entails counting the words in each utterance (sometimes in each sentence) across a piece of conversational text and calculating the mean for each partner. For example:

Mother: Hello Peter./
Did you have a good day at school today?/

Peter: Alright/

Mother: Did you have a nice lunch?/
                   Did you eat it all up like a good boy?/
Peter: Yea/
                   Mother's MLU = 27 words/4 utterances = 6.75
                   Peter's MLU = 2 words/2 utterances = 1.00

Clearly the mother is working very hard to get a response but Peter is barely responding.

Mean length of utterance (MLU) first became a widely accepted measure of children's language following Brown (1973) when he used morphemes to calculate the length of utterances in young English-speaking children. Some of his rules are straightforward; they require calculations to start on the second page of transcriptions, fillers (oh, ah, etc.) and unintelligible words to be ignored, and compound words such as birthday and quack-quack to count as only one. But his system also requires knowledge of morphology:

> Count as separate morphemes all inflections, for example possessive (s), plural (s), third person singular (s), regular past (d), progressive (ing). (Brown, 1973:54).

These could have been applied to the children acquiring English, but *ad hoc* judgements would have been necessary about what constitutes a morpheme in Welsh as no standard system is agreed. Even more crucially the core question remains about what counts as Welsh or as English.

Hickey (1991:566) discusses the advantages and disadvantages of MLU (morphemes) and MLU (words) at some length and uses both measures in her study of the language development of two-year-old Irish children. She concludes that the two versions of MLU are equally effective, provided they are used with caution, 'as an initial ordering of the data, which precedes a more complex analysis'. (p566, 1991). Crystal (1976) is amongst other researchers who have found the MLU (words) a useful measure when used in this way. Consequently, the older version of MLU was used, that which takes the word as the countable unit. Brown's other rules were applied; fillers were stripped from the script and compound words treated as single words. However, as recording and subsequent transcription did not start until the child was settled, all that which was transcribed was used, in its edited form, to calculate MLU.

For most purposes a sentence is an 'utterance', but the two are not synonymous. To utter is to give vocal expression and an utterance is the act of vocal expression. Thus a sentence or a word can be an utterance, but an utterance is not necessarily a sentence (or even a word). Although a robust measure, it is difficult to define precisely, but natural pauses in conversation, change of speaker, questions and exclamations all mark the end of an utterance. There is a danger in equating sentence and utterance too closely for two reasons. A sentence is a literary imposition on natural language, entailing rules such as the need for a verb. Much natural speech is supplemented with gesture and gaze and needs no such rules. Secondly, as Bloom (1973) has shown, to dignify a child's one-word utterance with the title 'sentence' is to imply that the child already knows a linguistic code for talking about relationships in the world. At the one-word stage they do show evidence of understanding quite a lot about relations between things. The key question is whether they have developed a code for expressing these – and that is not proven.

Roger Brown (1973) was one of the first to define clearly the most commonly used measure of the complexity of children's speech, the mean length of utterance (MLU). He transcribed many hours of children's speech and so was able not only to refine this measure on the basis of close examination of the speech of three children, but later to validate it using the language development of other children.

Using the second page of a transcription of a child's speech, he counted the number of utterances in a speech sample and then computed the mean number of morphemes per utterance. A *morpheme* is a unit of meaning, similar to but not conterminous with a word. An *utterance* is a speech event, similar to but not the same as a sentence, and usually marked by a pause in the conversation or a change of speaker.

This has served well as a simple way of making data from different children comparable and comprehensible. Brown (1973), realised, as had others before him, that to match children chronologically led to problems, whereas matching for MLU was comparing the same level of construc- tional complexity. He then separated the continuum of MLUs into stages of development, which were not stages in a Piagetian sense, but forced onto stages by the data. He commented:

> I decided to divide the total shared developmental stretch at five points as nearly as possible equidistant from one another in terms both of MLU and upper bound (UB) and draw 713 consecutive complete utterances from each child at each point for detailed linguistic analysis. The odd number, 713, was the accidental consequence of the size of the transcriptions from which the first samples were drawn. (Brown, 1973:56).

Thus, in Stage I the MLU is 1.75 with an upper bound of five words and Stage V is 4.00 with an UB of 13 words.

Brown (1973), found that when describing the process of language acquisition there was great commonality across children and a remarkably invariant order of acquisition. He was able to list the first 14 morphemes acquired, starting with the present progressive (e.g. *going*) through past irregulars (*gone*) and third person regulars (*he eats*) to contractible auxiliaries (*won't*). These processes go on beyond Stage V, but the order of development is primarily determined by the relative semantic and grammatical complexity of constructions. Despite the universality of early words, in terms of their sounds and soundability, Brown had some reservations about using his scheme with foreign languages. However, he did conclude that the developmental order of 14 morphemes is amazingly constant, that developmental rate varies widely, and that chronological age is a poor indicator, compared with MLU.

MLU was used on maternal speech in the motherese debate. Snow (1977b) used MLU to show that in early conversations with babies of three months to 18 months, the speech of mothers remained simple throughout that period. Furrow and colleagues (Furrow *et al.*, 1979; Furrow & Nelson, 1986) demonstrated that maternal MLU is correlated positively with the child's language growth, although Gleitman *et al.* (1984) suggested that this relationship only holds for the beginning of children's language development. This measure, MLU and the stages that are defined by it, has been used widely ever since publication of his work in 1973.

Stages

Brown went on to define and name a set of stages of language development which have also been adopted widely. Stage I is 'Semantic Roles and Syntactic Relations', a stage which he later described as 'made up of content words and (which) does lack functors'(1973:403). The MLU of this stage he defined as 1.75, that is, beyond the one word sentence, usually containing two morphemes. Stage II is called 'Modulation of Meaning' and requires two meaningful elements within an utterance, and an MLU of 2.25. Stage III is 'Modalities of the Simple Sentence' which refers to the use of negation, interrogation, and imperatives, etc. This stage has an MLU of 2.75. Stage IV has an MLU of 3.50 and involves embedding sentences in one another (e.g. I gonna get the book upstairs/). The final stage, Stage V, Brown calls 'Coordination of Simple Sentences and Propositional Relations'. It has an MLU of 4.00, but he states that at this level, the MLU is a less reliable measure of the stage of development than is the complexity of the language. Finally, he mentions that the grammatical tag question (*can't he?/*) does not occur until after Stage V.

The stages described independently by Crystal and his colleagues are those through which children progress as they learn to use the *grammar* of their language (Crystal, 1976; Crystal *et al.*, 1976).

He defines Stage I as the 'single-element stage' when the child's utterance comprises a single word such as *mama/ allgone/ ta-ta/ doggie/*. Although the child is clearly communicating, it is not possible to make grammatical claims at this stage. The child could be naming, commenting, requesting and so on.

At Stage II the child is putting two words together, but that still doesn't make meaning precise. *Allgone doggie/* while connecting the two concepts, could mean that the dog has gone, or that the child is telling the dog something else has gone.

By Stage III there are three elements in the child's utterance, though not necessarily the traditional subject-verb-object. Sentences like *mummy gone drink/ green car crash/* indicate a growing precision.

By Stage IV, when four or more elements are present, children can make themselves understood, although grammatical mistakes will continue to occur. At this stage a child might say *Sion felled on my bike/ do a proper picture mummy/ me want the 'nother box/*.

Stage V is typified by the use of clauses (*I said Mr Fixit wants the tractor/ she goes to bed and she does get up now and she has her breakfast/*).

Stage VI sees the consolidation of grammatical systems such as pronouns, auxiliary verbs and passives. Children can use sentences such as *you shouldn't do that mummy/ no the coffee was melted by the boy/*.

Crystal suggests that further stages can be identified, and that the acquisition of grammar continues to develop until adolescence. He (Crystal, 1976) says that for the normal population, Stage I occurs before age 18 months, Stage II between 18 and 24 months, Stage III between age 24 and 30 months and Stage IV is achieved by three years of age. Stage V develops around 42 months and Stage VI in the following year.

There is a good deal of agreement between these two schemes. The major difference concerns the earliest stages. Brown suggests that many two-word utterances (Stage II in Crystal's scheme), are still only at Stage I. However, the more generous criterion was adopted for this study; if a child was able to use two-word sentences, they were credited with reaching Stage II. MLU was used as a measure of developing language, not as a prerequisite for stage achievement. Table 1.1 lists the names and features of the two stage models for comparison.

Table 1.1 Stages in language development: Brown and Crystal compared

	Brown			Crystal	
MLU	Features	Stage	Features	Age (months)	
1.75	Semantic roles; syntactic relations (2 morphemes; content words; no functors)	I	Single element	by 18	
2.25	Grammatical morphemes; modulation of meaning (some plurals; differing intonations; early use of 'a', 'the' and 'in', etc.)	II	2 words together	18–24	
2.75	Modalities of the simple sentence (modulations such as negation, interrogation, imperatives)	III	3 or more element utterance; use of 'a' and 'the'	24–30	
3.50	Embedding one simple sentence in another (early embedding)	IV	4 or more elements; simple sentences; 'errors'	by 36	
4.00	Co-ordination of sentences; propositional relations (use of 'and' and 'but')	V	Clauses; embedding; use of 'and' and 'but'	about 42	
Later	Tag questions, etc.	VI	Pronouns, auxiliary verbs, etc.	about 48 onwards	

Brown's (1973) stages differ from traditional Piagetian stages, but are derived from them. He describes his stages as independent of the age of the child, and the features of each stage form a common, relatively invariate, developmental progression. However, whereas Piaget's stages required an act of adaptation or reevaluation before the next stage could be achieved, Brown's stages are markers in a continuing process. In describing his own stages, Brown says they are 'not known to be true stages in Piaget's sense; that is they may not be qualitative changes of organisation forced on the investigator by the data themselves.' (Brown, 1973:58). Rather they are intervals dividing MLU distribution. Furthermore, although he names his stages according to major new developments or elaborations of processes that occur in each stage, 'the whole development of any one of the major constructional processes is not contained within a given stage interval.' (Brown, 1973:59). Brown's stages are convenient descriptions of sections of a continuous, complex process.

Crystal (1976) did not use MLU to define his stage model. Instead, moving further away from Piaget, he suggests an approximate age level for each stage. Thus, by about 18 months when children are using single words they are at Stage I, between 24 and 30 months when they are using three-element utterances, they are at Stage III, and by four years old when they are using clauses, pronouns and different tenses, they are at Stage VI.

Crystal (1976) is critical of Piaget's stage theory, arguing that 'So far ... there have been few experimental studies of the way in which linguistic features can be shown to relate to these stages and as yet, the detailed relevance of Piaget's principles remains uncertain.' (1976:37). Instead of postulated internal processes, his stages are based on observed evidence of grammatical forms in the child's language.

For both Brown (1973) and Crystal (1976), stage development is a continuous process, whereas for Piaget stages are discrete. Piaget (1936) suggested that children develop internal cognitive structures which enable them to move from stage to stage. Brown (1973) describes apparently coherent sections of language development and leaves open the possibility of corresponding cognitive substrata. Crystal (1976) confines himself to description of observable behaviour alone. Putting aside speculation about underlying cognitive structures, the stage models outlined by Brown and Crystal provide a framework within which observable phenomena can be organised.

Cognition

Language and thought

It is commonly assumed that children learn about the world before they learn to use language. 'A child starts to learn his mother-culture even before he starts to learn his mother-tongue.' (Bullowa, 1979:9). What is not agreed is the extent to which this learning is the beginning of communication and hence of language, and to what extent this learning is the beginning of cognition and hence of thinking. The relationship between language and thinking has long been in dispute. Do cognitive and communicative abilities develop independently and if not, is the one a necessary precursor of the other? Can children think without language, and can they use language without some cognitive structuring of reality?

Thought first?

Piaget (1926) describes the growth of language as the extension of sensory-motor schemata onto speech patterns. Early sentences express a construction of reality which has been gained from active interaction with the world. The child thus represents those bits of the world that are most available, such as actions, schemata involving actors, locations, etc. Not everyone agrees. Sugerman-Bell (1978) believes that sensory-motor abilities are not sufficient for the onset of verbal communication. From her study of infants in home and institutional settings, she found no differences between the groups in their ability to perform simple motor tasks at the pre-verbal stage. Despite this early communication patterns were found in home but not institutional settings. She also found that institutionalised children had more difficulties with language acquisition.

Harris (1992), examined in detail the evidence for cognitive prerequisites for language. Looking first for analogies and correlations between sensory-motor intelligence and language development, he found none. Even Slobin's (1982) suggestion that cognitive development had a pace-setting function was not clearly supported. He turned next to aspects of language comprehension which have been linked with cognitive development and found that, on the whole, comprehension preceded expression. There is some evidence from Donaldson (1978) that expression can precede comprehension. Harris's point was that the one is not the necessary precursor of the other. Finally, he looked at language acquisition in bilinguals, (Harris, 1992). Following the suggestion that cognitive development dictates the order of acquisition of language, one would expect the order to be different for second-language acquisition. By and large this is not so, and language acquisition proceeds along the same sequence for both languages. He concluded that there was little evidence for cognitive prerequisites.

Language first?

Vygotsky (1962) in contrast, thought that cognitive abilities begin as social exchanges (such as language) which are internalised. 'Thought development is determined by language ie by the linguistic tools of thought and by the sociocultural experience of the child.' (Vygotsky, 1962:94). For him the starting point from which to understand development is social activity such as the 'sign system' (speech) which is used as a psychological tool to master higher mental processes. However, Hood et al. (1982) argue that he did not contrast learning and learning language, but saw both of these activities as part of the process of becoming a social, historical being.

The Sapir-Whorf hypothesis suggests that language constrains thought. The structures that exist within any particular language direct the thought processes of its speakers. Most quoted is the example of the Eskimos who have dozens of words for snow, the most significant feature of their environment (see Slobin, 1974 for details of this concept, expounded in detail in the 1950s). This is the strongest version of linguistic determinism, and few would subscribe to it now. However, there are some who suggest that language influences how we come to think.

Social context?

Macnamara (1982) proposed that children acquire language just because they already have lots of other skills, both social (such as the capacity for making sense of situations involving human interaction) and cognitive (such as a grasp of meaning, primitive hypothesis testing and inference). He recognised that long before language emerges, children are making sense of the world and making sense in the world. As Halliday had said 'By the time a child produces language he has already been meaning for a long time.' (Halliday, 1975:140). This making meaning takes place within a social context, and it is these cognitive and social skills which pave the way to learning language.

Perhaps it is not possible to extricate the parts played by language, cognition and social context in the development of the child. Social relationships facilitate the growth of thought and speech, thinking clarifies social and linguistic meaning, language explores thought and society. Like a three legged stool, all parts are essential.

Society

Cultural constraints

The socialisation process that turns out the all-American boy, or the inscrutable Chinese, begins at birth. It would be inappropriate to do more than look briefly at this, but the pragmatics of a language, as well as its structure define how the language can be used. There is an excellent example in Givon (1985). He describes how, unlike the Western child, most American Indian children are not expected to talk to adults, but to listen.

> Only the oldest and the wisest ..were traditionally expected to indulge in long deliberations. Even there the goal of deliberation is profoundly different from what we are accustomed to in Western cultures ...The goal of deliberation is not to convince .. Rather it is to create a spiritual consensus. (Givon, 1985:1025).

For children themselves, they must learn the meaning ascribed to actions and feelings by their culture. Initially mothers mark these actions for their children, teaching them the socially defined requirements of a situation (Shotter, 1979). Children are taught to wave bye-bye and play peek-a-boo before they are a year old, and before they go to school they know that completing a jigsaw is a socially significant event usually followed by praise. Similarly, they learn the meaning of speech events and the socially acceptable (and unacceptable) contexts for those events.

Pragmatics

Children learn how and when to use which sort of language, that is, to use language pragmatically. For linguists this usually means developing communicative intent. Dore (1974) described the 'primitive speech acts' of children at the single-word stage as evidence of communicative intention. The child knows how to use language purposively, to greet, call, protest or label. Developmental pragmatics also includes the child's skill as a conversational partner. Two-year-olds can repair miscommunications (Shatz & O'Reilly, 1990), can manage the topic of conversation (Foster, 1986), can integrate old and new information, and use queries, negations and reference, (Ochs & Schieffelin, 1979).

As children develop beyond the one-word stage, their pragmatic knowledge increases (Dewart & Summers 1988). This knowledge includes knowing how to use polite forms, to take turns in conversations, to use a pretend voice and to find ways of winning an argument. They also know what sort of language to use with whom. At as young as two years old, children are sensitive to the relative power of the speaker and to social distance (Ervin-Tripp, 1982). She used an American sample so there may be cultural differences, but the children were more likely to use imperatives with their mothers than with their fathers, to use directives with their siblings and to speak politely to strangers. Learning language and learning to use language in context appear to be inseparable.

Fathers

It is usually mothers who guide the social and language learning of their children, and as such they have received much attention. Until the mid-1970s, parent–child relationship almost always referred to the mother, but since then there has been much more interest in and acknowledgement of the role played by fathers in the family (for example, Beail & McGuire, 1982). They most often play a supportive, second carer role, and so some of the differences in their relationships with their children relate to lack of familiarity, both with children and with child-care routines.

Almost all studies have shown differences between the language used by fathers and that used by mothers. Fathers' speech is less repetitive (Giattino & Hogan, 1975) and more directive (Engle, 1980). They interrupt more often (Blank-Greif, 1980) and fail to acknowledge children's comments more frequently (Tomasello et al., 1990) than do mothers. There are also similarities. Both parents adapt their speech to accommodate small children (Rondal, 1980) but fathers are less able to continue to adapt as the child develops (Engle, 1980). McLaughlin et al., (1983) suggest that these adjustments are more similar than different, but that mothers are more skilled at 'fine tuning' their language to that of the child.

Fathers' language is characterised by declaratives, imperatives and interrogatives, and full of new information and challenge. In contrast, mothers' language is reflective, responsive and integrative and often imitated by the child. It has been suggested that the two parental styles are complementary (Rondal, 1980; McLaughlin et al., 1983; Tomasello et al., 1990) the last authors arguing that fathers provide a linguistic bridge between the familiarity of the home language to the language of strangers. There is also evidence that females have a greater aptitude for second-language learning (Carroll & Sapon, 1959).

Summary

After an excursion into theories and theoretical considerations, this chapter looked at ways in which the development of language has been described and classified. Linguists and psychologists approach the enterprise from different directions, but they can both learn from each other.

A great deal has been discovered about the abilities of small children, especially about their ability to communicate and to respond to communication. Before they are three years old, children are using language and not just words, and are sensitive to pragmatic cues in the language environment. It is doubtful if these achievements would be possible without the rich interactive environment provided by a primary caregiver, usually the mother. The mother–child (or father–child) relationship is the context for learning about reciprocity, as language partner as well as playmate. Debate remains about the relationship between language and cognition, and about what counts as language. Different workers have emphasised the actual words of the child, the child's communicative intent or the child–mother dialogue.

The chapter ends with an excursion into the wider community of the child. Each cultural community has its own mores. As they grow up, children learn what expectations the community has of them, and in particular how they are expected to behave linguistically. Their father will probably act as the bridge between the familiar home setting and the outside world. The influence of fathers has only recently been acknowledged, but they have a language style that is both different from that of women, and possibly more stimulating for the developing language user.

It is not clear at this point how much of the research into early child language can be extended to the study of bilingual children, or better still, to the study of the range of children acquiring language in a bilingual environment.

2 Where Do You Find Bilingual Children?

Introduction

Bilingualism

Bilingualism is international and so children become bilingual all over the world. The field is extensive, and has been widely studied from the perspectives of sociology, history, human geography and politics, as well as the more obvious disciplines of education, linguistics and psychology. This book deals with the early stages of childhood bilingualism, but some of the issues in the wider world of bilingualism and multilingualism need to be acknowledged in order to put the work in context.

From the start it is well to recognise that government policies affect not only what individuals and communities can do, but also the climate in which they can do things. Some countries have one official language, some have two, and some have avoided the issue (although one language is usually assumed to be the most important). There are countries which have tried to accommodate the needs of minority groups and their languages through legislation, while others ignore their existence. It is in the field of education where this has been of greatest significance. Some countries have tried to facilitate the assimilation of immigrants and others have encouraged the continuation of a multilingual culture. The former can lead to language shift, assimilation, and even to the loss of a language. However, Fishman (1991) has optimistically suggested that languages can be regenerated, and that liberal national policies can facilitate multiculturalism. For a wider discussion of the issues see Fishman (1991) and Lyon (1993),

Communities

Children are brought up in families within communities of monolingual, bilingual and multilingual speakers. The family and the community are the important contexts for the young language learner. There have been some sociological studies of bilingual populations, and the argument has been made that the culture of the community is dependent on its language. This has not taken account of the groups where, despite the loss of a native language, the community retain a group identity within the host, second-language culture. Jewish communities across the world provide such examples. (See Ross, 1979; Schumann, 1986; Mackey, 1988 for further discussion of cultural issues.) For the purposes of this book, bilingual communities are taken to mean groups of families within a locality wherein a sizeable proportion of the families speak two languages.

Families

The issue of what constitutes a bilingual family cannot be resolved so simply. There has been little research into kinds of bilingual family. Even within one community bilingual families differ according to who speaks which language/s within the home, how frequently they do so, and which, if any, of these languages is spoken in the community.

The rest of this chapter looks at the language environment of (potentially) bilingual children, namely their families and the wider community. It reports some of the earliest studies of bilingual language acquisition and commonplace bilingual families. Topics such as second-language learning and bilingual education are mentioned only briefly as they are beyond the scope of this book, but topics such as choice of language code and language switching are described and will be discussed in more detail in later chapters.

Bilingual Communities

Introduction

Britain is one of the few countries in the world where it is common to spend a lifetime using one language only. Throughout the world people need to accommodate other languages either by acquiring language bilingually or by learning the surrounding languages with varying degrees of proficiency. There is no common pattern. Even in places like Quebec where attempts are being made to ensure that two or more languages have equality of esteem, the situation is complex and fraught with tensions – as recent history shows.

In small communities the languages used are regarded as more or less appropriate, more or less important, more or less comfortable by the people who use them. Thus, a number of factors, both national and local, influence the incidence and prevalence of language use in an area. One of the factors is the attitudes of community members towards the languages available.

Attitudes towards languages

Immigrants and migrants are not always accepted by members of the dominant culture, who see them as competing for resources. They are most easily identified by their language which symbolises a whole way of life, both for themselves and for their hearers. While people whose native tongue is a minority language usually look favourably on the dominant language and attempt to learn it, a complementary attitude rarely exists. Speakers of a dominant language may not only look disparagingly at the speakers of a minority language, but may feel there is nothing to be gained by learning the minority language themselves.

Gardner and Lambert (1972) have suggested that there are basically two reasons which motivate people to learn a second language, integrative and instrumental reasons. Instrumental reasons include the pursuit of status, employment and other benefits exclusive to a linguistic group. Integrative reasons include the wish to become closely associated with members of the second language speaking community and to join in their cultural activities. Both reasons apply more to the minority than to the dominant language group. This model has received support from many workers (for reviews, see Gardner, 1985, 1991; Baker, 1992).

Families living in a bilingual culture are in a different situation again. Frasure-Smith et al., (1974) asked English-speaking parents in Quebec why they had chosen to send their children to a French medium school. Their reasons were primarily instrumental. They saw bilingualism as an added extra. The bilingual situation in Wales is similar to that of Quebec. Researchers in Wales have looked at child and adult attitudes to languages (e.g. Sharp et al., 1973; Lewis, 1975; Baker, 1985, 1992). Harrison and his colleagues (Harrison & Piette, 1980; Harrison et al., 1981) looked at some of the reasons given by Welsh speaking mothers for bringing up children to be Welsh speaking or not Welsh speaking, and they too found that instrumental reasons were associated with a monolingual English upbringing, while integrative reasons led to the transmission of Welsh. They also found that if the father was primarily English speaking then English was the language of the home (Harrison *et al.*, 1981). Thus, although the mother in such families was bilingual, her family was monolingual English speaking. Can such a family be called a bilingual family, or does a bilingual family require all of its members to be bilingual?

Bilingual families

Apart from sociological studies of bilingual populations, there has been little research into kinds of bilingual family. Even within one community bilingual families differ according to who speaks which language/s within the home, how frequently they do so, and which, if any, of these languages is spoken in the community.

One way of describing kinds of bilingual family is by the strategies adopted by parents to promote bilingual development in their children. Romaine (1995) and De Houwer (1990) have both described a few of the possible types. They have included differing kinds of language use within the family, which may or may not accord with language use in the locality. The most well-documented type is that where one parent uses only the minority language with the child while the other speaks to the child only in the language dominant in the community (e.g. Ronjat, 1913; Leopold, 1954; Taeschner, 1983). However, these are each reports of one or two children in particular families. Arguably, families who control the language input to children so closely are atypical. Romaine (1995) does add the suggestion that the type where children hear a mixture of two languages is a more common kind of bilingual family than is usually acknowledged. Although single cases have often highlighted issues in bilingual development relevant to all children (such as code switching, mixing and metalingual awareness), few studies have looked at bilingual development in commonplace family situations.

Families, or at least marriages, where each partner has a different first language are becoming more commonplace. Barbara (1989) presented evidence that in France cross-language marriages are increasing. More French women marry foreigners than do French men, the ratio being approximately 3:2. However, although he outlines many of the issues facing such partnerships, much of his book is anecdotal and adds little to the description of kinds of bilingual family, or of their language use. Giles *et al.*, (1977) found that in cross-language marriages the language with the higher status tends to become the language of the family. In her research with six couples in Australia, Harres (1989) found that the women were more likely to keep their German alive than were the men, and Clyne (1982) reports that in 1976 only 4% of German–English couples in Australia were successfully passing their German on to their children.

From a 10% sample of the Welsh Census data for 1981, Williams (1987) has been able to show that if both parents speak Welsh, 91% of their children speak Welsh, whereas if only one parent speaks Welsh this drops to 36% for Welsh-speaking fathers and 42% for Welsh speaking mothers. He does not make it clear, but these figures represent people who were asked if they *could* speak Welsh, not if they *did* speak Welsh. It is possible that many of the 'parents who speak Welsh' can do so, but rarely choose to do so. This gives no useful information about the language spoken in the home, or of the range of bilingual families that exist.

Language Background Questionnaires have approached the question of functional bilingualism, and a number have been created for the Welsh/English population (e.g. Sharp *et al.*, 1973; Baker & Hinde, 1984; Lyon, 1991). They have each attempted to classify speakers according to how much Welsh/English they use. Mostly questions have referred to the home situation, but questions about language use in, for instance, the school environment, have also been included. Baker and Hinde (1984) critically evaluated such questionnaires, pointing out that a major drawback is that equal weight is usually given to all answers, irrespective of the frequency with which a situation occurs, or the relevance and importance of a particular language usage. These are classifications of individuals and not of families. The current research (reported in Lyon, 1991) also uses a language background questionnaire, but uses classifications of individual parents to arrive at a classification of families (or more accurately, of couples).

Children and Languages

Early studies of childhood bilingualism

Parents in cross-language marriages were the first to study their own children, more or less systematically, and to report the progress of their child's bilingual language acquisition. One of the earliest systematic records comes from Ronjat who described the progress of his son, Louis (Ronjat, 1913). Wanting his child to be bilingual, he sought the advice of Grammont, a linguist, shortly after his son was born, and thereafter decided to adopt a one person-one language approach with him. Ronjat's wife used only her native German and he used French with the boy. His was a large household, with a range of servants and relatives speaking either German or French. The commonly used language alternated at various times in Louis' early life according to the household, but by age 38 months he was able to ask *about* language as well as use and understand simple French and German (Ronjat, 1913, Section 51:90 onwards).

Later, Leopold published four books of data about his daughter's bilingual language acquisition, this time English and German. He and his wife also adopted a one person-one language strategy with their child, and by age four Hildergard too could communicate in the two languages (Leopold, 1949ab, 1954, originally published 1939). With both children their mother's language was stronger, at least initially. Since then many scholars have recorded and reported the bilingual language development of their own children (e.g. Saunders, 1982; Taeschner, 1983; Fantini, 1985).

There are problems with all of these studies; they deal with special children. They are the children of linguists, or at least language-aware parents, and the parental relationships cannot be assumed to be unimportant in the development of a child's language. Although language samples are gathered in a natural context, this is rarely described. Parents have often adopted a special strategy to facilitate bilingual development, and there is rarely any measurement of child or parent language use. One of the few honourable exceptions is a study by DeHouwer, who takes an unrelated child as her subject, records her bilingual development in her natural surroundings, and describes some of the features of that environment (DeHouwer, 1990).

DeHouwer takes pains to define bilingual first-language children as those exposed to two languages from within a week of birth. There is evidence that babies recognise sound systems neonatally, if not prenatally (Genesee, 1989). However, external presentation is not the same as internal assimilation. A baby *can* distinguish sound patterns, but infrequent input lacking saliency may not be noticed. Can babies be called bilingual because two languages are spoken in their presence? When, in fact, can children begin to be called bilingual? As soon as they use a word in the second language? When parents think they understand both languages? Given such problems of definition, McLaughlin's (1978) approximate boundary at age three has great heuristic value. But it still needs to be questioned.

Acquiring language bilingually

Most children do not have to learn to be bilingual but become so naturally. The most widespread route to bilingual language acquisition is also the most unnoticed; there is one language for the home and one language for the wider world. This is the common situation with immigrant families, but as a result of circumstances rather than by design. The immigrant mother tongue is the first language used, and so the child's bilingualism may be acquired, or may be learned as a second language after school entry.

Romaine (1995) reviewed types of bilingual acquisition reported in the literature. She describes six types of language background, and comments that the 'mixed languages' type is probably more common than it seems from the literature. The work described in this book supports that view. In this type of family, parents who are bilingual and who may live in a bilingual community have no rigid language rules, but mix languages and code switch. All of Romaine's types are described in more detail in Chapter 5.

Where parents have consciously attempted to ensure that their child acquired language bilingually, the one person-one language method (as adopted in the early studies) has been the most popular. In this way, each parent in a cross-language family can communicate most comfortably with his or her child. In practice, the 'one person-one language' type is probably less common than it would seem from the literature. As Romaine comments 'The majority of detailed longitudinal studies (of bilingual acquisition) deal with elitist or additive bilingualism.' (Romaine, 1995:169). Other specific strategies have been tried in attempts to facilitate bilingual language acquisition and second language learning.

Schmidt-Mackey (1971) has described critically a number of cases where differing approaches were used, adding telling comments from her own experience. There were three languages in use when she was a child, first German and Hungarian and later Serbian. Although she learned all three successfully, she comments that the emotional elements involved cannot be easily quantified. Her parents used only German with her and did not realise that she had learned Hungarian until she was four years old. Hungarian was the language that they used with one another. It always seemed more appealing than German, and she felt excluded by their use of it when she was expected to use German.

Reports of the one person-one language formula (for example, Swain & Wesche, 1975; Volterra & Taeschner, 1978; Dopke, 1992a), have come almost exclusively from well educated, well motivated, cross-language parents throwing doubt on its wider applicability. DeHouwer (1990), following an extensive review of studies of bilingual first language acquisition, concludes that, although the 'one person-one language' principle is most often recommended, there is no evidence that it is better or worse than any other style of language presentation. In all of these strategies there is a risk that the dominant language in the cultural environment will gradually predominate in the child's language (see also DeHouwer, 1995, for a discussion of parental discourse strategies).

An account of what is known about *how* children acquire language bilingually is detailed later. There seems to a general consensus that it is possible for young children to acquire language bilingually with relative ease, although this cannot be assumed, as Itoh and Hatch (1978) have indicated. At first, children may mix or borrow words from both languages, but later they keep them separate. They may notice that they are using two different languages and soon learn which language to use with whom, becoming distressed if someone addresses them in 'the wrong language'. They also manage the switch from one language to the other and quickly learn to ask for a translation if they are stuck for a word they know in the other language. Their bilingualism at a later age is not so well documented. Many lose their bilingualism as they grow up. A child who had a German nanny and was bilingual in English and German at age five, one day refused to answer in German as it was a language for babies, and deeply regretted her action as an adult (Freed, 1961).

The language environment

Children do not just learn languages in isolation. They learn to use language in a social context. The naming game that infants play with their mothers has two major components, getting to know about the nature of the world and getting to know about the structure of social discourse. Infants learn how to signal that they want to communicate, that they do not understand, that they want attention and so on. These early speech acts are the beginning of an extremely complex learning process necessary for communicative competence. It includes learning the meaning of words, but that includes the word's pragmatic meaning, as well as its semantic meaning. Language is embedded in society, and so the child learning language is learning both social and linguistic facts and how they are related.

This aspect of bilingual language development was not commonly considered until recently. When Redlinger reviewed the field in 1979, of 51 studies there were six which took a sociolinguistic perspective. Fantini (1985:2) set out to provide 'an extensive investigation into the developmental sociolinguistics of bilingualism' by describing the development of his son, Mario. He then described the social factors which influenced the language choice of his bilingual son, and his choice of linguistic style in communications. Dopke (1992ab) lays great emphasis on the social environment in which languages are learned. She suggests that children acquire sociolinguistic rules before they acquire structural language rules. Finally, in a wide-ranging chapter reviewing the 'Interactions between parents and children in bilingual families', Goodz (1994) concludes that the conversations between parents and children are more important than precise language separation. Encouraging the child's active participation in the social and sociable act of communicating is most likely to facilitate that child's acquisition of the language/s that he or she is hearing.

Language code and language switching

Bilinguals (and multilinguals) are able to choose the language of their discourse as well as the code and style of communication. Researchers are intrigued by the way such speakers can keep their languages separate, and so occasions when they choose between them have come in for especial scrutiny. Monolingual speakers choose differing language codes according to features of the immediate environment. Farris (1992) suggests that even the use of 'babytalk' by carers can be seen as a form of code-switching. Ervin-Tripp (1968) listed the following features of code-switching; setting and situation (whether you are at a lecture or shopping), actors (whether you are with a peer or an elderly clergyman), topic (sport or a business agenda), and the function of the interaction (invitation or impression management). Using colloquial speech in a formal setting with an outsider represents a set of choices intended to lead to maximum discomfort!

Ferguson (1977), described a related situation where there coexist two codes (or two languages) which have separate and different functions. This is known as a diglossia, and he gives Switzerland, Greece and most Arab countries as examples. A high and a low variety of a language exists, such that the high language is never used for more mundane purposes, and the low language is only used for common everyday speech. Church services, and 'good' literature use the high code, whereas the low code may not even have a written form. These ideas have been applied to the bilingual situation where one language is regarded as the more complex and worthy, and the other is the language of the street. In the USA, immigrants tend to devalue their native language in favour of the majority language, which is often the only language they are allowed to use for official purposes. However, this is rarely a true diglossia. Although their native language is the language of the home and English the language of work, English can also be used at home, especially amongst the children, and Spanish may well be the language of the church (McLaughlin, 1987).

Factors influencing which language a bilingual chooses are similar to the features listed for code choice by Ervin-Tripp (1968). Most important seems to be the person to whom one is talking. Bilinguals use their first language with speakers of that language, and their second language with people who speak their second language. It is rare for two bilinguals to use their second language with one another unless a third person is with them who could not otherwise join their conversation. The formality of the situation, the topic under discussion, the age, sex and status of the participants and the function of the event all influence language choice in bilingual adults.

Code-switching in bilinguals and multilinguals is the switch to a second language in the middle of a first-language conversation. It usually involves a part or a whole sentence which is inserted into the first language. Language switching occurs most frequently when the speaker knows that his or her partner is also multilingual, and is associated with discussions about subjects first learned through the medium of the second language. It is also used to emphasise a point, to convey a feeling tone, or even to exclude (or impress) another listener (Heller, 1988).

Children develop a sensitivity to language choice early. At age three, Louis objected to his father answering him in German. His father was a person with whom he spoke French (Ronjat, 1913). With children, the person-language bond is the first language choice made. Lanza (1992), maintains that children as young as two years old can code-switch. The phenomenon she describes is more usually called language mixing, but her subject, Siri, mixed her languages with an apparent sensitivity to context. Siri used less mixing with her mother (who used English) than with her father (who used Norwegian), even though she was dominant in Norwegian. An examination of the scripts suggests that, whereas her mother's communicative style fostered monolingual English use, her father's style accommodated both language outputs from the child (Lanza, 1992).

Many researchers have reported that bilinguals as young as four years old choose their language to accommodate their partner, and that they will move to their second language if the partner proves to be less fluent in the first (e.g. Fantini, 1978). If there are no clues associated with the person, they choose their language by the setting or by its function; Fantini also reported how his small sons used the 'wrong' language deliberately on occasion to amuse or to startle their relatives.

Children will also switch to their second language to repeat themselves thus ensuring they are understood, or to attract attention. On the other hand, if they are answered in a switched language, usually the 'wrong' language for that person, they may well protest, (Fantini, 1985:68). Older children switch languages for similar reasons, but less often for translations and more often by topic. By secondary school age they will have begun to language switch for reasons associated with increased socialisation, such as establishing their group membership and influencing peers, (Harrison & Piette, 1980). In such a situation, children who cannot make a similar switch will be excluded from the peer group.

The child who learns a second or subsequent language also needs to learn to communicate, to use his or her second or third language in as natural a language environment as possible. It is difficult to learn the pragmatic uses to which French people put their language in an English classroom. An accepting social setting is particularly important for immigrant schoolchildren acquiring communicative competence in their second language (Fillmore, 1991). The child needs natural models in a variety of natural settings where the range of language use and linguistic styles can be observed and their social meaning understood.

Second language learning

Older children and adults who learn a second language can become bilingual, but unless they make use of their second language and use it with reasonable competence, they are not usually classified as bilinguals. As well as research into education for bilingual and minority language children which will be discussed in the next section, there has been a great deal of research into the teaching of second languages in a formal setting (for example, Dulay et al., 1982; Ellis, 1985; Klein, 1986). That body of work is not central to this book apart from studies of factors which help or hinder the learning of a second language and may therefore be relevant to the difficulties faced by migrant and immigrant families, such as English-speaking incomers to Wales.

A second language is most successfully learned where there is the possibility for learners to use their language to communicate naturally, thus emphasising the importance of language as a functional skill. They also need time to listen without the need to respond, in much the way that infants do before they start to speak. As previously discussed, the learners' attitude to the language, and to the language teacher will affect their motivation to learn, and people who are more self-conscious will be less able to tolerate the mistakes that are inevitable in the learning process. Thus affective characteristics of learners and situational factors determine the rate at which a second language is learned (Dulay et al., 1982; Ellis, 1985). Dulay and her colleagues have argued that there exists a natural sequence of development in the learning of a second language which is not influenced by these factors, but which is arguably common to first language acquisition. Learners make the same series of mistakes, and correction by a teacher does not necessarily help. They also learn routines, patterns of speech which they can adapt to the immediate situation. Finally, as found in other work, understanding the feelings, beliefs and thoughts of the people who speak the new language helps greatly. That is 'successful language learning is more likely when learners succeed in acculturating' (Ellis, 1985:292).

Bilingual education

The education available to children born into a multilingual society varies widely. At one extreme there is submersion. Children who are monolingual in the minority language have been expected to attend schools where all teaching is through the medium of the dominant language. This was the experience of many immigrant children in the USA, and some prosper – but many do not. In recent years, following legislation, attempts have been made in the USA to ease the entry of these children into mainstream schooling through 'transitional' facilitation programmes. These programmes use two languages initially, that of the child and English, and may also teach English as a second language (Cummins, 1984). Cummins calls this 'Majority language bilingual immersion', but it is usually termed 'Transitional bilingual education'. After three years the child is expected to be ready for mainstream education (through the medium of English). Both of these methods lead to the assimilation of children into the dominant culture with consequent loss of skills in their first language.

By contrast, attempts were made in Canada to encourage the continuation of a multilingual society. The type of bilingual education often adopted is the 'Minority language bilingual immersion' programme. The most well-documented of these was the St Lambert project (Lambert & Tucker, 1972; Swain & Lapkin, 1982; Cummins, 1984). In St. Lambert, Quebec, French is the dominant language and a group of monolingual English parents wanted their children to become competent bilinguals. Consequently, these monolingual children had a French teacher for their first two years, and were educated through the medium of French. They were allowed to speak English, and their English background was respected. As they proceeded through the school, English was introduced as a second medium for education, and by grade six they were competent bilinguals with English language skills which matched those of a control group (Lambert & Tucker, 1972).

A crucial difference here is the status of the minority language. French and English are the official languages of Canada, although the province of Quebec is monolingual French for official purposes. Nonetheless, English is a respected language. Other Canadian provinces have also provided bilingual education programmes to encourage the maintenance of languages other than English and French, languages they term 'heritage languages'. These programmes have been less effective (Cummins, 1984).

In England, there are many ethnic minorities, and provision of education for their children has been similar to that in the USA. As skills in the English language are viewed as essential both in school and at work, most policies have been aimed at helping the transition of pupils to mainstream English medium education. English as a second language is taught in some schools, but maintenance of the child's first language is usually left to the family.

In Wales, the situation is quite different. Although there are groups of immigrant non-English-language speakers, especially in the south, over the years Wales has received a large migrant population of English speakers. The native language of Wales is Welsh, but not all Welsh people speak their native language. The debate is between the use of Welsh, which is spoken by the minority, and the use of English which is the majority language. The distribution of Welsh speakers and of education policies which accommodate Welsh is uneven. In Gwynedd in North Wales, primary education is through the medium of Welsh. Whichever their first language, children enter a school where their classteacher is bilingual and where the amount of English used will vary according to the languages spoken by the children. It approximates the 'Minority language bilingual immersion programme' for the monolingual English children, and aims to maintain the Welsh language and to produce bilinguals. There has been too little research into the effectiveness of this approach, and all the aforementioned reservations about measurement do not make that an easy task. However, evidence so far indicates that the English language skills of neither group are adversely affected, and that the Welsh-speaking children become bilingual as do some of the English-speaking children. Some bilingualism is gained without loss (Baker, 1988b).

Summary

A wide variety of language situations exist nationally and internationally, some which tend to promote bilingualism and some which seem to lead to language loss. In this overview of issues relating to bilingual communities, few studies have emerged that addressed the question of language use by families in a bilingual environment or the consequent classification of types of family.

National policies are important factors, but local attitudes can also influence whether or not parents use a particular language with their children, how much effort they put into learning a second language, and how much encouragement they give to their children in a bilingual school. The integrative-instrumental model described by Gardner and Lambert (1972) has received support across a range of situations.The present study used a questionnaire to assess the language use of parents and included questions about parental attitudes to Welsh and English (Lyon & Ellis, 1991). Although the language of children is the primary focus, it was seen as important to describe the background against which the children's language was acquired.

Early studies of child bilinguals were all special children with language aware parents. Even later studies, conducted by non-related researchers, have tended to chose individual children from middle-class families who wish to encourage bilingualism. The strategy most often recommended to them is the 'one person-one language' strategy, and this and other strategies have been described. Historically, the social environment of the child and of the family has largely been ignored, but there are now a few studies that attempt to remedy this situation.

Children from cross-language marriages are likely to acquire language bilingually, the children of migrants from rural areas are likely to pick up the dominant language through broadcast media and local children, and the children of immigrants may face education in a foreign language they have never heard. These are crude examples, but they highlight the differences in child bilinguals. Furthermore, the bilingualism of individuals, both adults and children changes over time.

Thus, children become bilingual across the world in many communities and this can play a major part in the families into which they are born, and in their later lives at school. Bilingualism occurs within a complex, multi-layered context, but from the child's point of view the family is where it all begins, and it is with individual families that this book is largely concerned.

3 What is Meant by Childhood Bilingualism?

Introduction

It would be helpful at this point to be able to turn to a theoretical framework within which to understand childhood bilingualism. Unfortunately no single theory exists. This chapter looks at theoretical approaches from allied fields that have proved useful in elucidating issues in this area, and then makes some suggestions.

Before turning to theory, current practice is described. Definitions of bilingualism come first, followed by descriptions of some of the concepts in common use. The contentious issue of measurement is acknowledged as is the emerging interest in multilingualism. The rest of the chapter is then devoted to theoretical considerations.

Definitions

'Bilingual' is one of those words which most people use, but which eludes unambiguous definition. 'Multilingual' has a more recent history and will be examined later. Bilingualism is connected with the speaking of two languages or expression in two languages and it can be used to describe societies or individuals. For the individual, this description gives no indication of the balance between the languages either in terms of knowledge of them or in terms of their respective usage. There are two issues here. Firstly, are bilinguals defined by the *amount* of their two-language use and/or knowledge? Are you 'more bilingual' if you know (or use) more of your second language? And secondly, which is a better measure of someone's bilingualism, *use* or *knowledge*? In the field of language acquisition, Saussure (1916) first described *langue* (the knowledge of language) and *parole* (the use of language) as interacting but separate aspects of language development. Knowing is not the same as doing. Many of us from English-speaking backgrounds were taught a second (probably

European) language at school, but notoriously few of us use it, even on holiday.

Baetens-Beardsmore (1982) suggests that bilingualism can only be seen as a continuum along which people know and use two languages to varying degrees. Children acquiring the beginnings of two languages before the age of three are sometimes defined as primary bilinguals, whereas those who learn a second language later are secondary bilinguals. Dodson (1983) calls these children 'developing bilinguals'.

Concepts

The bilingual acquisition of language, both simultaneous and sequential, and childhood second language learning are all included in the term 'childhood bilingualism'. In simultaneous bilingual language acquisition children have been exposed to two languages from birth. Those who are exposed to one language initially, and come into contact with a second language during infancy, are said to acquire their languages sequentially. Evidence from Grosjean (1982) indicates that language use and other psychosocial factors have more influence on later bilingual development than whether acquisition was simultaneous or sequential.

The term 'acquisition' is usually reserved for languages not learned formally, and this natural acquisition of a second language is contrasted with second language learning (2LL). As an older language user, however much the second language (L2) is used, the language a child acquires first (L1) remains the mother tongue, but L2 may become the preferred language' See Skutnabb-Kangas (1981) for a full discussion of the meanings of 'mother-tongue'. Finally, the terms 'receptive' and 'productive' bilingualism are almost self-explanatory. People described as receptive bilinguals understand some of the second language they hear before they begin to use it productively. An important convention is McLaughlin's (1978) suggestion that in either case if infants use two languages by the age of three, they can be said to have acquired language bilingually. This is useful shorthand and has been adopted by many researchers. However, even within this group there are differences, and it is not always easy to keep the distinction between these children and young second-language learners. These conventions span the knowledge and use dimensions. A wider discussion of these issues can be found in Grosjean (1982); Cummins (1984); Lyon (1993).

Measurement

Traditionally language knowledge has been assessed usually in rather formal settings. On the whole, however, the results have been unsatisfactory. Fluency has also been used to measure bilingualism, but has been criticised by Grosjean. He studied language usage and quotes Malherbe in support:

> It is doubtful whether bilingualism *per se* can be measured apart from the situation in which it is to function in the social context in which a particular individual operates linguistically. (Grosjean, 1982:50)

The performance of any one individual will vary not only from language to language, but also according to who they are talking or listening to, what they are reading and writing and where they are at the time (Fishman, 1965).

Apart from observational approaches, the main attempt to measure language use has been with Language Background questionnaires (for example Baker & Hinde, 1984; Lyon, 1991). Subjects have been asked to indicate which language they use with whom or in which situation, and to what extent a particular language is the only one they use in certain circumstances. Even straightforward questions such as these are not without hazard. The range of situation probed, the frequency of that experience for the subject, and the methods of scoring can all distort the final picture, especially if answers are summed to give a global score. These difficulties and more are discussed in detail in Baker (1985, 1993).

Multilingualism

Almost all of the issues raised about the definition, description and measurement of bilingualism apply to the concept of multilingualism. By broadening the description of a person's language range some of the tension implied in 'bilingual' is released. If you have a number of language systems available through which to express your ideas, the question of which is your better, or stronger or even preferred language becomes less of a competition and more of a choice. The definition of a 'multilingual speaker' as someone who speaks more than one language is uncontentious, and does not have undertones of balanced/unbalanced, or dominant/non-dominant. None the less, it may still be necessary to describe multilingual speakers and to measure competence in their various languages, if only for occupational and educational purposes.

Children who have been exposed to more than two languages from a very early age have been studied even less frequently than have young bilinguals, probably because of the complexity and diversity of such situations. Many of the issues are the same. Is there interference between languages; is language acquisition simultaneous for all three (or more) languages, or is it sequential? What counts as effective use of a language system and can it be measured in the same way for all languages? Some case studies have appeared that throw up many more questions (for example, Hoffmann, 1985; Helot, 1988), and an edited book by Vedder (1995) looks at some of the broader issues of multicultural child development. However, here, as in the area of bilingual language acquisition, there is still much groundwork to be done. This book concentrates on language acquisition in bilingual children, while acknowledging that many of the findings will be relevant to multilingual children. Both groups of children display amazing language skills, and researchers have turned to them hoping that the process by which they learn to communicate can throw light onto the fascinating complexity of 'normal' language acquisition.

Theories

Borrowed theories?

Theories specific to childhood bilingualism are few and incomplete. Possibly theories in related areas can be used to elucidate issues in childhood bilingualism. Theories of language acquisition were discussed in the first chapter. Skinner and Chomsky raised fascinating questions about the process of language acquisition, but gave few hints that could be used in the bilingual field. Piaget and Vygotsky provided more starting points. Both emphasised the importance of the social dimension, and both observed the behaviour of real children! It has been possible to build on Piaget's (1959) Stage Theory of Development (following the work of Brown, 1973), but his theory says nothing about how a second language might develop, or about the features in the environment that would facilitate its development. Vygotsky, in contrast, did comment on childhood bilingualism, suggesting that children with two languages had a cognitive advantage (Vygotsky, 1962; Hood et al., 1982). Unfortunately he did not expand that idea which, like many of his ideas, has acted as a framework for the creative thinking of others rather than offered suggestions about how children become bilingual.

Chomsky's (1965) Theory of Universal Grammar has been productive in the field of second language learning. It has led to the Interlanguage Theory which postulates internal mechanisms to explain second language learning. 'Interlanguage' is a construct used to describe an approximate language system which is unlike either the learner's first or target language. It is seen as developing with the child's growing second language skill, and providing the basis for hypothesis testing about what does and does not work in the new language (Selinker, 1972). This concept can be fitted into Chomsky's theory. He saw children as *discovering* the rules of grammar despite inadequate input and little correction of their output. Second language learners, using interlanguage, also face a lack of negative feedback and a paucity of linguistic input.

Dulay and Burt (1974, 1978) tried to show that there is a natural sequence in all language acquisition, and to apply that to young bilinguals. Such a finding would support the interlanguage hypothesis, but unfortunately there are methodological difficulties with their work relating to the instrument they devised, the Bilingual Syntax Measure, and to their error analysis (McLaughlin, 1987). The methodological problems in exploring order and sequence in second language learning has been examined in detail by Ellis (1994). He suggests that, although some trends are evident, inter-learner variability and intra-learner variability make it difficult to find strong evidence of an order in second language acquisition. Not all features of second language acquisition are developmental, and acquisitional sequences are not rigid. Ellis uses the term 'acquisition' to mean acquiring the use of a second language irrespective of the age of the learner. In this book the term 'language acquisition' is reserved for young children acquiring language/s informally, usually at home. The term 'language learning' is used for more formal and structured attempts to learn a second (or third or fourth) language.

Most researchers using the interlanguage model have looked at the experiences of older child or adult second language learners, rather than at second language acquisition by pre-schoolers (Ellis 1985). In this they have been encouraged by recent challenges to the traditional notion that there is a 'critical period' for language acquisition, after which children cannot acquire language for the first time (Lenneberg, 1967). As McLaughlin (1987:108) says: 'the Universal Grammar approach (has) generated useful predictions about the course of interlanguage and the influence of the first language.' Despite the lack of interest in preschool children so far, it might be possible to extend the interlanguage concept to explain how young children develop two languages.

The Monitor Theory has also been used primarily to explain the second language learning of adults and older children, but has been sufficiently influential to require a brief description here. Krashen (1981) proposed a general theory of second language acquisition, comprising a set of hypotheses. Initially, the most central of these was the notion that there is a mechanism which monitors the language produced by the second language learner. The monitor edits language production using learned rules. While acquisition is seen as an unconscious process, learning a language is a conscious (even a self-conscious) process. He also postulated a natural sequence for the acquisition of grammatical features, that language acquisition proceeded via 'comprehensible input', and that an 'affective filter', can block or facilitate acquired competence in the second language (Krashen, 1981, 1982, 1988; Dulay et al., 1982).

McLaughlin (1987) has been one of its strongest critics, arguing that its definitions are imprecise, it has little predictive value and it is largely untestable. He does acknowledge that some of the teaching implications have proved very useful in the classroom. But a useful tool is not the same as a useful theory, and it has little to say about pre-school children.

Acculturation theories

Two further, related theories have emphasised the importance of the social-interactive dimension. Again they apply more to older children and adult learners than to young children, but are described here briefly for their relevance to the parents of children in this study (see also Lyon & Ellis, 1991).

Lambert's (1974:96) Motivation Theory suggested that 'linguistic distinctiveness is a basic component of personal identity.' As such, learning a second language has implications for the self-perception of the learner. While acknowledging that natural aptitude and intelligence played a part, his theory has focused on affective influences such as attitudes. He suggests that there are basically two kinds of attitude towards learning the language of another culture: one integrative and one instrumental. By integrative is meant a positive, personal interest in and identification with the target language and its culture. By instrumental is meant an interest in learning the target language for the sake of the benefits and practical advantages it can bring (Gardner & Lambert, 1972; Lambert, 1974; Gardner, 1985). Integrative reasons are usually stronger than instrumental ones. As Baker says: 'Canadians learn French and people in Wales learn Welsh predominantly for friendship, for social and cultural reasons.' (1988a:168).

Schumann's (1978) Acculturation Theory emphasises the importance of integrative motivation. He states that: 'the degree to which a learner acculturates to the target language group will control the degree to which he acquires the second language' (1978:34). Acculturation is more easily achieved when the learner has a positive attitude towards the cultural values associated with the target language and hopes to become assimilated into that culture. In turn, the target culture can facilitate the process by its attitude to learners and its willingness to share social and cultural activities. Acculturation is more likely to succeed when the number of learners is small and the first language of the learner shares equality of esteem with the target language (Schumann, 1978, 1986).

On the other hand, research into language change in Wales has suggested that economic advantage and status were the main reasons given by Welsh bilinguals for choosing to speak English (Williams, 1979). Instrumental or 'Machiavellian' reasons were also given by parents in Canada for sending their English speaking children to French immersion schools (Genesee *et al.*, 1976). Soh (1987) later took the debate a stage further and suggested that these basic motivations are not mutually antagonistic, but are independent variables. She also suggests that language use is an important factor in second language competence.

These theories aim to explain the features in the environment, and the factors in the individual which promote or predict second language acquisition. They do not address the question of *how* children acquire two languages.

Theories of Bilingual Language Acquisition

Three theories will be discussed here, although one is usually called a model (the Threshold Theory), and is usually discussed in connection with classroom bilingualism. However, before examining that model, two other, related theories will be discussed, the Gradual Differentiation Theory, and the Separate Development Theory.

The Gradual Differentiation Theory

Merrill Swain (1972) was the first worker to suggest that children acquiring their language in a bilingual setting acquired not one or the other language spoken locally, but 'Bilingualism as a first language' (the title of her PhD thesis). She suggested that there are no fundamental differences between a child's acquisition of one language and their acquisition of two. All children learn language using one language store, and later bilingual children separate this into identifiable language systems according to the speaker-situation, much as monolingual children learn to separate codes within their native language according to the speaker-situation (Swain, 1971, 1972; Swain & Wesche, 1975).

Supporting this comparison, there is evidence from Ervin-Tripp (1982) of the use of two codes by two-year-olds when they addressed their siblings and strangers differently; and in parallel, Vihman (1985) reported the separation of two language systems by a boy of the same age (25 months). However, the two languages/two codes analogy is not an appropriate explanation of the mechanisms involved in bilingual language acquisition. Using a language requires knowledge about grammatical systems. Using a code requires knowledge about the social environment. A set of rules cannot be equated with a set of situational cues.

Volterra and Taeschner (1978) later proposed a three-stage model for the Gradual Differentiation Theory. Initially the child has one lexical system with words from both languages. Next the child recognises that there are two lexical systems but uses both in one syntactic system. Finally, the child has two linguistic codes each comprising a separate syntax and lexicon. The Volterra and Taeschner model uses evidence of language mixing for support, and most researchers who have reported mixing take the view that children in a bilingual setting have one language store and progressively separate their languages, (e.g. Swain & Wesche, 1975; Volterra and Taeschner, 1978; Redlinger & Park, 1980; Vihman, 1985; Schlyter, 1987).

There are two important issues here; firstly whether the first syntactic system used by the child is a truly mixed syntactic system, or is an approach to one of the available grammars; and secondly whether language mixing is significant as claimed. If the postulated first syntactic system is a mixed syntactic system, as Volterra and Taeschner (1978) suggest, then the child is bilingual from the start (a simultaneous bilingual). This sounds very much like Swain's (1972) bilingualism as a first language. If, however, the child acquires one grammar into which words (mostly nouns) from two lexicons are inserted, then arguably he or she is monolingual in the beginning, for however short a time. As to the significance of language mixing, those who support the Separate Development Theory, see it as no more than evidence of limited, immature, language use (Genesee, 1989; DeHouwer, 1990, 1995).

The Separate Development Theory

An alternative theory postulates that bilingual children develop separate linguistic systems from the beginning, or at least from very early in their language acquisition, and that they remain separate apart from some borrowing of words and phrases (e.g. Padilla & Liebman, 1975; Lindholm & Padilla, 1978; Meisel, 1989; Genesee, 1989; DeHouwer, 1990, 1995).

Following their study of three children in their second and third years, Padilla and Liebman (1975), suggested that children use two systems that are distinct phonologically, lexically and syntactically from the beginning. They found little mixing. Lindholm and Padilla (1978), found that only 2% of utterances in their corpus (from children nearly three to six years old) were mixed, and that the structural consistency of utterances was maintained. However, it is possible that children progress beyond the stage of frequent word mixing by age three, and so an overall low level of mixing in their older subjects is unsurprising.

Genesee (1989) argued that mixing in the early stages of language acquisition could be explained by a number of general linguistic features such as lexical borrowing and over-extension, features not confined to bilingual children. Arguing for children's ability to separate syntactic systems, Genesee (1989) goes further and cites phonetic evidence to show that infants of a few weeks old can discriminate between the language spoken by the family and a foreign language and prefer the familiar one, and, perhaps more tellingly, between phonetic contrasts in unfamiliar languages.

Meisel (1989:35) concluded that 'an individual exposed to two languages from early on should be capable of separating the two grammatical systems without going through a phase of temporary confusion'. He offers no argument against a common lexicon, but suggests that there has been a lack of clarity in the literature, due to the over-extension of the word 'mixing'. Instead he suggests that the term 'fusion' should be used for those rare instances when children fuse two grammatical systems, reserving 'mixing ' for the failure of pragmatic competence evident when children use the 'wrong' word or phrase.

There appear to be two variants of the Separate Development Theory. In the strongest version, all language systems, phonology, syntax and lexicon, are distinct from the beginning of language production (Padilla & Liebman, 1975; Lindholm & Padilla, 1978; Genesee, 1989). In the weaker version, there may be an initial common lexicon, but the two syntactic systems develop without confusion (Meisel, 1989; DeHouwer, 1990, 1995). In both versions, early language mixing is not very significant, does not undermine the notion of separate language development, and can be seen as immature pragmatic awareness.

Two theories compared

Figure 3.1 represents these two theories diagrammatically. The labelling beneath stages on the two models is suggested by the author. According

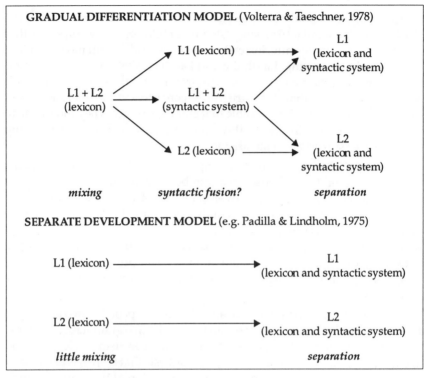

Figure 3.1 Two models of bilingual language acquisition

to this figure, if children in a bilingual setting acquire their bilingualism as one system which they separate into two, there will be evidence of language mixing other than borrowing, and evidence of syntactic systems that have features of both languages in question. If, on the other hand, children differentiate their languages from the beginning, there will be little evidence of mixing, or confusion between syntactic systems.

However, two other aspects of early bilingualism are not hereby taken into account. It has been suggested that the developmental dimension has been largely ignored in these studies and that, if attention were focused on the language of subjects over time, the language differentiation process would be more evident (Redlinger & Park, 1980). It has also been suggested that context is rarely reported. The mixing evident in the speech of small children may well be a reflection of the speech they hear (Genesee, 1989). Parental language input is hardly ever monitored. Even parents adopting the one person-one language strategy may be providing contexts that foster or discourage language mixing (Lanza, 1992).

Neither theory predicts the course of children's subsequent bilingual development, or suggests how their two languages may influence one another. Both assume that the child sooner or later achieves two differentiated language systems. As Arnberg and Arnberg (1985) note, that cannot be assumed. In the early school years, some bilingual children are struggling, and difficulties in differentiating two languages may be a cause. The third theory to be discussed does make suggestions about the process of the child's development of two languages. It also suggests how the development of one language may affect the development of the other.

The Threshold Theory

The Threshold Theory is different from the two theories discussed so far. It focuses on an older age group (school children rather than pre-schoolers) and, as well as offering a description of the process of becoming bilingual, this theory purports to describe the effects of becoming bilingual.

The Threshold Model was originally suggested by Cummins (1976) and Toukomaa and Skutnaab-Kangas (1977). It has been further developed by Cummins, and it is his version that will be described here (Cummins, 1978a, 1987). He suggested that the development of a second language was dependent on the level of a child's first language competence at the time of exposure to the second language. When the first language is dominant and prestigious, it will not be disadvantaged by the child's second language learning. Lambert (1974) termed this situation 'additive bilingualism', a second language is added without cost to the first. On the other hand, when the first language is less prestigious than the second, the first language may be poorly established when the second language begins to dominate, to the detriment of the first. That situation he called 'subtractive bilingualism' (Lambert, 1974). The first situation is typified by English-speaking children who add French to their language store, and the second by Hispanic children in the United States whose attempts to learn English are often at the expense of their first language. Cummins states that:

> The Threshold hypothesis assumes that those aspects of bilingualism which might positively influence cognitive growth are unlikely to come into effect until the child has attained a certain minimum or threshold level of competence in his second language. (Cummins, 1978:858).

He goes on to postulate that there are two thresholds, the lower threshold is sufficient to avoid the negative effects of bilingualism, but the

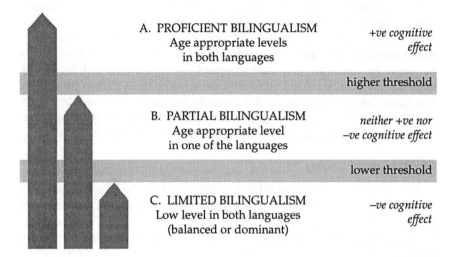

A. PROFICIENT BILINGUALISM
Age appropriate levels
in both languages

*+ve cognitive
effect*

higher threshold

B. PARTIAL BILINGUALISM
Age appropriate level
in one of the languages

*neither +ve nor
−ve cognitive effect*

lower threshold

C. LIMITED BILINGUALISM
Low level in both languages
(balanced or dominant)

*−ve cognitive
effect*

Figure 3.2 Threshold Theory: The cognitive effects of different kinds of bilingualism (from Cummins, 1987)

higher threshold is necessary to reap the positive benefits of bilingualism (see Figure 3.2).

One of the main precursors of this model was the work of Skutnabb-Kangas and Toukomaa (1976) in Sweden, which identified groups of minority language and migrant children with less than native-like ability in their first language, as well as in Swedish. These children were failing at school, and gave evidence of low cognitive skills. Social and motivational factors may well be interfering with their bilingual development, but they appear to be suffering from the detrimental effects of bilingualism, and can be seen as unable to cross the first threshold.

Since Lambert's (1974) description of additive and subtractive bilingualism, many researchers have been able to show the cognitive advantages of additive bilingualism. For example, Duncan and DeAvila (1979), showed that proficient bilinguals performed better on a range of cognitive tasks than did either monolinguals or less well developed bilinguals, thus supporting the hypothesis of an upper threshold. It is possible that the causal link is reversed; children who do well on cognitive tasks may be more able language students.

Some bilingual children may be failing because of social circumstances and/or poor motivation, and some bilingual children may be succeeding because of superior intellectual ability. Nonetheless, this model fits much of the available data concerning the effects of bilingualism on cognitive abilities, and has proved very useful in educational practice. However, as Baker (1992:137) comments, the problem is 'in precisely defining the level of language proficiency a child must obtain in order firstly, to avoid negative effects of bilingualism and secondly, to obtain the positive advantages of bilingualism'. What characterises either threshold?

The model does not purport to explain informal bilingual development, but might potentially do so. It is possible that children who are developing bilingually need to reach a certain level of proficiency before they are able gradually to differentiate their two languages, or that they need to develop to a certain level in a first language before the second language can be acquired as a system. Further thresholds might also be a useful way of conceptualising subsequent normal bilingual development.

Issues in Child Bilingualism

Borrowing

Much of what had been called language mixing could more appropriately be called, borrowing (Poplack et al., 1989). Foreign words (such as hamburger, dungaree, par excellence, et cetera) inserted into English dialogue are often not recognised as non-English; it is easier to recognise those English words borrowed by others. Bilingual speakers tend to be a little ashamed of using borrowed words, feeling it marks an inadequacy in their expressive repertoire, and recently (July 1994) some French politicians have tried to make it illegal to use English words and phrases as part of normal French speech. However, it is extremely common, and can enrich a conversation when the speaker can best express an idea in this way. Unlike the switch to a second language, it may be the only word or phrase borrowed by a monolingual speaker. The present author has used words and phrases from ten or more languages, but has only used three language systems. Borrowing is part of the process of creative language use which enriches all living languages and it includes 'Franglais' (French–English) and 'Wenglish' (Welsh–English) word mixes.

Poplack et al. (1989), in their study of the language of adult bilinguals, found that borrowing could be identified as a phenomenon separate from code-switching in communities where two languages were in contact. They found that much of the borrowing comprised words for new objects or new ideas, what has been called 'cultural borrowing'. Adult borrowing and code switching were the topics of Myers-Scotton (1992), research in parts of Africa. She differentiates the two by frequency of occurrence (borrowings are more common), and the degree to which the word or phrase has become part of the matrix language. Unlike Poplack, she thinks there is a continuum from borrowings to code-switches, rather than distinct categories (Myers-Scotton, 1992; see also 1988, 1993).

Language mixing and borrowing

The picture is not so simple where children are concerned. When they start to use language there is a long period of single word usage and children living in a bilingual culture acquire words from both languages, from whatever language is heard. It is not clear whether this should be called 'mixing' or 'borrowing'. The term 'mixing' is generally used, and many researchers have reported that young children do mix words from two languages as discussed earlier in connection with DeHouwer's (1990) study (see also Swain & Wesche, 1975: Volterra & Taeschner, 1978: Redlinger & Park, 1980: Vihman, 1985: Arnberg & Arnberg, 1985: Schlyter, 1987). Unfortunately 'mixing' is rarely defined, and its significance is disputed according to theoretical background. But, despite some variation between studies, it seems that language mixing occurs in about a quarter of the utterances of children when they are about two years old, and decreases to less than 10% at about three years of age (Redlinger & Park, 1980; Vihman, 1985; Schlyter, 1987; DeHouwer, 1990; Goodz, 1994).

From many researchers comes the finding that single content words are mixed most frequently, as reported earlier in DeHouwer (1990). Vihman (1985:316) suggested that at the stage when children are increasing their lexicon, 'we may surmise that he (the infant) was not concerned with the difference between language source, contexts or interlocutors'. In other words, she suggests that children acquire their own unique lexicon as a single store.

Swain and Wesche (1975) recorded slightly older children, over three years old, and reported little mixing at this later age (confirmed by DeHouwer in 1990). However they did report occasional mixing within the utterance, and even within the verb. Two of the examples they give are 'Elle est giving the ball.' and 'Y veut to keep it, her.' Similar examples were reported by Volterra and Taeschner (1978). Meisel (1989:37) suggests that this might more properly be termed 'fusion (of grammatical systems)'. He prefers to reserve the term 'mixing' for the failure of pragmatic competence evident when children use the 'wrong' word or phrase. If Lanza's (1992), child (reported earlier), is code-switching, the mixing she still uses with her monolingual mother is an example of pragmatic incompetence. Meisel

(1989) also comments on how few of the studies under discussion define what they mean by grammatical structures or the mixing thereof. There may well be occasions when errors and inaccuracies in a child's language are due to immature speech development rather than to language mixing (Dulay & Burt, 1974).

Just as surprising is how rarely studies state what they take as evidence that a young language learner is bilingual or is becoming bilingual.The tendency is to call children acquiring language 'bilingual' if they happen to have speakers of two or more languages around them. The acquisition of L2 words or phrases in a child's lexicon is hardly sufficient reason to call him or her bilingual. Such a term is more appropriately applied to children who can express themselves in two languages, and who give evidence of having two syntactic systems, however rudimentary. Goodz (1994) goes some way towards meeting this problem by calling them 'bilingual-to-be' children. Her research, using 13 children from French/English bilingual homes, attempts to clarify the nature of mixing in language learning children. She does not think that mixing can be equated with confusion between two languages, but rather with the child's powerful need to communicate (Goodz, 1994).

Throughout these and other studies there is general agreement that mixing occurs, but little reference to the criteria used to define 'mixing'. Swain and Wesche (1975), Redlinger and Park (1980), and Lanza (1992), omitted negatives and affirmatives (largely on the grounds that their linguistic provenance was ambiguous). Volterra and Taeschner (1978) had categories of words which they called 'IG' and 'EG' (Italian-German and English-German), words that are close in form and meaning, and Lindholm and Padilla (1978) noted that the similarity of some words made categorising difficult.

It is not clear from this work, or from the work of other studies, how this issue has been handled. Is the word or the utterance the unit of mixed-ness? Most studies use utterance, but do not define how an utterance is classified. Would 'dolly wants a diod (drink)' count as a single mixed utterance, or as a speech sample with 25% mixing? And how are words defined as mixed? The Welsh word 'doli' and the English word 'dolly' sound and mean the same. How, for instance, are proper names, or international words such as 'okay' and 'hi!' classified, or are they discounted? Lanza (1992) comes nearest to using the word as unit of mixedness. She defines 'turn to talk' as the unit, but in the case of her two-year-old subject, this was often a single word. She defines words as mixed if they contain morphemes from two languages; she does not explain how words not obviously English or Norwegian are handled.

The term 'mixing' means the taking and combining of things from separate sources. It is possible that the language children hear is already mixed, and that some of it at least contains borrowed words. Too little interest has been paid to the source of children's language, except in those families sufficiently well organised to be able to adopt a one person-one language strategy with their children, as did Taeschner (Volterra & Taeschner, 1978). Parental language is not reported in most of the studies above, although Redlinger and Park (1980), reported that parents said they did not mix their languages. Bilingual speakers are not always aware of the language they use. Genesee (1989) suggested that language mixing in young children could be related to mixed parental language, and Arnberg and Arnberg (1992), suggested the role of parental/social input had been underplayed.

Lanza (1992) and Goodz (1994) are exceptions. Lanza suggests that the language context of the young bilingual is of primary importance. As reported earlier, Siri's language mixing varied according to whether she was talking with her father or her mother (Lanza, 1992). Goodz, in her study of 13 children, reports that although the parents of these children were trying to adopt a one person-one language strategy, they often modelled mixed utterances for them. Patrick's father replied in English that yes, it was a 'camion' (truck), and his mother corrected his 'pinetree' to 'pineapple' within a French utterance 'Non, ce n'est pas un pinetree, Patrick, c'est un pineapple'. (Goodz, 1994:72). In this study he was not alone in having mixed uttering parents. Thus, children using mixed utterances, however they are defined, may simply be learning the language use of their parents.

Language awareness and metalingual awareness

The issue of language awareness is dealt with in greater detail in Chapter 9, but some writers have seen it as an important factor in the development of bilingualism. Although supporting the notion of a single linguistic system at an initial stage, Vihman (1985) suggested that subsequent differentiation of languages was associated with language awareness. Arnberg and Arnberg (1985), in reporting that differentiation takes place sometime between the child's second and third year, commented that those children who become aware of both languages rarely mixed their languages. Finally Vygotsky (1962) was the first to suggest that, in learning that their language is one of many systems, bilingual children become aware of their linguistic skills.

Many terms have been employed to describe this phenomenon, and the terms 'language awareness' and 'metalingual awareness' appear to be used interchangeably. In describing the language use of small children it is difficult to avoid imputing more knowledge and awareness than can be justified. Children quickly learn by trial and error how to get what they want from their parents without knowing how they do this. Thus, perhaps the clearest examples of language awareness is talking about talking.

McLaughlin (1984) criticised the concept of language awareness, commenting that, without criteria, to say that the child who separates language systems has language awareness is a circular argument. The Arnbergs (1992) responded to this by devising a test of language awareness. Language awareness was judged by a simple word naming task, repeated on separate days in separate languages. Children who substituted a word from the 'other' language were deemed to be less language aware than those who acknowledged that they did not know the right word.

Cummins (1987:67), in a review of the studies relating bilingualism and cognitive development, found that bilingual children showed more evidence of metalingual awareness than did monolingual children. However, he felt that 'the phenomenon of metalingual awareness (was) still inadequately understood and the literature (was) devoid of instruments whose construct validity (had) been demonstrated'. Since then, Bialystock has gone a long way towards providing valid measures of metalingual skills, (Bialystock & Ryan, 1985, 1988; 1991b, 1992). In 1985, Bialystock and Ryan outlined a 'Metacognitive framework for the development of first and second language skills' (title of paper). They claimed that two components of linguistic awareness (and other language tasks) could be identified, analysis of linguistic knowledge and control of linguistic processing. The first they described as the skill component, responsible for organising and understanding language implicitly or explicitly. The second they described as the executive component, responsible for directing attention appropriately and integrating new information.

Subsequently Bialystock (1988), used metalingual tasks such as the Arbitrariness of Language Task to compare monolingual and types of bilingual children. In this task children are told of a special place where the sun has been called 'moon' and the moon has been called 'sun'. They are then asked to retell a sun/moon story making appropriate substitutions. As hypothesised, most bilingual children performed better on tasks involving cognitive control, and fully bilingual children performed better on tasks involving analysis of knowledge. Although her subjects were slightly older children (between six and seven years old), she was able to demonstrate that bilingualism influences the development of linguistic awareness. Later, she has cited evidence that younger (age three to five), bilingual children consistently performed better than monolinguals in tasks requiring high levels of selective attention (Bialystock, 1992). For this she used a Lego/Duplo Tower Task where children had to compare the quantity of blocks despite gross disparity in their respective sizes. Other evidence to support these findings has been reported by Gonz and Kodzopeljic (1991) who used pre-school children. They suggest that bilingual experience directs attention to the essential aspects of the environment and fosters an analytic approach to tasks such as reading.

Although there is less evidence concerning younger children (below age three), it would seem that Vygotsky (1962) was correct in his supposition, and that children who are or are becoming bilingual are more likely to develop language awareness and other metalingual skills than are monolingual children, or at least to do so at an earlier age. What, then, is the wider significance of metalingual abilities? There have been claims in Bialystock's work that metalingual skills are indicative of more general cognitive ability. Van Kleek (1982:261), who used a Piagetian framework to examine studies that reported linguistic awareness in children, postulated that 'cognitive reasoning abilities provide the bases for all metalinguistic skill development'. Therefore evidence regarding bilingualism and intelligence will be examined next.

Bilingualism and Cognition

'Bilingualism is an experience that has major consequences for children's intellectual development' (Bialystock,1991a:5). Initially, Bialystock had been interested in the literacy skills of bilingual children and began experimenting with metalingual tasks as a means of explaining some of the inconsistent findings regarding bilingualism and cognition.

Palij and Homel (1987) reviewed the early studies of the relationship between bilingualism and intelligence and found that virtually all writers until 1962 concluded that there were at least some negative consequences of bilingualism, mainly associated with verbal intelligence. Bilingualism was thought to dissipate the stock of available intellect. Then, against their expectation, Peal and Lambert (1962) found that children who were balanced bilinguals, measured on tests standardised in both French and English, performed significantly better on tests of verbal intelligence than did monolingual children. Others have replicated their findings (see reviews by Cummins, 1984; Palij & Homel, 1987; Baker, 1988b).

The greatest pressure for research on this question has come from education, and most of that in Canada or the USA. In both countries as many as 50% of a school population may not speak the language of the school, and earlier emphasis on the assimilation of all children into English medium education produced what has been called, pejoratively, 'semilingualism'. Critiques of the term can be found in both Skutnabb-Kangas (1981) and Baker (1993). These children have poor skills in English as well as underdeveloped skills in their first language. Thus, to find that there were positive correlates of at least some kinds of childhood bilingualism led to a reappraisal of education policy (Grosjean, 1982). As Baker (1988b) has suggested, many factors are involved in this debate. The positive effects have been found using children whose linguistic development in both languages is balanced, and it could be that more intelligent children become more balanced bilinguals. Parental attitudes may play a part. Those who wish their children to be bilingual are more likely to encourage their child's bilingual education. And children may be more motivated to become bilingual in a society that values bilingualism.

Turning to work with younger children, Bialystock (1992), showed that bilingual children consistently performed better than monolinguals in tasks requiring high levels of selective attention. This she defines as a metalinguistic skill which is central to cognitive functioning. Bilingual children between the ages of three and five were shown to have the advantage over monolingual children in tasks requiring high levels of control of attentional processing. While emphasising the need to identify the degree and type of bilingualism children had achieved before making comparisons with a monolingual sample, she suggested that if bilinguals develop these cognitive skills differently from monolinguals, then differences should be evident in oral, literate as well as metalingual tasks.

In the bulk of studies, including that of Peal and Lambert (1962), subjects were school-age children. This is understandable for at least three reasons: the education authorities have the problem of helping bilingual children who are underachieving; the school population is more accessible and provides greater opportunity for matching subjects; and the reliability of intellectual assessment with preschool children is dubious. None the less, research remains to be done with the pre-school child. A similar comment can be made about research with children learning more than two languages. It would be fascinating to know if the benefits that seem to accrue to bilingual language acquisition are enhanced or diminished in the multilingual home.

Children in Wales

Turning nearer to home, there has not been a great deal of research into the bilingualism of children in Wales, and even less into that of pre-school children. What little there is tends to be either linguistic (for example Ball, 1988) or educational rather than psychological. There have been studies of the education system in Wales (for example Dodson, 1967, 1985; Dodson & Price, 1978), and of the bilingualism of its pupils, (Sharp et al., 1973; Price-Jones, 1982; Baker, 1988a). The most comprehensive work in the area is that of Baker (1985) which, as well as describing the overall language situation in Wales, examines education policy, how bilingual education works in practice, curriculum development, and the influence of the media and the microcomputer on schools in Wales.

There is also some research on attitudes to Welsh expressed by children. Sharp et al. (1973) found that whereas all schoolchildren tended to have a mildly positive attitude towards Welsh just before the start of secondary schooling, this became less positive during the subsequent four years as attitudes towards English became more positive. Price-Jones (1982) looked at children of about the same age and his findings were similar, findings he associates with the use or non-use of Welsh language mass media.

Reasons given by adults for their attitudes to the Welsh and English languages formed part of a later report by Lewis (1975), who had been involved in the Sharp et al. project of 1973. There has also been work on the measurement of language use, language ability and classification of language background (Sharp et al., 1973; Baker & Hinde, 1984; Baker, 1985). The language background questionnaires reported above were designed for schoolchildren. Those used in the present study were designed for the parents of small children.

There has been occasional reporting of the Welsh–English language development of individual children, such as Harrison and Thomas (1975), Bellin (1984) and Evans (1987); but Harrison et al. (1981) appears to be the only study which includes a group of young children in their home setting. Their project set out to discover why bilingual mothers in Wales did not bring their children up to be bilingual speakers. They interviewed 300 bilingual mothers of children ranging from less than a year to more than 16 years old, in six areas of the principality. The interview schedule asked about maternal language use, maternal opinions, individual child development, child preferences, and a number of demographic questions. It is an interesting descriptive study, but reports mainly in percentages and uses only simple analyses of the data.

The child born in the North West of Wales will almost certainly come into contact with both Welsh and English by the time he or she is old enough to attend nursery school. Although English is the dominant language in Gwynedd, and the 1991 census indicated that the percentage of people who can speak Welsh has fallen from 63% to 61% since 1981, the percentage of children between the ages of three and 15 who can speak Welsh has increased from 69.3% to 77.6% (Office of Population Census and Surveys, 1992). This is probably due to the policy of the local Education Department regarding Welsh medium schooling. Thus, parents of such children, whether Welsh speaking or not, whether Welsh by birth or incomers, will have the opportunity to enable their children to become bilingual. It is within this population that the research reported here was conducted.

Summary

Theories of bilingual language acquisition do not abound! Aspects of theories of monolingual language acquisition have some relevance, as do theories from the field of second language acquisition. However, of most interest are the competing theories of Separate Development and Gradual Differentiation which will inform the debate in subsequent chapters. Similarly, the Threshold Model, although usually applied to 2LL, can illuminate the process of developing bilingualism.

Other issues in child bilingualism have been discussed, and although many of these issues may well relate to multilingual children and families, it is acknowledged that even less research has been conducted in that area. Children in a bilingual situation do use words from different languages. Mixing may occur but in some children there is remarkably little confusion. The significance of mixing is disputed. The bilingual's languages are differentiated, but it is not clear how or what facilitates the process. Bilingual children do seem to have the edge, at least metalingually, but the extent and the implications of that advantage remain unclear. The theories and models that do exist have suggested some interesting issues, but have not greatly clarified the picture. As Arnberg and Arnberg comment, this is not simply a theoretical pursuit. In a bilingual world the more that is known about the mechanisms of successful bilingual acquisition the more effective the interventions on behalf of children who are not succeeding (Arnberg & Arnberg, 1985).

4 How can Child Language be Studied?

Introduction

Approaches to the study of child language

As suggested in the previous chapter, the study of bilingual children and the language they use is not only of theoretical interest. Most of the world's children grow up learning more than one language, and so the more we understand about how they do so the better we are able to help them discover the advantages of using two or more languages and avoid the confusion that so many predict. But child language is not an easy subject for study. This chapter will look at some of the approaches that have been adopted and at some of the pitfalls.

When studying children's language, there is more to be observed and recorded than can be handled in a meaningful way, at all stages of development. Modern technology has added to the problem. If you decide to videotape an interaction, where do you point the camera/s? Where do you place the microphones? Do you record indoors or outside? If you collect data from a group of children, how do you define them – by age, developmental level or background? Of necessity, all these decisions exclude data. The problems become even more complex when questions of data analysis are addressed.

As the focus of this book is the child in a bilingual setting, only studies which address that dimension are discussed here. However, many of the comments are pertinent to the more general field of child language. Fortunately, that subject is so fascinating that there are a great many researchers adding their findings from a range of perspectives. At least some of these pieces are relevant to the bilingual jigsaw.

Case study and questionnaire approaches

Mention has already been made of the many early single case studies of bilingual language acquisition and at some of the advantages and disadvantages of these studies. Single, special children may not be representative, but they can provide fine-grained information about the process of bilingual language acquisition.

Although at one remove from the phenomena, data gathering by questionnaire can provide a range of data from a more ordinary population. These approaches are discussed first as they have a bearing on the research reported in detail later in the chapter and in subsequent chapters of this book.

The Anglesey Project

Finally, this chapter describes in detail how the Anglesey Project used features from the case study approach as well as two different questionnaires to obtain data from a representative sample of children and families in North Wales. This sets the scene for a number of questions asked in the rest of the book about which concern the bilingual acquisition of language in young children.

Approaches to the Study of Child Language

Case studies

The classical studies were described in the previous chapter, namely those of Ronjat (1913) and Leopold (1949ab; 1954). Since then there have been many others. When Redlinger reviewed the area in 1979 she found 51 studies, many written by academics reporting the bilingual language development of their own children, although interest by other researchers was beginning to grow. A number of researchers (for example Swain 1972; Padilla & Liebman, 1975; Redlinger & Park, 1980) recorded the language of unrelated young bilingual children for shorter periods. For the most part they were looking for data concerning specific issues, such as whether bilingual language acquisition was a simultaneous or sequential process.

Of those who reported more extensively on their own children, Saunders (1982) and Fantini (1985) are two of the most remarkable. Saunders is a scholar of the German language, married to a German wife and living in Australia. They decided to teach their sons both German and English, and succeeded well enough to move the boys to Germany when he was offered a lecturing post there. Both boys continued their education in a German-speaking school. Fantini (1985) is a linguist who takes a sociolinguistic approach when reporting the bilingual development of his son, Mario. Unlike many studies, he has recorded Mario's language from birth to at least age ten, and has noted the effects of his son's language partners on his use of Italian and English over the years. Both write as much for the guidance of other parents as for academics.

A recent case study

More recently, DeHouwer (1990) has recorded the bilingual development of Kate, a child unrelated to herself. Even here the researcher has chosen a special child, a child with relatively wealthy, language aware parents, who had adopted a deliberate strategy to foster their child's bilingualism, and who had exposed her to at least two different language environments. This study is of especial interest as it avoids some common pitfalls while illustrating others.

DeHouwer, (1990) recorded Kate's developing language/s from age 2.7 to 3.4 years, for one hour at intervals of approximately two weeks. Recording sessions took place in Kate's home, and usually comprised her conversation with DeHouwer and whoever else was in the room: Kate's mother was often in the adjoining room, but most sessions included some English and some Dutch interactions. DeHouwer deliberately chose a naturalistic setting as best representing the child's language, but did not control the participants in the sessions.

From the recordings, mean length of utterance (MLU) was calculated for Kate's speech. As with earlier researchers (e.g. Hickey, 1991), DeHouwer did not follow Brown's (1973) criteria for MLU strictly, arguing that they entailed too much data interpretation, especially if the language was not English. She is one of the few researchers (Schlyter, 1987, is another) who reports separate MLUs for each of the child's languages. Mixing occurred in about 5% of Kate's utterances, and was constant across languages and sessions.

Almost all mixed utterances (89.4%) comprised one-word insertions and almost half of these (46.4%) were nouns. DeHouwer suggests that this could reflect the limitations of Kate's language production generally. It could also be 'borrowing', a term already discussed in detail. However, she thinks not, saying that 'a word may be tagged in memory as belonging to both languages without the child realizing in any way that it in fact belongs to only one'(DeHouwer, 1990:106). That implies two word-language stores. She found that Kate knew (had used?) the lexical equivalent in up to half of the cases, so she discounts the idea that words are borrowed to fill a lexical gap. Instead she suggests mixing could be due to the increased availability of a word recently used, the differing perceptual saliency of words, the greater frequency of some word use, the fact that some words are learned earlier, or a simple slip of the tongue. DeHouwer adopts an information processing model for bilingual language acquisition, using the idea of an internal 'monitor' which notes discrepancies in language choice, etc. (Lindsay & Norman, 1977). The child's underdeveloped monitor simply makes the wrong choice.

In conclusion, DeHouwer (1990:339) claims that 'the morpho-syntactic development of a pre-school child regularly exposed to two languages from birth which are presented in a separate manner proceeds in a separate fashion for both languages'. She does not mention lexical development, although she comments earlier that the bilingual child has 'a bilingual lexicon, and two closed linguistic rule systems' (DeHouwer, 1990:114). Thus, she supports the Separate Development Theory. The mixing that was found is seen as peripheral. Greater mixing could indicate transference which represents evidence of an initial common language that must separate gradually, that is the alternative, Gradual Differentiation Theory. Both of these theories were discussed in the previous chapter.

This study avoids some of the weaknesses of earlier studies: it takes an unrelated child as its subject, it measures the language use of the child and her partner, (DeHouwer, 1990), it looks in detail at issues such as language mixing and language switching, and it uses a familiar, normal setting. But it is still the study of a single, special child, and although more details are available about the language environment, the language of Kate's parents is not analysed. There is no indication either of how words shared by Dutch or English are dealt with, and there is no comparison with other children in similar or different settings.

Questionnaires

One of the problems with questionnaires is to assess the extent to which the respondents are representative of the population under scrutiny. If the population is within an institution (such as a school), then those in authority can insist that everyone completes the form. They cannot ensure that everyone completes it with the same amount of care and honesty. If the population has a greater degree of freedom, then all those who take the trouble to answer may well answer honestly, but nothing can be said about those who do not reply. Non-response may mask indifference, hostility or just forgetfulness.

As described in an earlier chapter, language and culture are closely associated, and so to ask questions about someone's language may raise questions in their minds about cultural (or political) issues. In Wales, there have been few language questionnaire studies published (Sharp *et al.*, 1973; Harrison *et al.*, 1981; Baker & Hinde 1984; Lyon, 1991; Lyon & Ellis 1991). The Sharp *et al.* questionnaire asked 10, 12 and 14 year old schoolchildren about their attitudes to the two languages. The Baker and Hinde questionnaire aimed to classify schoolage children according to their language background. Neither had a great deal to say about the factors associated with bilingual development. The Harrison et al questionnaire used selected mothers and open-ended questions to ask why bilingual mothers in Wales do not produce Welsh speaking children. This study did try to choose representative families, but does not make it clear how they decided that a family was monolingual or bilingual. The report is descriptive rather than statistical, and gives few clues relevant to bilingual language acquisition.

Both the Lyon papers (Lyon, 1991; Lyon & Ellis 1991) report on the Language Background Questionnaire described in more detail next. It questioned parents in an attempt to describe the language background into which babies were born.

Questionnaires do give the researcher the opportunity to collect a large amount of data relatively easily. These data are then available for statistical analyses which can reveal relationships not previously apparent, or can confirm or refute suspected relationships. However, interpretations of these relationships are still necessary, and so close observation of phenomena may still be needed to support and give life to the grosser number crunching exercise.

The Language Background Questionnaire

The Language Background Questionnaire was devised by the author for use in the Anglesey Project described later in this chapter. In the absence of available information, it was an attempt to map the distribution of kinds of monolingual and bilingual families on Ynys Mon (Anglesey), an island off the coast of North Wales. The questionnaire is addressed to the baby's mother and asks for information about her own and the child's father's background (see Appendix I). Questions about current and past language use are asked, followed by questions asking for an opinion about the Welsh language, and for demographic details. The questionnaire is written in both English and Welsh. Questions concerning language use use a five-point scale. These questions cover both with whom the language is used and was used, and in what situations it is and has been used. For example:

Q 1.   At present, which language do you use ... with people at work?

Q 5.   When you were a child in primary school, what language did you use ... with your sisters?

The questions of opinion are fewer, specifically:

- Whether they describe themselves as speaking Welsh;
- How much Welsh they want their child to learn;
- Why they want their child to learn Welsh (or not);
- How important they think it is for children to learn Welsh;
- How much they think Welsh will be used in the future;
- Where they hope their child will choose to live;
- Whom they hope their child will marry.

Demographic questions ask about the presence or absence of a partner, the age band and socioeconomic status of each parent, the numbers and ages of other children, the length of time the parents have lived on Ynys Mon (Anglesey) and about the child's grandparents. There are also questions inviting comment.

Some of the questions have proved less fruitful than others. Opinions about the future plans of their children elicited only bland replies; parents felt the children must decide for themselves when the time came. Perhaps future research can establish whether that remains so as the children reach adulthood! Questions about grandparents have been surprisingly unproductive, as has that concerning the length of stay on the island. Maybe grandparents only become a factor to be reckoned with when the children are old enough to talk to them.

The open questions have provided a wealth of information about what happens in bilingual families. Though more difficult to quantify, they are to be recommended in all questionnaires for two main reasons. Firstly, allowing respondents to express opinions on the subject of the questionnaire maximises the response rate. Secondly, and more importantly, such comments can identify areas of relevance overlooked by the researcher.

The Language Development Questionnaire

This questionnaire, QII, was compiled to check the progress of families in the Anglesey Project three years after the birth of the babies who were the subjects of the project.

The current language use questions from the Language Background Questionnaire, QI, are repeated. Included are those which ask about thinking, reading and watching television as are questions about whether and how parents want their child to learn Welsh (see Appendix II). The further questions ask about the language used for activities shared with the three-year-old child, such as talking, reading and watching television, and the language heard by the child from a number of sources (such as peers, grandparents, etc). Parents are asked about the child's language development and about the acquisition of nine key aspects of Welsh and nine of English on a three point scale, for example:

Q 6:   Does your child: NOT YET SOMETIMES OFTEN
        say things are 'big' or 'little'   ....
        say things are 'mawr' or 'bach' ....
(Appendix II).

The questionnaire is produced bilingually, so this question also appears as:

Q 6:   A yw ei plentyn: DIM ETO WEITHIAU YN AML
        dweud bod pethau yn
           'big' neu 'little'   ....
        dweud bod pethau yn
           'mawr' neu 'bach'   ....
(Appendix II).

Thus the development of both languages in each child can be represented.

Finally demographic questions are asked including questions about who else lives with the child (father, younger siblings, etc.), whether either or both parents work, and what child care arrangements exist. Again, parents are invited to add their own comments, and again these have proved very illuminating, as will be seen in the next chapters.

Whereas the Language Background Questionnaire was devised to try to map the bilingual situation of families in a given population, the Language Development Questionnaire had the more limited aims of verifying earlier findings and obtaining a broad measure of general language development.

Advantages and disadvantages

Questionnaires allow the researcher to obtain data from a wider range of subjects than from a single or a small number of case studies. They also allow more questions to be asked than do large-scale population surveys. Furthermore, with the use of open-ended questions and attention to free comments, much serendipitous insight can be gained.

In contrast, the fine-grained detail available during the scrutiny of the development of individual children is forfeit. There are advantages in both methods, and a combination of both approaches is arguably the best solution allowing for depth of insight and breadth of vision.

The Anglesey Project

Overview of research

The original aim of the research project described here was to look at the development of language in children from bilingual backgrounds. On Anglesey in North Wales, both Welsh and English are spoken extensively, but language use varies widely from area to area. If comparisons were to be made it was essential to be able to define the kind of linguistic background in which children grew up, and so the first step was to survey language use in a large number of families on the island.

All families into which a baby was born in a 12-month period received the Language Background Questionnaire, QI, as described in the previous chapter. From the returns, families were defined as mostly Welsh-speaking (WW), mostly English-speaking (EE), having a Welsh-speaking mother and non-Welsh-speaking father (WM), having a Welsh-speaking father and a non-Welsh-speaking mother (WF), or having both parents with both languages in their background (MM). MM, the least cohesive group, was not used in all analyses.

Once the groups were defined, two representative families were chosen from each group for further study. Eight recordings were made of communication between these 10 mother–child dyads from age 15 months to three years, and a recording was made of the father–child dyads at age three for comparison. The focus was on pre-school children before they were routinely exposed to language influences outside of the home. The results were analysed quantitatively and qualitatively and the children were also assessed psychometrically and descriptively.

About three years later, the Language Development Questionnaire, QII, was sent to those families who replied to QI. This too was described in the previous chapter. These data were used as the normative sample against which the children from the small group could be compared. They were also used with data from QI to identify factors predicting language use.

The Language Background Questionnaire: QI

The questionnaire was sent to the mothers of all babies born in one year on Ynys Mon (Anglesey), North Wales. This is a part of Wales where the Welsh language is used widely and where, according to the 1981 census, 61.6% of the population is Welsh speaking (Office of Population Census and Surveys, 1983).

In the year from 1 March 1988 to 28 February 1989, 963 children were born on the island but the numbers available reduced to 927, mostly by mothers who moved away: 417 questionnaires were returned, representing 45% of possible returns. According to Oppenheim, between 40% and 60% return rate is to be expected from a postal questionnaire (Oppenheim, 1966). It is quite encouraging that, at such an important time in the family's life, almost half of the mothers found time to complete and return the questionnaire. Only 52 questionnaires were answered in Welsh, representing 12% of those returned, although a great many more families can be classified as Welsh speaking (as will be seen by the later analyses). However, many Welsh-speaking parents have commented that they were glad the questionnaire was in Welsh as well, although they find it easier to complete most official forms using the English version.

Data were obtained from the Welsh Office concerning this population and were used to compare those returning the questionnaire with those not returning it. There were no significant differences in socioeconomic status, maternal age, or in the sex of the baby. For the whole sample, most of the parents (85% of mothers and 89% of fathers), were between 20 and 39 years old. About a third of families (37%) had no other children. Just under half of the women and just over half of the men had been born on the island, but about a quarter of all parents had lived there less than five years.

The mean scores of the language usage questions were used to classify parents. Initially, the mean scores of mothers and fathers were calculated separately, and each was assigned to a primarily Welsh-speaking group (W), a Mixed group (M) or an almost entirely English-speaking group (E). It should also be noted that when 'English' or 'Welsh' parents are described, this refers to their language usage, not their culture or nationality. The sample was then divided into five groups of differing couples:

WW = Welsh couples (N = 93)

WM = Welsh mother and non-Welsh father (N = 36)

WF = Welsh father and non-Welsh mother (N = 46)

EE = English couples (N = 132) and

MM = Mixed couples (N = 77),

(where one or both partners have a mixed language background).

Table 4.1 Allocation of couples to groups

		Mother		
		Welsh	Mixed	English
	Welsh	WW	WF	WF
Father	Mixed	WM	MM	MM
	English	WM	MM	EE

WW = Both parents speak primarily Welsh.

WM = The mother speaks primarily Welsh and her husband does not.

MM = Mixed language background for one or both parents.

WF = The father speaks primarily Welsh and his wife does not.

EE   = Both parents speak primarily English.

Recordings

For the small sample, the aim was to select mother–baby dyads to represent the five types of family defined by the language use of parents from the Language Background Questionnaire, and to make audio recordings of the vocal interactions between these mothers and babies at three-monthly intervals from approximately 15 months of age to three years old. These were subsequently transcribed, annotated and analysed. The development of the language of these children was formally assessed at the end of the second year and of the third year when a non-verbal test of intelligence was also administered.

It was decided that in order to match subjects, they would be chosen from the pool of first children with both parents living with them. This was to exclude the influence of other children and ensure the influence of a mother and a father. Those with very young parents (below 20 years of age) and those with older than average mothers (over 40 years of age), were also excluded. Next to be excluded were those who might not remain for three years, namely those with the RAF, and those who had lived on Anglesey only for a short time. A list of those remaining was examined for practical constraints, and families living in the more inaccessible parts of the island,

and also those known to the experimenter were excluded. Ten children were needed, two from each kind of family.

A letter was sent to appropriate families asking if they would be willing to take part in further research. These letters were sent out in batches over a nine-month period and, as two babies were found to fill a slot, no further families of that kind were approached. These 10 children were the subjects for this second part of the study.

There followed an initial semi-structured interview which took place when the baby was about a year old. Mothers were asked specifically about the child's early attempts at communication, the family's language background, and about her own ideas for the future of her baby. The sample was not matched for socioeconomic status. Parents were unsure how they would describe themselves; some said working class and some middle class. These perceptions did not match their class as defined by Census Office on the basis of occupation. However, none of the families could be described as either needy or wealthy, and standards of child care were uniformly high. All 10 families lived in a house on their own except one and they were in the middle of building a house and living with paternal grandparents meanwhile. Eight of these were owner occupiers, one was considering buying the house they lived in and one had a house which went with the job. All of the fathers were in full employment and seven of the mothers had temporary or part-time jobs during the course of the study. Only two said they did not want more children, and five had a further baby before their first child was three years old. Five of the fathers were very closely involved with their baby from birth, the others adopting a more traditional paternal role and only starting to play with their children once they became more independent. Some of the children's names have been changed to protect their identity, and only their first names are used. The children chosen were:

Nerys	WW family
Iwan	WW family
Becky	WM family
Emyr	WM family
Gareth	MM family
David	MM family
Nia	WF family
Mathew	WF family
Llywela	EE family
Michael	EE family

The children were recorded at approximately three-monthly intervals from about 16 months old to just over three years old at the last maternal session. The session with fathers took place about a month later. All the sessions took place in the child's home, in the part of the house where the child usually played. The mother had been asked to play with the child as she would do normally, using ordinary commonplace games and pastimes. The mother was also told that the experimenter would try not to respond to the child at all, and not to speak during recording. On occasion this proved impossible. Sometimes mothers naturally included the experimenter in the conversation and no reply would have been impolite; sometimes the child's overtures where irresistible. However, both mother and child soon became accustomed to the silent observer, and rarely appeared to notice when the tape recorder was switched off or on.

The sessions took about 75 minutes on average. Generally, about 40 minutes' recording was made in a session. On the second and sixth session, the experimenter took novel toys (a teddy, a doll, a bed and a bath) and at the fourth and eighth sessions the child had the small toys of the Reynell test to play with. On other occasions, mothers read from story books, built things, held children up to see what was outside, talked about family photos, played with small toys, drew pictures, and got drinks for their children. None of the mothers ran out of ideas for games with their child and all appeared to enjoy the sessions as did the children.

While the mother and child were engaged in playing, copious field notes were made to catch the train of events. This required attention to the gross physical activity of both participants, and to fine motor activities such as pointing, looking, nodding and a variety of other gestures and non-vocal clues to communication.

The data

The sections of the tapes selected for transcription and later analysis were those representing the best or most voluble examples of the child's vocalisations. As the children got older, they were chosen to include the sections best illustrating the pragmatic aspects of mother–child interaction. It was apparent from the beginning that some of the pairs were more silent than others, and so the quantity of material transcribed varied.

The transcripts were typed in a standard format with three columns, the first for maternal vocalisations, the second for child vocalisations and the third for accompanying or intervening actions thus:

M: What're you doing?/	C: Dolly/ Dolly bed/	PICKS DOLL UP DOLL TO BED
M: You're putting dolly to bed/ are you?/	C: Yeah/ Dolly bye-byes/	ADDS BLANKET TURNS AWAY
M: Is she tired?/	C: mmm/ C: Mum/	LOOKS AT M
M: What?/	C: Mum sweetie/	APPEALING

A new line indicated when an utterance initiated a communicative interaction, and a slash indicated the end of each utterance. An utterance does not need to be a sentence. It could be defined as a phrase that carries a message. Thus, a vocative such as 'Mum' is an utterance if it is a call for attention, but is not a separate utterance in 'Mum sweetie'. (Gutfreund *et al.*, 1989). As each utterance was subsequently given a new line, 'line' and 'utterance' are used synonymously.

The data were retained in two forms, in standard format, referred to as the *script*, which included vocalisations and accompanying actions (as in the example given above) and in an edited form, stripped of all detail except words and utterances, the text. From the standard format it was possible to identify dynamic sequences of mother–child interaction from the script, to highlight the pragmatic nature of these interactions, and to assess the level of language development for comparison with normative data (at least for the English-speaking children) using the work of Brown (1973) and Crystal (1976). This is discussed in more detail later.

Most dialogue includes a lot of 'fillers', sounds which have no intrinsic meaning but which indicate that the partner is listening, prompting, or reacting appropriately to the speaker. Examples are usually written as 'oh!', 'ah' or 'mmm?' and so forth. These, together with other extraneous detail were stripped from the scripts, making it possible to compute word and utterance counts, mean length of utterance (MLU) and ratio of mother/child words and utterances for each transcript. From this text it was also possible to assess the use of Welsh and English in each session by identifying words and utterances as Welsh, English or Common.

Measures

It was fortunate that a group of speech therapists was concurrently producing a standard version of the Reynell Developmental Language Scales in Welsh (Huntley, 1986). Consequently it was possible to administer this test at ages two and three to all 10 of the small sample, either in the original English or else in Welsh. There are difficulties with this test, the greatest being the antiquity of the picture cards which are supposed to evoke spontaneous language if enough has not been heard in the test situation. However, it is a standardised test with reasonable reliability which produces an Expressive and a Comprehension score for children from age 18 months to seven years (Reynell, 1987).

As can be seen from Table 4.2, apart from one child, the children's language development was within the average range.

Table 4.2 Scores from formal assessments of small sample

		2 yrs (Reynell)		3 yrs (Reynell)		3 yrs PIQ
		Expr.	Comp.	Expr.	Comp.	
Nerys	WW	27.00	29.00	37.00	36.00	93
Iwan	WW	28.00	23.00	39.00	40.00	130[a]
Becky	WM	24.00[b]	26.00	40.00	34.00	90[b]
Emyr	WM	27.00	25.00	34.00	42.00	97
Garth	MM	27.00	28.00	42.00	50.00[a]	120[a]
David	MM	23.00[b]	22.00[b]	34.00	31.00[b]	97
Nia	WF	28.00	31.00[a]	49.00[a]	47.00	100
Mathew	WF	27.00	22.00[b]	34.00	32.00[b]	101
Llywela	EE	28.00	27.00	46.00[a]	52.00[a]	115
Michael	EE	28.00	27.00	—	—	—
Mean		26.70	26.20	39.44	40.44	104.78
SD		1.77	3.16	5.43	7.84	13.64

The Reynell Development Language Scales were administered twice, at about two years old and again at about three years. They comprise an Expressive scale (*Expr.*) and a Comprehensive scale (*Comp.*). The Performance subtests of the Weschler Preschool and Primary Scale of Intelligence (WPPSI-R) were also used at age three to give a Performance Intelligence Quotient (*PIQ*).

[a] indicates more than one SD above the mean of the group.
[b] indicates more than one SD below the mean of the group.

The Performance half of the Weschler Pre-school and Primary Scale of Intelligence (WPPSI-R) was also administered at about age three to monitor non-verbal intelligence. This is the most widely used standardised test of intelligence, and can produce a verbal as well as a performance, or non-verbal score for children from age three years (Weschler, 1991). Given that these children were only just old enough, there may be some floor effects. Also from table 4.2 it can be seen that the mean score was 104.8. All scores except two fell within the 'Average range of Intelligence' of 100±15 points. Two boys had scores of 120 and 130 respectively, and the latter was becoming bilingual by the time the test was made. Overall these two tests indicate that the small sample chosen was within the average limits for the general population.

Mean length of utterance (MLU) and Stages of Language Development (Brown, 1973) were described in an earlier chapter, but a summary table (Table 4.3) is reproduced here as a reminder. Stages and MLUs were used to classify the children's language at each session.

Dictionary of common words

Whenever two languages are in close contact, a great deal of borrowing occurs between them. Single words are borrowed most frequently and, in the course of time, become assimilated into the second language (Grosjean, 1982). English, for example, is full of borrowed words such as restaurant, shampoo, abseil, anorak, ruse, patio. The syntactic structure of conversations usually enables one to say that someone is using one language rather than another, but words develop before syntax. When children use words which are currently shared by more than one language, it is very difficult to decide which language is being learned, or whether one or two language systems are developing. Consequently it was found necessary to list the words common to both Welsh and English that were being learned by the children in this study (Appendix III).

For the purposes of this study, there are five types of Common word. Proper names comprise the first type and include the names of popular characters such as Postman Pat and Swperted. Baby words such as wow-wow, quack-quack (cwac-cwac) and bye-bye (bei-bei) form the second type, and foreign and/or technical words the third. This last group includes words such as video (fideo), and okay, an American importation into both languages. All words which sound very similar and which have the same meaning in both languages are defined as Common. These include words such as bus\bws, car, Dad, doll\dol, lot, right\reit, train\tren, top, yea\ia (see Dictionary of Common Words Appendix III for

Table 4.3 Stages in language development (as in Chapter 1): Brown and Crystal compared

	Brown		*Crystal*		
MLU	*Features*	*Stage*	*Features*	*Age (months)*	
1.75	Semantic roles; syntactic relations (2 morphemes; content words; no functors)	I	Single element	by 18	
2.25	Grammatical morphemes; modulation of meaning (some plurals; differing intonations; early use of 'a', 'the' and 'in', etc.)	II	2 words together	18–24	
2.75	Modalities of the simple sentence (modulations such as negation, interrogation, imperatives)	III	3 or more element utterance; use of 'a' and 'the'	24–30	
3.50	Embedding one simple sentence in another (early embedding)	IV	4 or more elements; simple sentences; 'errors'	by 36	
4.00	Co-ordination of sentences; propositional relations (use of 'and' and 'but')	V	Clauses; embedding; use of 'and' and 'but'	about 42	
Later	Tag questions, etc.	VI	Pronouns, auxiliary verbs, etc.	about 48 onwards	

complete list). Criteria for inclusion in the dictionary were that they were found both in the data collected, and in either Y Geiriadur Mawr (1986), the standard Welsh–English Dictionary, or else in Y Geiriadur Lliwgar (1979), a popular Welsh Children's Picture Dictionary, as well as in an English Dictionary. Mostly these are nouns, but include some adjectives, adverbs and prepositions. Lastly, a group of 'Wenglish' words have been included. There are some words which do not appear in either the formal or informal dictionaries of Welsh words, but are English words used locally and changed to conform with Welsh syntax. These are almost all verbs and have a Welsh alternative. Although cwympo is to crash and nofio is to swim, families often use crashio and swimio. Martin Ball in Bristol (1988) has suggested that the transition of words from one language to another is a process and that some words are still in transition. Where English and Welsh are the languages in question he calls English words used creatively like this with Welsh syntax, 'Wenglish'. Theoretically this term could cover words in transit from Welsh to English.

Utterances were similarly defined as Welsh, English or Common, but the criteria were more difficult to define. If the structure of the utterance was clearly Welsh or English, then the inclusion of Common words makes no difference. If the utterance was composed entirely of Common words and no clues were obtainable from the structure, then it was called Common, and if the utterance included words from both languages with no clear structural clues, then it was defined as Common. Both of these last events tended to occur only in immature utterances, for example, 'dadi car stop ia?/' ('daddy car stop yea?'/) uses only Common words, and 'Mr Fixit 'di mynd and gone to bye-byes/' uses structures from both Welsh and English. Once the child had progressed to simple sentences, classifying lines was usually straightforward.

Much of a child's early language consists of baby terms and proper names which fall into the 'Common' category. They also delight in naming objects, and many of these names for things are the same in both languages. Consequently, a large part of the early language used by children in this study, whether from primarily Welsh- or English-speaking families, has been classified as 'Common', that is shared by the two languages.

Language Development Questionnaire: QII

The Language Development Questionnaires were posted to all families who had responded to the first questionnaire, 418 in all. To check the accuracy of reports of father's language use, two questionnaires were sent to each family with the request that parents complete them separately.

They were sent out in batches to coincide with the third birthday of their children.

Of the 418 families who responded to the first questionnaire, 178 responded to the second; also 16 of the original responders are known to have moved out of the area and it is likely that more have done so. Thus, a return rate of 44% of possible families is within reasonable expectations. Of those returning, 124 families included two questionnaires, one from each parent, and they provide the data for most of the subsequent analyses. One of the single questionnaires came from a father and the rest came from mothers. In some analyses, the group of 177 mothers are used.

It is not possible to say why more families who were willing to co-operate on the first occasion did not feel able to do so three years later. It is possible that the enthusiasm felt at the time when a new baby joins the family has waned by the time a toddler is making constant demands for attention. On the other hand, life events such as illness, death and divorce must make a questionnaire like this seem irrelevant.

Those who replied were compared with the rest of the population who gave birth in the year in question, using the data made available by the Welsh Office. There were no significant differences between the two samples in terms of maternal age or sex of child, and, if the returns are bifurcated, exactly 48.2% of both the responding and non-responding groups were from Socio Economic Status (SES) groups 4 and 5.

Couples were again allocated to a Language Background group using the procedure described for the first questionnaire. The results were as follows:

- 38 WW, primarily Welsh-speaking couples;
- 15 WM, Welsh-speaking mother and non-Welsh-speaking father;
- 5 WF, Welsh-speaking father and non-Welsh-speaking mother;
- 33 EE, mostly English-speaking couples;
- 33 MM, couples with a mixture of languages in their backgrounds.

Data regarding background group membership were compared with those from QI. To check the validity of these groupings it was necessary to calculate the proportionate agreement between the allocation of the fathers, the mothers and the couples on the two occasions. The proportionate agreement was above 81% in all three comparisons, and the kappa value, the co-efficient of agreement, ranged from 0.76 to 0.82, well within the limits of acceptability (Youngman, 1979).

The primary aim of QII was to sample the language development of the base population. Answers to the 'Aspects of Language Development' questions were computed for both Welsh and English, and then subtracted to give a Bilingual score. A child using all and only the nine aspects of English would score 27 for English, and 9 for Welsh ('not yet' counts as 1) and so their Bilingual score would be 18. A child whose first language was English but who was acquiring some Welsh as well, might score 24 for English and 18 for Welsh ('sometimes' counts as 2) giving a Bilingual score of 6. Thus, the nearer a child's Bilingual score approached zero, the more balanced was their two-language development. These data were then split into three language development groups, those who were monolingual or tending to be monolingual in English (+18 to +7) those using the two languages fairly equally (+6 to –6) and those who were monolingual or nearly monolingual in Welsh (–7 to –18). For the sake of brevity they are referred to as the 'English', 'Bilingual' and 'Welsh' groups of children. The numbers in each group are as follows:

English   N = 79
Bilingual   N = 57
Welsh   N = 41

These data were cross-tabulated with answers to the questions and with the language development groups as outlined above. Data were also analysed on the basis of gender of respondent, and free text comments were similarly ordered as for the first questionnaire.

Finally, a number of regression analyses were performed to look for predictors of language development. These used the four 'aspiration' variables and the maternal, paternal and couple language group variables from the first questionnaire as independent variables, and the language development, child-use and child understand variables as dependent variables.

With hindsight, it would have been useful to replicate more of the questions from the first questionnaire and omit the child care questions which have not proven helpful. In particular questions concerning parents' self-perception as a Welsh speaker, opinions about the future of Welsh and about the current importance of the Welsh language could have indicated whether changes are occurring in parental attitudes.

Summary

Initial discussion centred on the advantages and disadvantages of case study and questionnaire approaches to the study of children's language acquisition (monolingual and bilingual). This prepared the ground for a description of the Anglesey Project. The three phases of this longitudinal research project were described in some detail, and the use made of these investigations will be described in the subsequent chapters. In the main, a series of questions will be asked of the data and evidence gathered from every available source, that is from any part of all three sections of the study. Each question acts as a focus and as a boundary for the data. Overall an attempt will made to deal with each question within a strictly bilingual framework, and to identify those answers in which the bilingual dimension is important. It is seen as a search for clues, not only about how children acquire language bilingually and how that differs, if at all, from monolingual language acquisition, but also for what predicts a child's language.

5 What Language Backgrounds are There?

Introduction

Describing bilingual families

This chapter might also be called 'What is a Bilingual Family?' The description is used widely but without a great deal of precision and, apart from sociological studies of bilingual populations, there has been little research into kinds of bilingual family. It is argued here that, as a minimum, it is a family in which two or more languages are used regularly. Thus, families who use one language most of the time but use a second language once a week in church or chapel are included, as are families where only one parent uses a second language, perhaps for work. In both examples, the use of two languages defines the family as bilingual.

As discussed earlier, to know a language is not the same as to use it. There is not much point describing a family as bilingual simply because both parents studied a second language at school, or even at university. They may never refer to that knowledge in the bustle of family life. Furthermore, most people cannot say how much they know of a language, or how well they know their own first language. It does not take a linguist to know that 'were drove in a road the car' is ungrammatical, or to re-order correctly the adjectives in 'the metal red heavy old large box', but people surprise themselves when they can do this. Knowledge of a language is difficult to quantify and may be irrelevant. Language behaviour, in contrast, is easier to describe and only occurs when needed. For a second language to be relevant to family life it needs to be used.

There are many ways of using languages differentially. Communities may employ different languages for different purposes, but the rules are usually reasonably overt. Latin was used for Roman Catholic church services until a few years ago, but not for gossiping afterwards, for example: and many countries have an official language for formal occasions and one or more vernacular languages. Even within one community, bilingual language use in the family develops in a less ordered way (with a few exceptions). Bilingual families differ according to who speaks which language/s within the home, how frequently they do so, and which, if any, of these languages is spoken in the community. In reporting strategies adopted by parents to promote bilingual development in their children, Schmidt-Mackey (1971) and Romaine (1995) have both described a few of the possible kinds of bilingual family.

Family bilingualism

Romaine (1995) suggested a typology of bilingual acquisition in childhood based on earlier suggestions by Harding and Riley (1986). Confining herself to reported studies, she describes six types as follows:

(1) Type 1. 'One person-one language'
    This type is well documented and epitomised by Ronjat (1913) and Leopold (1939; 1949). Parents who are competent in two languages each speak only one language to the child. One of the languages is usually the dominant language of the community.

(2) Type 2. 'Non-dominant home language'
    Here the language of one parent is that of the community, but both use only a non-dominant language at home and the child hears the dominant language only in the community (e.g. Fantini, 1985).

(3) Type 3. 'Non-dominant home language without community support'
    Parents share a language which is not the dominant language in the community (e.g. Haugen, 1969).

(4) Type 4. 'Double non-dominant language without community support'
    Parents have different first languages which both differ from the language dominant in the community and use their first languages with the child (e.g. Elwert, 1959).

(5) Type 5. 'Non-native parents'
    The parents share a first language which is the community language, but one of them always uses a second language with the child (e.g. Saunders 1982).

(6) Type 6. 'Mixed languages'
    Parents are bilingual and the community may also be bilingual. They use a mix of both languages with the child. This is a less clear-cut type (e.g. Burling, 1959).

The studies cited are each reports of one or two children in particular families. Arguably, families who control the language input to children so closely are atypical. Romaine (1995) does add the suggestion that Type 6, where children hear a mixture of two or more languages, is a more common kind of bilingual family than would appear from the literature. Although single cases have often highlighted issues in bilingual development relevant to all children (such as code-switching, mixing and metalingual awareness), few studies have looked at bilingual development in commonplace family situations.

A classification that more nearly fits commonplace families was suggested some years ago by Schmidt-Mackey (1971). She described dichotomy and alternation as the two basic strategies employed to foster bilingual language development, and then sub-classified them as follows;

(1) 'Dichotomy-person'
    This is the familiar 'one person-one language' strategy first suggested to Ronjat by Grammont in 1913.

(2) 'Dichotomy-place'
    This strategy too is commonplace, though adopted by necessity as much as by intention. It is found where the language of the home is different from that of the community, and as such describes the circumstances of the children of immigrants. These strategies can work well.

(3) 'Dichotomy-time, topic, activity'
    Under this heading is included staging (wherein the second language is introduced only when parents are confident that the first is well established) timing (where, for example, languages are changed from day to day) and topic (where the language is predetermined by the activity). All versions of this strategy have proved difficult to implement.

(4) 'Alternation'
    Alternation is the alternating use of both languages, either freely or conditioned. The topic or activity may evoke one rather than another language, or a monolingual guest may dictate the language of a particular conversation.

Alternation, like Romaine's Type 6, probably comes closest to describing commonplace bilingualism. However, as it is a less controlled and more varied kind of situation, it is less easy to report and so has received less attention. As Schmidt-Mackey, who clearly does not think much of restrictive strategies, comments: 'At least in some cases alternation does not lead to disaster.' (1971:139)

The importance of input in language acquisition

In the ordinary, non-controlled bilingual environment described above as 'Mixed' or 'Alternation', it becomes very important to describe accurately the quality and quantity of the language input to the child. If one or both parents mix their languages, a child is likely to learn to mix languages. If one or both parents use very little of a second language, the child likewise may rarely use that language. And if everyone within a child's hearing borrows regularly from a dominant language, then the child's language will be full of borrowings.

DeHouwer (1990) and Goodz (1994) provide two of the rare studies which look in detail at the language environment of the child (although DeHower's subject, Kate, is also a special child whose parents are middle-class professional people). DeHouwer charts the time Kate spends with each member of the family and in a variety of situations, and notes the language used on each occasion. She does not, however, record the actual language used by Kate's partners, and so any evidence of models for borrowing and mixing is unavailable.

Language Use in a Community

Language backgrounds

For the Anglesey Project parents were asked about their language use. It is the language used that children hear (and presumably learn). The Language Background Questionnaire allows parents to be classified according to their use of Welsh and English across a number of situations (Lyon, 1991). This was sent to a cohort of the mothers of babies born in one year (1988–1989), and couples were distributed as shown in Table 5.1.

Table 5.1 Distribution of couples, broken down by language use

		N	(%)
Welsh	(WW)	93	24.2
Welsh mother	(WM)	36	9.4
Mixed	(MM)	77	20.1
Welsh father	(WF)	46	12.0
English	(EE)	132	34.4
Total sample		384	100.0

Following classification as mainly Welsh speaking (W), mainly English speaking (E) and those using a mixture of languages (M), five groups were defined; Welsh-speaking parents (WW), English-speaking parents (EE), couples with a Welsh-speaking mother and a non-Welsh-speaking father (WM), couples with a Welsh-speaking father and a non-Welsh-speaking mother (WF) and finally mixed language couples (MM). According to the definition at the beginning of the chapter, all of the WW couples are bilingual, as are those in the WM, MM and WF groups. Although Welsh is the language of choice, English is used for some situations in all of these families, if only for communicating with monolingual English neighbours. Monolinguals are commonly English speakers and English speakers are commonly monolingual.

Language use in Welsh families

When classified into couples, less than a quarter of the replying families were classified as primarily Welsh speaking, and about a third were classified as primarily English speaking. However, that does mean that by including mixed language partnerships, in almost two-thirds of the families in the sample the Welsh language was used to some extent in some situations by at least one of the partners. Although the range of two-language use is wide, two-thirds of these families are providing a bilingual environment for their children.

There were some similarities in the language use of couples in the EE and WW groups. Both kinds of family had a main language which they used virtually exclusively with their own parents, with their children, at church or chapel and at work, much as one would expect. In the past they had used only their main language for most encounters, and mostly their friends shared their language. However, WW couples communicated with friends in their second language more frequently than did the EE couples, either because they have a linguistically wider range of friends or because they are more linguistically accommodating.

Some Welsh is used in four of the five types of family, but only Welsh-speaking couples (WW) use Welsh frequently. Even where one partner is primarily Welsh speaking (as in WM and WF groups), the cumulative effect is for that language to be used less in a range of situations than if both partners had been first language Welsh speakers. All of the people in the survey can speak English. Thus, the need to communicate easily and quickly means that a couple will tend to rely on their common language when together, and in over 75% of families this is English.

Preference for one language is more clearly evident in some situations than others. If Welsh is spoken at work, or with children, this encourages the use of that language by infrequent Welsh speakers. Shopping and conversation with neighbours or friends, on the other hand, is almost always conducted in English by the English-speaking couples and by English-speaking partners. Welsh-speaking mothers are more adaptable. They will use English with friends, neighbours, when shopping and at work. There seems to be more adaptation towards English language usage than towards use of the Welsh language.

Viewing, reading and thinking by parents

In the questionnaire, three questions were asked concerning parents' preferred language for reading, thinking and watching television. The majority of programmes shown on a fourth television channel in North Wales (S4C) are in Welsh. Although those on other channels are never in Welsh, a choice of medium does exist.

Even so, 76% of the total sample almost always watch English-language television, with just 6% preferring mostly Welsh television (Table 5.2). Doubtless the content of programmes has a major influence on these choices.

Table 5.2 Language used for watching television by parent and by language background group (QI) *(for notes see next page)*

		Almost always and mostly Welsh		Half and half		Almost always and mostly English	
		M	F	M	F	M	F
WW	N = 90	21%	19%	41%	39%	38%	42%
WM	N = 35	6%	0%	38%	3%	56%	97%
MM	N = 74	0%	0%	12%	13%	88%	87%
WF	N = 43	0%	12%	22%	37%	78%	51%
EE	N = 132	0%	0%	1%	1%	99%	99%
Total	N = 374	6%	6%	19%	17%	75%	77%

Notes for Table 5.2
WW = Parents are both primarily Welsh-speaking.
WM = Welsh-speaking mother and non-Welsh-speaking father.
MM = Parents have a mixed-language background.
WF = Welsh-speaking father and non-Welsh-speaking mother.
EE = Parents are both primarily English-speaking.

About a fifth of the WW group mostly choose programmes in Welsh, but over two fifths mostly choose programmes in English, the rest swopping channels. Welsh mothers in the WM group and Welsh fathers in the WF group behaved less like parents in the all-Welsh group than in other circumstances; fewer Welsh parents from cross-language partnerships watched mostly Welsh programmes than did those married to Welsh-speaking partners. Watching television is usually a joint enterprise. Therefore it is likely that, unless both parents want to watch a Welsh-medium programme, it is easier to choose an English-medium compromise.

The English language also dominates most people's reading. Table 5.3 shows that 86% of the total virtually always read in English and that

Table 5.3 Language used for reading by parent and by language background group (QI)

		Almost always and mostly Welsh		Half and half		Almost always and mostly English	
		M	F	M	F	M	F
WW	N = 92	17%	14%	23%	24%	60%	62%
WM	N = 35	12%	0%	17%	0%	71%	100%
MM	N = 76	0%	1%	3%	4%	97%	95%
WF	N = 46	0%	12%	4%	21%	96%	67%
EE	N = 132	0%	0%	0%	0%	100%	100%
Total	N = 381	5%	5%	8%	9%	87%	86%

WW = Parents are both primarily Welsh-speaking.
WM = Welsh-speaking mother and non-Welsh-speaking father.
MM = Parents have a mixed-language background.
WF = Welsh-speaking father and non-Welsh-speaking mother.
EE = Parents are both primarily English-speaking.

includes about 60% of the WW group. Just 16% of that group mostly read in Welsh. Here mothers in the WM group and fathers in the WF group did behave like parents in the WW group. This is, however, a complicated choice. A lot depends on the range and quality of literature available in the two languages, and a similar point holds for television programmes.

Predictably, there were significant differences in the language preferred for thinking (Table 5.4). Most parents in the WW group tended to think in Welsh, as did 68% of the mothers in the WM group. Mothers in the WF group tended to think in English (about 84%) as did fathers in the WM group (94%). All of the EE parents thought in English almost exclusively.

Table 5.4 Language used for thinking by parent and by language background group (QI)

		Almost always and mostly Welsh		Half and half		Almost always and mostly English	
		M	F	M	F	M	F
WW	N = 92	89%	84%	4%	11%	7%	5%
WM	N = 35	68%	6%	17%	0%	14%	94%
MM	N = 76	5%	7%	5%	13%	90%	80%
WF	N = 46	5%	49%	11%	37%	84%	14%
EE	N = 132	0%	0%	0%	0%	100%	100%
Total	N = 381	30%	28%	5%	10%	65%	62%

WW = Parents are both primarily Welsh-speaking.
WM = Welsh-speaking mother and non-Welsh-speaking father.
MM = Parents have a mixed-language background.
WF = Welsh-speaking father and non-Welsh-speaking mother.
EE = Parents are both primarily English-speaking.

Apart from an occasional look at Welsh television, the English-speaking couples used English exclusively: they thought in English, read in English and watched English language television. Taking the other extreme group, the majority of the Welsh-speaking couples thought in Welsh, but only a minority confined their reading to the Welsh language and or mostly watched Welsh language television. By and large the Welsh-speaking partners in the cross-language partnerships made similar choices. The clearest difference between the groups was found in their choice of language for thinking (that is, if choice is the most accurate description). All English-speaking couples think in English virtually all of the time and most Welsh-speaking couples think in Welsh virtually all of the time.

Talking to One Another

The influence of gender

As one might expect, the Welsh couples and the English couples speak to one another in their main language. In families where the mother is Welsh speaking and the father is not (WM), they almost always use English. More Welsh is used in WF families where the father is Welsh speaking and the mother's first language is not Welsh.

There are interesting comparisons to be made between the women in the WM group and those in the WW group. The latter have partners who are primarily Welsh speaking whereas the former have not. There is a difference of up to 30% between those in the WM group and those in the WW group who use mostly Welsh in all the situations listed except with their own parents. One can understand that those in cross-language partnerships will have more friends who are monolingual English speakers. It is more surprising that fewer of these women use mostly Welsh when shopping, at church or chapel and with children. This predominance of English would suggest that the influence of a non-Welsh-speaking partner is wide-ranging.

This influence is primarily the influence of the male partner. Almost 30% of the Welsh-speaking men in the WF group use mainly Welsh with their non-Welsh-speaking partners. Far fewer Welsh-speaking women in the WM group (19%) use Welsh with their non-Welsh-speaking partners. Perhaps women are just better at learning a second language. What little evidence there is in the literature on second language learning supports the suggestion that this might be the case (see, for example Carroll & Sapon, 1959).

The influence of language

Caution is necessary in interpreting these results. The language itself appears to ave a greater influence than gender. More mothers in the WM group (75%), and more fathers in the WF group (57%) spoke to their English-speaking partner in English than fathers in the WM group and mothers in the WF group used Welsh with their Welsh-speaking partner (17% and 27% respectively).

Language and gender

This evidence further indicates that the father has more influence on language use in the home. When he is the Welsh speaker, he is spoken to in Welsh by his non-first language Welsh wife in about 27% of WF couples, whereas when the mother is the Welsh speaker she is spoken to in Welsh by her non-first language Welsh husband in only 17% of WM couples. Conversely, when he is the English speaker he is spoken to in English by his Welsh-speaking wife in 75% of WM couples, whereas when the mother is the English speaker she is spoken to in English by her Welsh-speaking husband in only 57% of WF couples.

If those in groups WF and WM who reported using both languages equally are included with the 'Almost always' or 'Mostly Welsh' couples, the effect is clearer. More than 43% of Welsh-speaking fathers in cross-language marriages use Welsh at least half of the time to their wives and 39% of them are spoken to in Welsh at least as often by their wives. By comparison, in the WM group, 25% of Welsh-speaking mothers use Welsh at least half the time with their husbands and only 20% of them are spoken to in Welsh at least as often by their husbands. That is, two-fifths of primarily English-speaking women use a substantial amount of Welsh with their Welsh-speaking husbands, whereas only one-fifth of primarily English-speaking men communicate similarly in Welsh with their Welsh-speaking wives. The women who completed this questionnaire emerge as more likely to accommodate their husband's main language than he is to accommodate theirs.

In the factor analysis reported earlier, the language used by these parents with their mothers in the past had a similar high factor loading to that of the language they used with their fathers. This indicates that there is little difference between using Welsh with your father or your mother as a child. Both are significantly associated with becoming a Welsh-speaking adult. In the group of couples where each has a mixed language background, the gender effect is not evident. Nearly 90% of fathers spoke to their partner in English almost all of the time and almost 90% of mothers spoke to their partner in English most of the time.

Thus, with the exception of the quarter of the sample in the Welsh (WW) group, the vast bulk of all conversations for couples from four out of five kinds of background are in English. Further details of this study can be found in Lyon (1993).

Summary

There is no generally accepted classification of bilingual families. Romaine (1995) has suggested a typology of strategies used by bilingual families based on published reports. However, the classification suggested by Schmidt-Mackey (1971) appears more relevant to commonplace bilingual families. The importance of language input to the growing child was also discussed, highlighting the need for descriptions of parental language.

A classification is suggested here based on the preferred language use of each parent across a number of situations. This gives two primary language groups (WW and EE), two cross-language groups (WM and WF), and a mixed (MM) group. This classification was used in the Anglesey project and showed that only a quarter of the couples in the sample used Welsh frequently and in a wide range of situations, while about a third used virtually no Welsh. Some Welsh was spoken in the remaining two-thirds of families and this varied according to the situation. Factors influencing choice of language use include cross-language partnerships, gender of Welsh speaker, and some specific situations. Most of the time primarily English-speaking women with Welsh-speaking partners will tend to use Welsh with children or at work. In contrast, Welsh-speaking women married to primarily English-speaking men will tend to use English in most situations.

The majority of subjects in the Welsh-speaking groups thought mainly in Welsh, while all of the subjects in the English-speaking group thought in English. It was this which most clearly differentiated the groups. Most of the subjects in the mixed groups also tended to think in English.

Reading mainly in Welsh was the choice of 14% of Welsh speakers only (38 or 265 subjects), with almost everyone in the other groups reading mainly in English. More people chose to watch some Welsh language television than to read Welsh and they came from all groups. However, the bulk of the total sample watch English language programmes almost exclusively, and read English almost exclusively. These figures partly reflect available choices. Even with a channel broadcasting many programmes in Welsh, the greater part of television is transmitted through the medium of English. Reading material in Welsh is similarly limited.

Finally, the suggestion arises in the data that fathers have a more influential role in choice of language use within the family than do mothers. This will be discussed further in a later chapter.

6 What Opinions Do Parents Hold About Language?

Introduction

Attitudes and opinions

The amount of energy we have available for any enterprise is influenced by our dislike or enthusiasm. Enthusiastic parents can encourage and enrich the development of their children, but virtually all children develop language, whether or not parents take an interest in the process. Similarly, in a bilingual setting children will pick up words and phrases from two or more languages; but now there is a choice and with choice come opinions and attitudes. Languages are associated with the people who use them and the contexts in which they are used. A mother who was humiliated by teachers because of her poor English may go to a lot of trouble to ensure that her child goes to a Welsh-medium school. The father who always thought that his Welsh-speaking grandparents were rigid and old fashioned is unlikely to put much effort into encouraging his child to learn Welsh. Parents can ensure that their children are exposed to two languages and encourage their use, or they can avoid and discourage acknowledgement of any language other than their native language.

As shown in the work of Gardner and Lambert (1972), the attitudes and opinions of adults towards languages play a major part in whether they themselves become bilingual or not. Sharp *et al.* (1973) showed that the attitudes of bilingual adolescents change, as does their language use. By age 14, their attitude towards English became more favourable and towards Welsh less favourable. Correspondingly, their use of English increased and of Welsh declined. These results were confirmed by Price-Jones almost a decade later (Price-Jones, 1982). Thus, the attitude of the speaker affects the

the speaker affects the use or non-use of two languages by older children and adults. The language use of younger children is affected by the attitudes of their parents (and teachers).

Because of the paucity of research, the focus of this chapter is on the work carried out by the author in this area.

The questionnaires

In the Anglesey Project, the Language Background Questionnaire described earlier (QI) was used. This had a number of questions included to gauge the attitudes of parents towards the Welsh language. They were asked how much Welsh they wanted their child to learn and invited to give reasons for their answers. They were asked how important they thought it was for children to learn Welsh and for their opinions about the future of the Welsh language. Finally, they were encouraged to add comments and most of those who did spoke of their thoughts and feelings about the language and culture of Wales.

Three years later QII was sent to the same parents and some questions were repeated. They were again asked about the amount of Welsh they wanted their children to learn and asked to give reasons for their answers. Further comments were also invited. Many of the comments charted the progress of their children, but many more were expressions of opinion about the Welsh language.

Some further information was gathered in the process of selecting subjects for the small sample. In the informal setting of a face-to-face interview, the mothers talked freely about their aspirations for their children, their partners' opinions about Welsh, and about their own feelings of Welshness. These data are selective, but illustrate the depth and divergence of opinion that exists. It may not be a general phenomenon, but in North Wales everyone has an opinion about the Welsh and English languages and their relationship to one another.

Parents in North Wales

Language expectations

The question about how much Welsh parents wanted their children to learn was structured so that to be 'fluent' appeared as a step further than 'to learn Welsh at school'. The other options were 'to pick up some Welsh' or 'to learn only English', although space was left for respondents to specify alternative options.

The majority of parents (86%) wanted their children to learn Welsh at school, or to be fluent in Welsh (Table 6.1). Only about 5% (almost all from the EE group), wanted their children to learn only English. In the EE group there was less overall enthusiasm for Welsh learning by their children, although 71% wanted them to learn Welsh at school or to be fluent. This group does not necessarily comprise only English-born incomers. Many Welsh-born parents from Welsh cultural backgrounds use virtually no Welsh, and so were included in the EE group. None the less, this high proportion of support for the teaching of Welsh comes from parents with English cultural as well as Welsh cultural backgrounds.

Table 6.1 Parental choice of child language (QI) by language background group

	English only		Some Welsh		School Welsh		Fluent Welsh	
	M %	F %	M %	F %	M %	F %	M %	F %
WW	0	0	0	0	2	2	98	98
WM	0	0	6	6	3	8	92	86
MM	3	3	16	9	23	22	58	66
WF	0	0	4	2	20	15	76	83
EE	14	15	15	13	46	45	26	26
All	5	6	9	7	24	23	62	64

Replies shown as the percentage of mothers (M) and fathers (F) in each group.

The pattern of replies in the cross-language groups differed greatly from the EE group, and more nearly matched the WW group. However, 95% of Welsh-speaking mothers in WM and 98% of Welsh-speaking fathers in WF wanted their children to learn Welsh at school or to be fluent. Virtually all families with one or more Welsh-speaking parent wanted this for their child. Rather more of the families with a non Welsh-speaking mother chose school Welsh for their child, which may relate to views about mothers being responsible for teaching the 'mother tongue' at home. The influence of parental gender on the language in the home will be discussed in a later chapter.

A sizeable minority of all the Welsh speakers wanted their children to learn their Welsh from school (5% of all Welsh-speaking mothers and 18% of all Welsh-speaking fathers). It may be that parents are just choosing the easiest option, or it may reflect the lack of confidence demonstrated in the following comment: 'I can use better Welsh than I use in everyday speaking.' (Mother in WM group).

Reasons for wanting children to learn Welsh (or not)

Although respondents were asked to give reasons why they wanted, or did not want, their children to learn Welsh, not everyone did so, and some gave many reasons. The English-speaking group contributed more than any of the rest.

These reasons were originally grouped into seven categories, most of them positive (Lyon & Ellis, 1991). In the light of results from the second questionnaire, they were re-examined and grouped into eight categories, largely so that comments emphasising the importance of learning both languages could be identified. Previously such reasons had been included in Group 2 ('Generally a good Idea') and Group 4 ('Good for Communication').

Questionnaire One (1989)

(1)   Both languages are important

This 'both languages' group included general positive comments about being bilingual and comments (mostly from Welsh families) stressing the importance of learning English:

'I think it's good for children to be bilingual,' or again
'I would like my child to speak both Welsh and English fluently.'

(40 comments, 9%)

(2)   Generally a good idea

Some simply stated that it would be an advantage to be able to speak Welsh, without elaborating:

'It will make them a better person.'

(67 comments, 16%)

(3) Job prospects

The next group felt that Welsh speaking would enhance their children's future job prospects:

'Because he'll be classed as Welsh-speaking for getting a job.'

(56 comments, 13%)

(4) Good for communication

The need for good communication in a second language to help children to fit into the local community were the reasons in the next group:

'So that they can converse with friends who are Welsh-speaking and can understand Welsh if spoken to.'

(50 comments, 12%)

(5) Unfocused comments

Some ignored the question as such and commented on the means of learning, or on their own language experiences:

'He should learn Welsh at school because children learn better with other children.'

(56 comments, 13%)

(6) Keep back the English

One small group of answers expressed anti-English feelings:

'Mae gormod o Seuson yn byw yn Cymru, rhaid cael madal a nhw.'
('There are too many English living in Wales, we must get rid of them.')

(3 comments, 1%)

(7) Irrelevant or unnecessary

There were also some who were opposed to their children learning Welsh. Mostly it was felt to be unnecessary or irrelevant:

'Welsh is a backward step,' or
'My husband is in the RAF and so we are only visitors here.'

(45 comments, 10%)

(8) Welsh identity and heritage

However, the largest group of replies related to having a Welsh identity:

'It is important for her to have strong roots and an appreciation of her heritage,' and

'Am ein bod ni yn Gymraeg, nid Saeson.'

(Because we are Welsh not English.)

(113 comments, 26%)

Thus, the set of reasons given most often by all subjects were related to a feeling of Welshness. People wrote that they were proud of their heritage, that Welsh was their mother tongue, that all of their friends and family spoke Welsh, that their child had been born in Wales and that it was important to keep the language alive: 'Gwlad neb iaith, gwlad heb galon.' (Land without a language, land without a heart) (Mother in WW group).

Table 6.2 Types of reason given for wanting (or not wanting) children to learn Welsh by language background group

1989	WW (%)	WM (%)	MM (%)	WF (%)	EE (%)	All (%)
1. Both languages important	9	24	11	21	1	9
2. A good job	6	10	18	14	21	16
3. Better job prospects	2	10	22	10	16	13
4. Good for communication	6	0	12	12	18	12
5. Unfocused comments	16	16	8	14	13	13
6. Keep back the English	2	0	1	0	0	1
7. Irrelevant or unnecessary	0	5	5	2	22	10
8. Welsh identity and heritage	60	36	23	26	8	26
	100	100	100	100	100	100
Number of comments	89	42	92	42	165	430
Number of subjects	93	36	77	46	132	384

Results are from QI, completed shortly after the children were born in 1989. (Revised 1993.) Figures are given as percentage scores in each group.

Predictably these were the reasons given by the majority of the WW group, but they were also the reasons chosen most often by the cross-language groups (WM = 36%; WF = 26%) and by those from a mixed language background. The feeling behind many of the replies was that the answer was so obvious that it almost did not need to be written: 'because we're Welsh!'

The group of comments that did not answer the question could not be analysed further, and the anti-English and irrelevant Welsh groups require little further explanation. They came from monolingual Welsh and English groups respectively and from only a handful of families.

Enhancement of future job prospects was a popular reason given, especially by the EE (16%) and MM (22%) groups. In Gwynedd, most posts in local government require the ability to communicate in both languages, and in many other jobs throughout Wales that skill is an added advantage. Parents in these two groups are either not frequent Welsh-language users, or else do not speak Welsh. They have been made aware of the disadvantage entailed and therefore it is realistic for them to wish to ensure that their children learn Welsh.

A relatively large proportion of the replies also cited the ability to communicate and to fit into the community as reasons for learning Welsh. Again the groups less competent in Welsh chose these reasons, 12% of the MM group and 18% of the EE group. Possibly these parents have been made aware of communication difficulties, and have felt like outsiders. Parents in the cross-language families (WF and WM) most frequently cited the importance of both languages as a reason for their children to learn Welsh. Presumably this is because cross-language partnership increases the salience of bilingualism.

The importance of children learning Welsh

Parents were asked to assign an importance to their children learning the Welsh language on a four-point scale from 'unimportant' to 'very important'. In the total sample, 80% felt it was quite important or very important. There were a few don't knows, but only 18% felt it was unimportant or not very important.

It was not surprising to find that few in the WW group (about 4%) felt that it was not very important for their children to learn Welsh, or that 78% felt it was very important. Even more support would have been predicted. Most of those who said it was unimportant came from the EE group, but 17% of them dissented, saying it was very important. The majority of this group, as every group in the sample, felt that Welsh learning was either quite important or very important.

Expectations for the Welsh language

Overall, the majority expect that the Welsh language will be used about the same amount in the future as it is at present (56%). About 28% believe it will be used less than English or will be replaced by English, and 15% believe it will be used more or that it will replace English. As one might expect, those believing that Welsh would be used more in the future came mainly from the WW group (25%), and also from the Welsh-speaking men in the WF group (24%), but not from the Welsh-speaking women in the WM group (only 6%). The obverse pattern was similar, but not completely so. Those who believe Welsh will be used less comprise the non-Welsh-speaking men in the WM group (36%), the non Welsh-speaking women in the WF group (31%) and men in the EE group (34%).

There is a tendency for people to expect that things will go on much the same as they have in the past, although the evidence for the overall decline of the Welsh language between the census of 1971 and that of 1981 (and even 1991) does not support this optimism. Of those who think there will be change, more think that the language will be used less than think it will be used more. In particular, the non-Welsh-speakers think it will diminish, if there is a change, whereas the Welsh speakers are evenly divided,(with one exception). Those that thought the Welsh language would be used more, or might even replace English in the future were largely Welsh speakers. However, Welsh-speaking women married to English-speaking husbands do not fit the pattern. More English-speaking women think Welsh is on the increase than do this group. A similar relation does not appear in the responses for the fathers. Welsh-speaking men, whether married to Welsh-speaking women or not, are more likely to believe Welsh will be used more than are English-speaking men, much as one might expect. It would seem that to marry a non-Welsh-speaking partner is more likely to decrease your optimism about the future of the language if you are female than if you are male.

Three Years Later

Are language expectations the same?

The second questionnaire was distributed three years after the first. In this, parents were again asked about the amount of Welsh they wanted their children to learn, and Table 6.3 shows how they responded. Again the majority of all families wanted their children to learn Welsh at school or else to be fluent in Welsh (88% overall). Virtually all parents in families with a Welsh-speaking partner wanted their children to be fluent in Welsh, as did more than 80% of parents with mixed language backgrounds. Understandably, the English-speaking parents were not as whole-hearted as the rest. However, even in this group, a third of mothers and more than 40% of fathers wanted their children to become fluent Welsh speakers, and only 8% of mothers and 16% of fathers didn't want them to learn any Welsh.

Table 6.3 Second questionnaire, QII (n = 122). Amount of Welsh learning wanted for thie children by language background (children now age three)

	English only		Some Welsh		School Welsh		Fluent Welsh	
	M %	F %	M %	F %	M %	F %	M %	F %
WW	0	3	0	0	0	0	100	98
WM	0	0	0	0	0	6	100	94
MM	0	0	3	3	13	10	83	90
WF	0	0	0	0	0	0	100	100
EE	8	16	31	16	28	27	33	41
All	3	6	9	5	12	11	76	78

Figures are percentages of mothers (M) and fathers (F) in each language background group.

There is more similarity than difference between these results and those obtained three years previously. About the same percentage of parents overall want their children to learn Welsh at school or to fluency (86% of mothers and 87% of fathers at QI and 88% and 89% respectively at QII). However, 14% more of both parents wanted them to be fluent on the second occasion. Maybe the parents have become more confident in their own ability to facilitate fluency, or maybe they have less faith in the schools' ability to do that for them.

On the second occasion, the EE families seem to be more satisfied with children only picking up some Welsh, and the MM families seem less satisfied with this option. Perhaps they were both being more realistic about what was possible, linguistically, given their respective back-grounds. The proportion opting for English only remained virtually the same; 5% of mothers and 6% of fathers on the first occasion and 3% and 6% respectively at QII.

Thus, it is clear that on both occasions the vast majority of parents wanted their children to learn Welsh.

Have reasons for wanting children to learn Welsh or not changed?

Again not all parents added comments or gave reasons for their choice of language learning for their children, and again the EE group is proportionally more verbose than the others. Comments were organised into the eight groups described earlier in the chapter, and many had a similar flavour (Table 6.4).

Table 6.4 Types of reason given for wanting (or not wanting) children to learn Welsh by language background group. Result from Questionnaire II, shortly after the children were three years old in 1992.

1992	WW (%)	WM (%)	MM (%)	WF (%)	EE (%)	All (%)
1. Both languages important	29	21	8	20	8	17
2. It is an advantage	2	3	13	0	8	6
3. Better job prospects	0	9	13	10	8	7
4. Communication	2	6	10	10	14	8
5. Non-reason comments	19	27	29	0	24	23
6. Keep back the English	5	0	0	0	0	2
7. Irrelevant or unnecessary	0	3	6	20	30	11
8. Welsh identity and heritage	43	30	22	40	7	26
	100	100	100	100	100	100
Number of comments	98	33	63	10	86	290
Number of couples	38	15	33	5	33	124

Questionnaire Two (1992)

(1) Both languages are important

The 'both languages' group of reasons was more in evidence this time:

' ...a siared Saesneg yn rhugl, dysgu Ffrangeg yn yr ysgol a codi rhywfaint ar ieithoedd Ewropiaidd eraill.' (...and speak English fluently, learn French in school and pick up some other European languages), and

'Eventually I wish my child to be as fluent in English as he is in Welsh.'

(49 comments, 17%)

(2) Generally a good idea

There were still some comments which merely stated that learning Welsh would be advantageous:

'I can see only advantages in bilingualism,' and
"rwyf eisiau'r plant fod yn hollol ddwy-ieithog.'
(I want the children to be completely bilingual)

(18 comments, 6%)

(3) Job prospects

Job prospects were again mentioned, but by fewer people:

'Not being able to speak Welsh is a disadvantage when it comes to getting a job, etc.'

(19 comments, 7%)

(4) Good for communication

Communicating with neighbours and generally fitting into the local community reappeared:

'To integrate into North Wales society fully she will need to speak Welsh.'

(23 comments, 8%)

(5) Unfocused comments

Non-answers were more in evidence, and people seemed to be happy to comment widely on the family experience of the two languages:

'The only reason for our lack of speaking Welsh is sheer laziness I'm afraid,' and
'I would find it extremely odd speaking English to a member of my family when Welsh is the first language.'

(67 comments, 23%)

(6) Keep back the English

Anti-English comments remained rare but were passionately felt:

'Fyddai ddim yn cyfnabod Saesneg yn iaith cyfreithlon yn Gymru' (We'll never accept English as an official language in Wales), and 'Tosa (nid oes) ddim fashiwn iaith a Saesneg 6 iaith wedi rhoi yn i gilydd iw hi. Trafoddaith fo adiriad o dros clawth Offa' (There's no such language as English, it's 6 languages put together. Send it back (?) across Offa's dyke).

(5 comments, 2%)

(7) Irrelevant or unnecessary

There were again a number of comments arguing that Welsh was irrelevant, unnecessary or positively confusing:

'Why should she have to be forced to learn a useless language when the rest of the entire world is learning ENGLISH!?' and 'English will take him further in the world than Welsh will.'

(33 comments, 11%)

(8) Welsh identity and heritage

Finally, the strength of the Welsh Identity comments remained high:

'Eisiau rhoi etifeddiaeth Cymraeg iddynt' (I want to give their Welsh inheritance to them), and 'Cymraeg yw iaith y cartref a'r wlad' (Welsh is the language of the home and the country), and again 'Cymraeg yn ei fam iaith a felly fe hoffwn iddo gael ei addysg yn Gymraeg' (Welsh is his mother language and so I want him to get his education in Welsh)

(76 comments, 26%)

The greatest number of reasons were in this last category (N = 76), and comprised more than 40% of the total comments in the WW and WF groups, but also 7% of the comments from the EE group. The generally chatty, non-reason comments formed the next largest category, and were well represented in all but the WF groups. People wrote about how their children were becoming bilingual, about what they thought of the local education policy, about the differences between their children's and their own experiences, and so on. Between them, these two categories covered virtually half of the total comments made.

The fewest reasons were anti-English (N = 5), and these five comments came from only two questionnaires. Job prospects, better communication and general advantage reasons made up less than 10% of the replies each, the EE group being more keen to communicate and the MM group more often looking to job prospects and general advantage.

The most frequent comment made by the EE group focused on the irrelevance of learning Welsh, but only the WW group produced no comments in this vein. The last category to be discussed is the one which became more evident as a theme in this second questionnaire, namely the reasons stressing the importance of both languages. They comprised more than 20% of comments in all three groups with a first language Welsh speaker, and 17% of comments overall. This accords with a finding by Williams (1979) that, although Welsh-speaking families want their children educated through the medium of Welsh, they do not want them to lose the advantages of speaking English as well.

Comparisons

Both at the time of the birth of their child and when that child was about three years old, the majority of parents wanted their children to become fluent Welsh speakers. On the first occasion, 63% opted for fluency and that had increased to 77% three years later. Many of the remainder wanted their children to be taught Welsh at school, with less than 14% wanting little or no Welsh learning for their children on either occasion. In t-tests (reported in detail in Chapter 10) there were no significant differences between the answers given by either parent on the two occasions.

Turning to the reasons given for the above question, Table 6.5 (overleaf) shows that, apart from a greater number of general comments, the biggest increase was in comments supporting the two languages, a jump from 9% to 17% of the total. Allegiance to the Welsh culture, dislike of the English and irritation with the Welsh language remained at similar levels.

The percentage of comments about the general advantage of speaking Welsh, and its usefulness in getting a job and in integrating into the neighbourhood, all declined. Wider sociopolitical forces may well account for some of this change. The worsening job market means that there are very few vacancies, and so the ability to speak Welsh can no longer be seen as a passport to full employment. On the other hand, anyone fluent in both English and Welsh is in the best position to take advantage of whatever opportunities do arise, wherever they arise.

Table 6.5 Types of reason given for wanting (or not wanting) children to learn Welsh

	QI 1989 (%)	QII 1992 (%)
1. Both languages are important	9	17
2. It is an advantage	16	6
3. Better job prospects	13	7
4. Communication	12	8
5. Non-reason comments	13	23
6. Keep back the English	1	2
7. Irrelevant or unnecessary	10	11
8. Welsh identity and heritage	26	26
	100	100
Number of comments	430	290
Number of couples	384	124

Figures given are the percentage of comments on each occasion.

This information, from a large questionnaire sample, gives an overall impression of the opinions of parents about the language environment of their children. Only a limited number of questions can be asked in a postal questionnaire. Thus, although the small sample can only provide answers from 10 more families, they can give more fine-grained information about the attitudes and opinions they hold.

Individual families

All families who volunteered to take part in the small sample were interviewed so that they could be matched as nearly as possible. This interview took place within a few weeks of the birth of the babies and, although informal, asked detailed questions about many aspects of the family and future plans. During this meeting, opinions about the Welsh language were expressed by most families incidentally, and these were all noted.

Throughout subsequent recording sessions, discussion was encouraged about the specifics of actual language use within the family, and mothers were asked about their thoughts concerning their child's language and about their opinions regarding the Welsh language in general. These too were noted informally. Although neither source is representative, the views recorded provide some clues about the interplay between attitude and action.

Inevitably there were differences amongst all 10 families, even between the two families in the same category. Michael's parents (EE) did not have any Welsh aspirations for him, whereas the other EE parents wanted Llywela to be bilingual eventually and were trying to learn Welsh themselves. By the eighth session, Llywela's mother reported that her teachers at Ysgol Feithrin (similar to a Nursery School) said that she understood a lot of Welsh and was using some Welsh words and phrases. Michael's mother could not recall hearing him use any Welsh words before they left the area when he was 33 months old. Both of the WW families (Iwan and Nerys) and Becky's WM parents wanted their children to have a Welsh future. For them all that meant living in Wales, probably marrying a Welsh speaker and being bilingual. Speaking Welsh as a first language was taken for granted, and all three said they would avoid a school that was 'too Welshy' and that they were anti-extremist. The other WM family wanted Emyr to grow up in Wales, 'but not to be stuck here'. They too wanted him to be bilingual. All four children were fluent Welsh speakers at age three, and all were said to understand some English at least and to use a few English words and phrases. There was some evidence that Iwan (WW) and Emyr (WM) were developing more syntactic skills in English as well, that is, were on the way to becoming bilingual.

The WF mothers both wanted their children to be bilingual and both tried to learn Welsh. Both husbands were strongly in favour of their children learning Welsh and put in a lot of effort to that end. At age three their first language was firmly English, but both children had some Welsh words and phrases, and seemed to understand simple Welsh addressed to them.

The biggest differences existed between the two families with mixed language backgrounds. All four parents could use both languages, but David's family was rarely heard to do so. His parents said they wanted him to have the best of both worlds, but did not want him to go to a Welsh school, and were afraid that learning Welsh would confuse him. He was effectively a monolingual English speaker at age three.

In contrast, Gareth's parents used both languages freely, and wanted him to be bilingual. This was despite grave reservations on the part of his mother about the Welsh language and being Welsh. She felt she was British, and she too deplored extreme nationalism. They decided to speak Welsh with Gareth as they felt it would be easier for him to learn English later, and Gareth did develop Welsh as his first language. However, by age 30 months he used English words and phrases, and by age three his mother reported that he would talk for 'a couple of hours' in English. As later chapters will show, he used both languages equally during the final session, and merits the descriptor 'bilingual' however it is defined.

Thus there are indications that a positive attitude towards bilingualism can facilitate bilingual language development. The three children who showed evidence of bilingual abilities rather than simply having some words and phrases in a second language, were Gareth (MM), Iwan (WW) and Emyr (WM). All three families had expressed the wish that their children become bilingual, and all three families had mothers fluent in both languages. However, many other families also said they wanted their children to be bilingual. Nerys (WW) and Becky (WM) also had mothers who were fluent in both languages, so those two factors are not sufficient to ensure bilingual development, although they may be necessary.

At the other extreme, it seems likely that a negative attitude towards bilingualism can restrict language learning. Michael (EE) and David (MM) had parents who were not in favour of bilingualism, and those two boys appear to have learned no Welsh before age three. Somewhere in the middle come the families who would like their children to be bilingual, but who do not have mothers fluent in both languages. Llywela (EE), Mathew (WF) and Nia (WF) fall into this group, and all three had mothers who wanted to learn Welsh and felt positive about bilingual education. These three children, like Nerys (WW) and Becky (WM) had acquired some words and phrases and some understanding of a second language by the last session. Unlike Nerys and Becky who had picked up English from playmates and from television, the parents of Llywela, Mathew and Nia had had to make positive efforts to expose their children to the Welsh language.

Summary

In both of the questionnaires, over 85% of all parents wanted their children to be fluent Welsh speakers or to learn Welsh at school. The 5% who wanted them to learn only English had dropped to around 2% on the second occasion. Thus, it seems that the local policy of education through the medium of Welsh enjoys the support of the majority of parents, whatever their language background.

Seven sets of reasons were identified in the comments on the questionnaires, and an eighth category included comments that gave no ostensible reason, but simply noted matters of interest. Reasons in favour were for improved job prospects, for improved communication, for general advantage, to keep the English at bay (it was not clear if that refers to the language or the people), and to preserve and maintain the Welsh heritage. The only reasons against learning Welsh were because of its irrelevance, and some chose to affirm the need to support both languages.

The reason most frequently given for that support was associated with feelings of Welsh culture and identity, again on both occasions. Many parents seemed surprised at the question, and wrote 'because we're Welsh!' A tiny minority wanted to be rid of the English, and a larger minority, mostly EE, felt Welsh was a waste of time. The proportion of these views also remained constant. Support fell for reasons associated with getting a job, with communicating better, and with general advantage, but there was a marked increase in reasons that emphasised the need for both languages, largely from the families which included a first language Welsh speaker.

In the first questionnaire, QI, at least 80% felt that it was either very important or quite important for their children to learn Welsh, but opinions were more divided about its future. Although over half (about 55%) felt it would be used about the same amount in the future as at present, only 16% thought it would be used more.

In the small sample, having a positive attitude towards bilingualism was seen to be insufficient to ensure that a child's language developed bilingually. Having a positive attitude and a mother fluent in both languages improved the likelihood that a child would become bilingual. It was also noted that more effort was needed to ensure the beginnings of Welsh language learning than English language learning, even when attitudes were positive. Negative attitudes were associated with an absence of second language acquisition, even at the single-word level.

7 A Close Look at the Language of Young Children

Introduction

Examination of the language background and of parental attitudes to two languages sets the scene for the entrance of the 10 representative children. Throughout the descriptions of their achievements which follow, it is important to remember the backcloth against which they each acquire their language or languages. In the early part of a child's life, parents act as models for a range of skills which children need to develop, and language is one of the most important if not the most important of all the skills they acquire. The fact that it is a commonplace acquisition can disguise its complexity. As discussed in Chapter 2 and again in Chapter 4, the very start of the whole process is still far from clear. How, why, when, where and with whom do infants begin to vocalise meaningfully, then to use words and then to fit them together? (See particularly Bloom 1973; Bruner, 1977; Newport *et al.*, 1977; Snow, 1977b; Dore, 1979; Barrett, 1985; Furrow & Nelson 1986; Kamhi, 1986; Murray & Trevarthen, 1986.)

Chapter 5 described the difficulties of studying the language of very young children and outlined the methods adopted in the Anglesey Project. One of the first tasks was to find ways of describing the language that the children in the small sample were acquiring. Were they learning the language predicted by their background? Had the influence of English become so pervasive that they were all learning some English at least? Was it possible for a child to be a monolingual Welsh speaker, at least to age three?

The development of communication

A formal language system is an important part of communication, but the roots of language are to be found in earlier, more primitive efforts to communicate (Clarke and Clarke, 1976). First efforts to communicate are seen most easily through the child's interaction with his or her mother. Although mothers in the study spoke to their babies in English or Welsh – albeit an adapted version sometimes called 'motherese' (see Snow, 1977ab) – the babies' early responses were largely unintelligible. It is probable that a linguist could have found evidence of future language systems in these early vocalisations. However, the emphasis of this book is on psychological processes and so these responses were interpreted as evidence of communicative intent on the part of these young children.

The development of conversation

Once the communication game was established within the mother–child dyads, attention focused on issues of control; who started conversations, who changed topics, who directed attention and on the simpler question of who said most. It is not always easy to decide who is directing a conversation as mothers are extremely sensitive to children's changing interests. The gross amount of speech for each mother and child can be calculated in both single words and utterances (such as sentences). When these are expressed as mother–child ratios (M/C) the changing pattern of control in the partnership can be seen clearly.

The dictionary

It was clear that the language system (Welsh, English or a mixture) used by each dyad differed and also differed at each session. Half of the pairs used almost only English and half used mostly Welsh. To assess this more accurately, attempts were made to classify first single words and then utterances as 'Welsh' or 'English'. Unfortunately, many words and phrases did not fit either category exclusively. Therefore, as described in the previous chapter, words (and subsequently utterances) have been classified as 'Welsh', 'English' or 'Common' for the purposes of the Anglesey Project. In this way it is possible to say what percentage of each 'language' was used by any person in any session.

The large sample

Data from the second questionnaire make it possible to look at what language/s a large sample of children were using at age three, and hence at the representativeness of the small sample. It is also possible to look for evidence of the 'one person-one language strategy' in a general, non-specialist population.

Becoming a Language User

Development of communication

In the early recordings, infants responded to the communicative attempts of their mothers with unintelligible vocalisations. These were all counted as a *response*. Often they were just sounds, or 'fillers' which filled a gap in the conversation. It was not possible to include movement, gaze or facial expression, although their communicative function is acknowledged. Similarly, all vocal communication by mothers was counted as a *response*, even simple exclamations and 'babytalk'.

In contrast, an *utterance* consists of one or more words. Fillers such as 'oh' and 'ah' and 'er' have communicative value, but are not words in a formal sense. Because of the problems entailed in counting words (for example is 'hasn't' one or two words?) utterances rather than words have been chosen for comparison with responses. In this way it has been possible to compute the responses and the utterances for the children and for their mothers. It was then simple to calculate the ratio of mother responses to child responses and mother utterances to child utterances for each dyad. These ratios were computed for every session.

Initially, when the children are about 15 months old, the mean ratio for utterances was 7:38. That is, the mothers produced over seven times as many intelligible communicative attempts as did their offspring. In contrast, a M/C response ratio of 2:75 is much more even-handed, with mothers working less than three times as hard as their babies. The scripts of these early sessions show that babies tended to fill the pauses in these 'proto-conversations' (Snow, 1977ab) with exclamations, imitations and babbling to which mothers responded as if to intelligible comment.

For example:

M: Do you want a drink?/   C: eh!/

M: Drink?/   C: aba aba ababababa/

M: aba aba aba/   C: aba baba/

M: I know all about that
   but d'you want a drink?/

M: drink/ say drink/

M: drink/
M: drink/
M: drink/   **C:** din/
M: that's right, drink/

    Mother: Response = 9   **Child:** Response = 4
           Utterance = 10   Utterance = 1 ('din')

    M/C (Responses) = 9/4 = 2:25
    M/C (Utterances) = 10/1 = 10:00

By the fourth session, the comparative ratios are almost equal at 1:25 for utterances and 1:20 for responses. In other words, little of what the child says is completely unintelligible and fillers had been largely replaced by simple utterances. Now there is little difference between an utterance and a response. At this time the children are about two years of age. Utterances still tend to be rather short, often comprising no more than one or two word 'sentences'. (But see Bloom, 1973 and Dore, 1974 for discussion of this contentious suggestion).

As the two ratios approach unity, the partners in the conversation become more equal. At the fourth session, mothers are still making more utterances (and responses) than their children, but at 1:20, this is approaching equality.

For example;

M: What are you doing?/   **C:** Dolly/
M: You playing with dolly?/   **C:** Yeah/ Dolly sleep now/
M: Dolly's going to bye-byes/   **C:** Dolly bye-byes/
                              C: Getting up now/
M: Oh she's getting up now/is she?/
M: What's she gonna do?/Play?/   **C:** That's dolly breakfast/
M: Oh!/
M: Does dolly like cornflakes?/   **C:** mm/
    Does she?/
M: Or does she like toast?/   **C:** yeah toast/ and marlamade/

    Mother: Responses = 8   **Child:** Responses = 7
            Utterances = 10   Utterances = 8

    M/C (Responses) = 8/7 = 1:14
    M/C (Utterances) = 10/8 = 1:25

There is a wide individual difference between the 10 dyads, especially in the first session. However, this does not appear to relate to the language background of the children. Initially the children with the highest M/C response ratios are from EE, MM, and WF families (Michael, David and Nia). These mothers had to work much harder to get any response from their children than those with the lowest response ratios, namely three from WW, WF and MM families (Nerys, Mathew and Gareth). The two with the largest M/C utterance ratios (Nerys and Michael) are from WW and EE families respectively, and those with the smallest utterance ratios are from MM and WW families (Gareth and Iwan). Utterances are included in responses, so that suggests that Iwan and Gareth moved more quickly to utterances than did the first two. However, it should be noted that, although Nerys was slow to use utterances, she was responsive to mother's utterances and responses from the start.

By the fourth session the range of M/C ratios is much narrower for both measures. The pairs of comparative M/C ratios are all close, suggesting that all of the children are moving to intelligible utterances from simple vocal responses. There still appears to be no relationship with language background, as one child from a MM background is making more than twice as many responses as his mother (M/C of 0.44) while the second MM child is the least responsive in the group (M/C of 1.73).

The Mother/Child ratio for utterances approaches that for responses as the sessions proceed and the children grow older. By the fourth session (when children are about two years old), they are so similar that further analyses of responses are not productive. Thus, it can be seen that these children learned to communicate intelligibly over the nine month period, and there is support for Newson's suggestion that they learn to communicate because their mothers treat them as conversational partners long before they are so in reality, and that they grow into that role (Newson, 1977). There seems to be no difference in this process between those from differing family backgrounds. Children learn to communicate whatever language is offered to them in the initial stages.

From the beginning of these recordings, the mothers worked hard to elicit a response from their babies, and from the beginning the babies responded. That both partners work hard to communicate is well documented. Bruner (1983) studied the use of referencing and requesting games in infant–mother dyads, and Halliday and Leslie (1986) followed this with evidence that both partners use imitation, modelling and reciprocity to keep the communication dialogue moving. Conti-Ramsden and Friel-Patti and Friel-Patti (1986) also showed that in children as young as 12–24 months, infants initiated new topics as frequently as did their mothers.

This study shows that by 24 months, children are almost equal partners in the dialogue. Their contributions may be shorter and simpler but they don't often miss their turn in the conversation.

Development of conversation

The 10 mothers in this study shared a keen interest in the development of their children but differed qualitatively in the ways in which they tried to encourage their children's growing skills. These differences were hard to quantify, they lead to a query about whether some styles of maternal interaction are more helpful than others in developing language and if some styles are more typical of certain language backgrounds.

Mother/Child ratios were computed for single words and for utterances with this in mind. These ratios show who is more vociferous in each session. By comparing the two measures, they can also be used to monitor the development of each child's language system. Throughout the study, measurements involving utterances are quoted in default, as they represent a more sophisticated use of language than do words alone. Both of these measures are examined *inter* and *intra* subjectively.

At first there is a steady increase in the child's participation in the sessions, from a mean M/C for utterances of 7:38 in the first session to a mean M/C of 0:90 at the seventh session. Even more marked is the change from a mean M/C for single words of 15:02 to 1:32 when the children were almost three years of age, indicating that their gross contribution to the conversations are becoming more even-handed. The eighth session did not follow the usual format. It began with formal assessments, consequently the initial enthusiasm was lost from the recordings and the children tended to be tired. Session seven is therefore the better indication of the group's progress and so is used for comparative purposes. Session Dad was a postscript session, recorded slightly differently, within the month following the eighth session. It is used for comparison with the last maternal session in Chapter 10.

Given the general trend, there are again wide differences between individual children which do not correspond to differences in language background. Llywela, one of the English-speaking children, has half of her scores well below the mean scores, as does Gareth, a child from a mixed language background. David, the second child from a Mixed background has scores that are consistently *higher* than others by more than a standard deviation. A score of one indicates an equal sharing of the conversation between mother and child. A higher score indicates that the mother's contribution is larger and a lower score indicates that the child is talking more than the mother.

There seems to be no pattern related to language background, except that the two from MM backgrounds are exceptional. One explanation lies in the style of maternal–child interaction. This was not tested or recorded formally, but subjectively it seemed that some mothers are better at allowing their children to take the lead in conversations and at following the interests of the child. Llywela's mother listened attentively to a convoluted story about a pepper pot trespassing and getting hurt (Session VIII); Iwan's mother did exactly as she was told when her son directed the building of a railway line (Session VI). On the other hand, David's mother spent a whole session trying to teach her son to attend to details on the cards of a lotto game which did not interest him (Session VIII). Gareth's mother was especially adept at following his lead, and this included his change from Welsh to English and back to Welsh. This phenomenon will be discussed in detail later.

As the children become older, the balance of the conversations becomes even-handed with the children producing almost as many utterances as did their mothers. Some produced more. Mothers still produce more words than their children, but only about half as many again on average. There seems to be no difference in this process between those from differing family backgrounds. Children learn to communicate and to have conversations using whatever language is offered to them in the early stages.

The Dictionary

General comments

Having established that these children are learning to communicate with their mothers, and that they are becoming equal conversational partners, the next question concerns the medium in which their conversations are conducted. This is not straightforward. All extraneous detail had to be stripped from the scripts, leaving only acceptable, intelligible words and utterances. 'Oh's' and 'ah's' and sounds of agreement or query ('mmm' and 'mmm?') were excluded.

It might be expected that, in North Wales, the language of mother and child conversations could be divided into Welsh or English words and then Welsh or English utterances. It might even be expected that some utterances would be a mixture of Welsh and English words. When the texts were examined, it soon became clear that a third language category is necessary. Many words are common to both languages and so they are called 'Common', and many utterances were a mixture of Welsh, English and Common words and so they too were called 'Common'. Criteria for these categories have been described and Appendix III shows the complete dictionary of Common words found in the texts examined.

The words and utterances in each text have been expressed as percentages of the total child or mother text. In general, mother and child scores are presented side by side. Unlike many studies, the Anglesey Project emphasises the social facet of language development, and mothers and the language they use are important aspects of the child's social setting. As indicated earlier, there is evidence that the language choice in any interaction, but especially in bilingual interactions, is strongly influenced if not directly predicted by the language choice of the other person (Ervin-Tripp, 1968). It is therefore safe to assume that maternal speech is an important factor in predicting child speech. Copies of transcripts, texts and details of the proportion of each language used by each child and mother in each session, presented by dyad and by session can be obtained from the author, through the School of Psychology, University of Wales, Bangor.

Children

In describing the language each of the 10 children acquired, averages become meaningless. They have been selected to represent differing backgrounds and so differences from one another are of greatest interest. Later, some parallels will be drawn between the development of some of the children, but initially it is most revealing to describe briefly the development of each child. As utterances can require the use of appropriate syntactic structures as well as single words, the data relating to utterances have been chosen as the more accurate reflection of language development.

(a) Nerys WW

Nerys is the first child from a primarily Welsh-speaking background. No more than 6% of her mother's words were English in any session and no more than 5% of her utterances were English. Apart from the third session, Nerys's language use mirrored her mother's use, and her use of Welsh grew to 83% of all her utterances and 86% of all her words by the eighth session. Both she and her mother used fewer Common words and utterances as she grew older. This phenomenon is observable in all of the subjects.

(b) Iwan WW

Iwan is the second Welsh-speaking child. His use of Welsh utterances rose to 92% and of Welsh words to 87%, and his use of English was at most 7% of his utterances. His mother used a lot of English in the second session only (12% of utterances and 15% of words) but otherwise used Welsh almost exclusively.

(c) Becky WM

Becky's mother is primarily Welsh-speaking and her father speaks mostly English. During the sessions, Becky's Welsh usage rose to 82% for utterances and 79% for words by the last session, although her progress was uneven. This was very similar to her mother's Welsh usage, but their overall language use was not similar; Becky's mother used more English (as much as 22% for utterances and 27% for words in the second session) than Becky who used more Common language and, as will be discussed later, objected violently when her mother tried to talk to her in Welsh.

(d) Emyr WM

Emyr's mother is also Welsh speaking. She used less English than did Becky's mother. Emyr achieved a 77% Welsh usage for utterances and 75% for words by the last session, although this may be an underestimate when previous sessions are considered. This reflects his mother's language use.

(e) Gareth MM

Both of Gareth's parents spoke a mixture of Welsh and English in the past. They decided to use Welsh mostly with Gareth, but they used English between themselves. His language development is the most interesting of all. His use of English and Welsh had become virtually equal for both utterances and words by the last session, despite his mother's greater use of Welsh.

(f) David MM

By contrast, David, who is the second child from a mixed language background, used virtually no Welsh after the initial session. His parents both spoke a mixture of Welsh and English in the past, but had decided to speak English with David. The only Welsh he heard was from one set of grandparents. Although David used more Common language than did his mother, he was in effect an English-speaking child.

(g) Nia WF

Nia's father is primarily Welsh speaking, and although her mother tried to use Welsh with her as a baby, these efforts gradually disappeared. Nia used no Welsh after the fourth session, and by the sixth session used English for 96% of her utterances and for 90% of her words.

(h) Mathew WF

Mathew's father is also primarily Welsh speaking and his mother was a bit more persistent in her efforts to use Welsh with him. None the less 89% of her words and utterances were in English at the last session, and Mathew's English usage was even higher. However, during the seventh session, he used Welsh utterances 10% of the time and Welsh words 8% of the time.

(j) Llywela EE

Both of Llywela's parents speak only English, although both had attempted to learn Welsh in the past. Her mother used virtually no Welsh with her and Llywela used none at all.

(k) Michael EE

Michael is also from an entirely English-speaking family. The family moved before the last session could take place, but neither Michael nor his mother used any Welsh during the seven recordings.

Sessions

The progress of these children was charted through the eight sessions. Initially the children could be divided roughly into those who spoke mostly Welsh and those who spoke mostly English. By the sixth session, however, Gareth was beginning to use more English, and by the final session he was using English and Welsh equally. From a mixed picture at the first and second sessions, the children were favouring one language more clearly by the fourth session, and by the last session they all appeared to be virtually monolingual with the exception of Gareth.

Four children, those from the WW and WM groups, all used less than 10% English and more than 70% Welsh (except for a 67% score from Nerys) from the sixth session onwards. The four children from the EE and WF groups and one of the MM children all used no more than 10% Welsh and more than 80% English over the same period. So, by age three, nine children in this small sample could reasonably be called monolingual, four in Welsh and five in English. Although the Welsh-speaking children all used a little English, only those in the WF group used a little Welsh, and only Gareth (MM) could be called bilingual.

Common language

Common language accounts for up to 76% (Iwan) of the children's utterances and 23% (Nia) of the mother's utterances in the first session. By the fifth session it is still accounting for over 30% of utterances by David and Nerys, but has reduced to less than 5% for Nia and Llywela. By the eighth session it accounts for less than 20% of any of the children's utterances, but all of the children still use some Common language.

The function of Common language is not clear. In some ways it mirrors the 'motherese' or 'Babytalk' (BT) that is so often referred to in the child language literature (for example Newson, 1977, 1979; Furrow et al, 1979). Motherese comprises short, well-formed, often repeated utterances which, it has been argued, promotes language acquisition (Newson, 1979). However, when Newport *et al.* (1977) studied motherese they suggested that it mostly entailed the use of action directives and little else. In this study, Common language does include the baby words included in motherese, and some of the words shared by Welsh and English are simple action directives (such as *stop*). But it also includes proper names, many non-action words that are shared, and utterances that use a mixture of Welsh and English. Therefore, it cannot be equated with motherese or BT as defined elsewhere.

In the early sessions, where naming and baby words comprised a large part of the dialogue, high Common language use is predictable. It was also predictable that, as Common language by definition includes simpler or mixed forms of syntax, children would progress beyond its use. One might expect that children from a monolingual background (WW and EE) would decrease the percentage of Common utterances in their speech as they learned one syntactic code only. This is not clearly supported. Although Iwan (WW) and both the EE children used less than 10% Common utterances in the last two sessions, so did Gareth (MM), and each of the WF children on one of the two sessions in question, whereas the second WW child always used more than 10% Common utterances.

The concept of a Common language allows the language acquisition of these children to be described developmentally. The function of Common language is not clear, but it may be that it shares with motherese a transitional role in the acquisition of language, whether of one or of two language codes. If attention is paid only to the amounts of Welsh and English in these children's conversations, then they do appear to be acquiring the languages predicted by their language backgrounds. Those from monolingual backgrounds (WW and EE) are using 5% or less of the second·language, both in words and utterances at the final session. The children from cross-language backgrounds (WM and WF) are learning their mother's language primarily, and used less than 6% of their second language at that eighth session. The position of the children from mixed language backgrounds could not have been predicted. David is developing as a monolingual English-speaking child whereas Gareth is arguably a 'balanced bilingual'. Evidence that will be presented later from the session with the subjects' fathers, broadly supports these statements. The monolingual children and one MM child used no more of the second language in that session than they did in the eighth session. Three of the cross-language children used more of their second language with the parent who used that language, and Gareth used Welsh, his father's preferred language, for the bulk of his conversation with him.

Thus, English is not as pervasive as is sometimes believed, and it is possible for children to acquire Welsh only in their early years.

Development in the Population

Statements about language development in the population have to be more guarded. They rely entirely on parental reports (which are naturally subjective and usually biased), of a limited number of aspects of Welsh and English language development. However, they are a useful indication of what is happening in the wider population.

Table 7.1 shows the percentage of children from this population who are said to use nine aspects of Welsh and nine aspects of English 'often'. Virtually half of these children use all nine aspects of English often, and around 70% use the simpler aspects often. At least a third of the same children were said to use all nine aspects of Welsh often.

Table 7.1 Percentages of the large population of children using aspects of English and Welsh

Aspects	English (%)	Welsh (%)
Single words	71	57
Many words	69	53
Two words together	71	55
Allgone–Wedimynd	73	48
Big/Little–Mawr/Bach	64	48
Colours	49	47
Sentences	66	48
Yesterday	49	34
Stories	53	43

NB Every child had a score for both English and Welsh aspects, and so each percentage is a percentage of the total (N = 177)

Apart from the first aspect, about half used the simpler aspects often. Thus, most of these children are learning English, and half of them are learning Welsh. These two sets of children overlap. Some children are developing monolingually in Welsh, some are developing monolingually in English and some are developing bilingually. Details of how these groups were separated can be found in Chapter 11.

Language Background has powerful influence on the aspects of Welsh and English the larger population of children are reported to use. Most of the WW children are not learning any English (apart from 'allgone' which is probably a poor choice). This fits with Nerys' position at age three, but Iwan is one of the minority. Gareth and David illustrate the MM group in this population beautifully: about half of the group are reported to use most aspects of Welsh, and that would be true of Gareth and not of David. Further, virtually all of the MM children appear to have mastered the simpler aspects of English, two-thirds of them using the more complex aspects as well. This description would reasonably fit both of the two boys in this group.

More than two-thirds of the WF group are said to use all aspects of Welsh, and that is at odds with the development of the two WF children in the small sample. Neither Mathew nor Nia was telling stories, talking about the past or even using sentences freely by the end of the project. Unfortunately, there were only six families in this category, and so figures for that group must be treated with caution.

Emyr and Becky more or less fit the pattern of the WM group, and Llywela, like almost a quarter of those in the EE group, had some single words in Welsh. Michael left the area, but was part of the majority of children from English-speaking backgrounds who use no Welsh before the age of three.

One person-one language

In QII, each parent was asked to say what language they preferred for reading, talking, and viewing with their children, using a five-point scale. These scores were added and a mean score computed for each parent. Thus it is possible to identify those families where both parents prefer to use only the same language (Welsh or English) with their children, those who use a mixture of languages, and those (of special interest) where each parent prefers to use a different language with the child. Table 7.2 shows that only in five of the 141 sets of parents who answered these questions does one parent prefer to use a different language from that preferred by the second parent. In four cases the mother prefers Welsh and the father English, and in the fifth case the converse is true. All five are families whose children were bilingual at three years of age, representing 11% of all of the bilingual children. (The procedures used to classify children as bilingual or monolingual at age three are described in detail in Chapter 11.)

Table 7.2 Languages parents prefer to use with their children by child language use at age three

	Welsh monolingual children	Bilingual children	English monolingual children	Totals
M = Welsh	34	10	0	44
F = Welsh	100%	22%	0%	31%
M = English	0	1	33	34
F = English	0%	2%	54%	24%
M = Welsh	0	4	0	4
F = English	0%	9%	0%	3%
M = English	0	1	0	1
F = Welsh	0%	2%	0%	1%
M = Both	0	30	28	58
F = Both	0%	65%	46%	41%
Totals	34	46	61	141

These five families appear to conform to the one person-one language strategy, but it is not known whether or not this is a deliberate strategy. It is also possible that some parents are deliberately using this strategy, and that because this puts them at odds with their preferred language, that fact is not evident in the data. It seems unlikely. Parents were invited to comment on their experience of bringing up bilingual children, and only one comment mentioned the one person-one language strategy. On this evidence, it is clear that the one person-one language strategy is not a common route to bilingualism in Wales.

Summary

When responses rather than words or utterances are used as the measure, infants as young as 15 months respond to at least a third of their mothers' attempts to communicate, and response in this context does not include gaze or movement or facial expression, but only vocal response. By age 24 months they respond to 80% of maternal communications (M/C of 1:25), mostly with intelligible words or utterances, even though their replies are short and simple. Thus it can be seen that children learn to communicate intelligibly over a nine-month period. This supports Newson's suggestion that they learn to communicate because their mothers treat them as conversational partners long before it is a reality, and that they grow into that role (1977). Bever (1982) suggests that children discover language for themselves. If this is so, then mothers spend a lot of time structuring the environment to make it easy for them to discover language through communication.

'Common' language makes it possible to include language that could not be claimed exclusively by either Welsh or English. While not fitting the descriptions in the literature for 'motherese', it is a language associated with young children, and decreases as children's first language becomes established.

It seems that in the wider population, most children are learning at least the simpler aspects of English and about half are learning the simpler aspects of Welsh. Very few of the children from WW backgrounds are learning English (except 'allgone'!), and, apart from single words, very few from EE backgrounds are learning any Welsh. At least half of the children from cross-language backgrounds are learning Welsh, but less than that are learning the more complex aspects of English. Most of those from mixed language backgrounds are learning English, and only about half are learning Welsh.

The children selected for the small sample appear to be reasonably representative of the population, with the possible exception of those with a Welsh-speaking father. This group is so small in the population (of respondents) that no conclusion can be reached either way.

A small group of families do seem to use a one person-one language strategy with their children, and those children become bilingual. However, it is not known if parents deliberately restrict their language use in this way, or if the data represent nothing more than chance preferences.

8 How Do Children in a Bilingual Community Learn Language?

Introduction

There is a considerable body of research showing how children's language develops monolingually. It is not nearly so clear how children's language develops in a bilingual culture. This chapter examines how the language of 10 children developed, and then makes comparisons with language development in the larger population. Particular questions ask whether stages of language development are the same or at least similar for children learning English, Welsh and a mixture of the two. Is it possible for children to develop language bilingually (bilingualism as a first language)? Are there qualitative differences in the way children acquire Welsh and English and if so what are they?

One factor needs to be borne in mind throughout, namely that age is *not* a reliable guide to level of language development. The 10 children whose development is explored here were aged from about 16 to 36 months during time of the study. They are discussed according to age and not according to pre-specified levels of language development.

Mean length of utterance

Once communication is established, there are widely used methods to describe how the monolingual child's language develops. The most popular, though not the least controversial of these, is the mean length of utterance (MLU). MLU for words was used in the Anglesey study, both to monitor the growth of language use, and to facilitate stage description. After all extraneous material was stripped from the early dialogues, a mean length of utterance (MLU) was calculated for each partner in each session.

Stages

Using MLU as a guide and examining the scripts, it has been possible to describe the stages of language development reached by each child at each session. The stages described by both Brown (1973) and Crystal (1976) are based on English language use. The work of Ball (1987) served as the basis for the stages suggested as equivalent in Welsh, but these must be treated with caution.

Development in the population

As described in the previous chapter, the second questionnaire asked about the development of nine aspects of language in English and of nine similar aspects in Welsh for each child in the base population. Thus, each child was assigned a level of development in each language, according to parental reports. Although a less reliable measure than objective observations, they provide a guide to the level of English, Welsh and bilingual language development in the young children of Anglesey.

First Measures

Mean length of utterance (MLU)

MLU is a measure of language proficiency. It is discussed in relation to stage of development in the next section, but here it is examined in relation to the mother–child dialogues. There is a steady progression in the children's MLU from a mean of less than two words per utterance (1.42 at session two) to a mean of over three words per utterance (3.09 at session eight). The mean scores for mothers show a slight increase, but stay between three and four words per utterance throughout.

Predictably, the children's scores (and maternal scores) conceal wide individual differences. All the children progress fairly evenly across the sessions, but the rate and level of this progress differs widely. Maternal scores remain steadier, but differ from one another. Becky's mother (WM) had a number of scores which were significantly lower than the average means, and Llywela's mother (EE) had three scores significantly higher than the mean of the group. Although it was clear during recordings that the latter used rather sophisticated language with her daughter, it was not obvious that the former was using especially simplified language.

Turning to the children's MLUs, Llywela's MLU was more than a standard deviation above the group on four of the six sessions shown, and it was clear at the time that she was following her mother's conversation easily. Gareth (MM) also had scores significantly above average, and Nerys (WW) had scores significantly below average. It was evident during the sessions that Gareth was producing longer utterances and that Nerys was producing almost monosyllabic replies and comments.

Amongst the children whose first language was Welsh, Iwan (WW) made the greatest progress, moving from an MLU of 1.88 at the second session to 4.53 by session eight, whereas Nerys (WW) only increased her MLU from 1.54 at session two to 2.08 (or 2.19 at best) by the end. In the English group, Llywela (EE) progressed from 1.55 to almost five words per utterance at age three, whilst David (MM) only moved from 1.88 to 2.42 in that time. Again there is no evidence of a relation with language background; the greatest and the least progress was made by the two WW children.

Gareth is of special interest as he was using both languages equally by the end of the study. His MLUs are not dissimilar to the rest. His progress is disrupted at or around the sixth session, just as he was beginning to use more of his second language. Examination of Table 8.2 (which appears later in this chapter) reveals that this pattern can be traced in the MLUs of other children; Llywela seems to have a setback at session five, Nia at session six and Iwan, Emyr and Mathew seem to have setbacks at session seven. Apart from Llywela, all these children became bilingual, although not all within the time limits of the study. It is suggested that this is the likely point at which these children noticed the second language in their environment, and that this threw them off their stride, as it were. They were aged between 31 and 34 months. As will be seen in Chapter 11, there is an association between bilingualism and language awareness and there is strong evidence that Gareth at least was aware of language itself before the age of 36 months. It is possible that children in a bilingual setting become aware of language and of the fact of two languages as early as the second half of their third year.

Stages

As noted elsewhere, MLU is a crude measure, and closer examination of the texts is necessary to assign stages of language development to each child at each session. A full description of stages as described by Brown (1973) and by Crystal (1976) is given in Chapter 1, but Table 8.1 (a repeat of Table 1.1) summarises the key features. Although many researchers warn against equating language development with chronological age, Crystal does suggest approximate ages for stages as can be seen.

Table 8.1 Summary of stages in language development: Brown and Crystal compared (repeat)

| | Brown | | Crystal | |
MLU	Features	Stage	Features	Age (months)
1.75	Content words; no functors	1	Single element	by 18
2.25	Modulation of meaning	2	2 words together	18–24
2.75	Negation, interrogation, imperatives	3	3 element utterance	24–30
3.50	Embedding one simple sentence in another	4	4 or more elements; simple sentences	by 36
4.00	Co-ordination of sentences	5	Clauses; use of 'and' and 'but'	about 42
Later	Tag questions, etc.	6	Pronouns, auxiliary verbs, etc.	about 48 onwards

Table 8.1 shows the stage assignment of each child at each session according to criteria from both Brown (1973) and Crystal (1976). MLU scores are included for comparison, but presence of key grammatical features are given greater weight. A child is assessed as having reached a stage when a number of examples of the use of pertinent grammatical features are to be found in the text. Uncertain instances were checked with the script; sometimes children at an early stage can imitate complex parental utterances perfectly.

Some aspects of the Welsh language make it difficult to be confident of stage allocation, despite reference to Ball (1987). For example, the tag 'yea?' or 'ia?' is part of the style of speakers in Wales, and does not appear to have the same value as a developmental marker as Stage 6 tag questions. Next comes an examination of the texts of individual children, followed by comparisons between them.

Nerys (WW)

Nerys was capable of two-word utterances from the fourth session onwards, with 'het hen'/'Bwgan Brain hapus'/'shish arall'/ ('old hat'/ 'happy scarecrow'/ 'other shish [fish]'). She was then about two years old, and was never a very communicative child. Only occasional examples of Stage 3 utterances were heard before the seventh session when Stage 4 utterances were also recorded. As well as the first three element sentences such as 'lle mae coch?' ('where's the red?') and 'dwi isio hair-dryer', The following were recorded: 'rhywbeth wedi newid yn fana' ('something has changed there') 'hogia bach hefo coech babi' ('little boys with a baby pram') 'ti'm 'di gweld hwna'('you didn't see that') and 'fi tynnu hwn o bocs' ('I'm taking that out of the box'), all stage 4 utterances. From the first session, Nerys used occasional words and phrases in English, such as 'bad boy' and 'no way!', and they were scattered throughout the recordings. No progression of English usage was noted.

Iwan (WW)

Iwan was at Stage 2 by the third session: 'yli bont'/ 'do eto'/ 'pont di disgyn'/ 'dau goch'/('look bridge'/'yes again'/'bridge fallen down'/and 'two reds'/). He moved to Stage 3 at least by the fourth session, and to Stage 4 by the fifth with utterances such as 'Jean rhywbeth i tren' ('Jean [take] something to the train') 'dafad arall 'di mynd yn fana' ('the other sheep went in there') 'a golau coch i tractor mynd'('and the red light for the tractor to go') and 'mynd i coedan arall nath hi' ('go to the other tree she did'). At the next session he had moved on to Stage 5, and it is possible that he reached a further stage before the end of recording, but it becomes more difficult to assign equivalent stages in Welsh as the child's usage becomes more sophisticated. The following examples are taken from the last three sessions and judged as being stage 5, but that judgement is conservative: 'lle mae ceffyl 'di dychryn Smot?' ('Where's the horse which frightened Smot?') 'a be di hwn yn cnocio ar coed' ('and what's that knocking on wood?') ''misio darllen llyfr i doli'('don't want to read the book for the dolly') 'un arall 'di disgyn ar ben Mam' ('another one fell on Mam's head') 'bysa fo'n eista cael bici' ('he must sit [down] to get a bici') 'f'isio cael hwna cyn i wydda mynd ar ol bwyta cae' ('I want to get that before the geese go back to eat the field'). He used single words and phrases in English from the second recording session, and at the seventh session a few Stage 3 examples were recorded, namely: 'stand well there' and 'will he drip?'. There was no evidence of this level of usage at the final session, only single element utterances again.

Becky (WM)

It wasn't till the fourth session that Becky reached Stage 2 with utterances like 'dim tatws' ('no potatoes'), 'isio potel' ('want a bottle') and 'mwy caws'('more cheese'). The following session produced Stage 3 examples; 'ti'n tynnu sgidiau' ('you take off shoes') 'moo-moo 'di bwyta bwyd' ('moo-moo ate food') and 'isio sws i fo' ('want to kiss it'). By the seventh session, when she was about 34 months old, Becky was using Welsh at Stage 4, with 'Becky doli isio ffisig' ('Becky's dolly wants medicine') and 'isio bwyd yn fana y gyd a llwy' ('want all the food over there [with] and a spoon'). From the third session or so Becky was using occasional English words and phrases, but their frequency hardly increased. By the end she was probably at Stage 1 for English.

Emyr (WM)

By the third session Emyr had reached Stage 2 with utterances such as 'dau golau' ('two lights') and 'hiya Nain'. He reached Stage 3 by the fifth session with 'fana mae'n gweld rwan'('he sees [from] there now') 'gael chips i tea' ('get chips for tea') and 'pushio fo fana fela'('push him there like that'). There were some words and phrases in English at this session, but not enough to score beyond Stage 1. At the seventh session, however, Emyr used a number of English utterances ('there allgone rwan'/ 'want a pillow I said') indicating that his English was at least up to Stage 3. At this time his Welsh was at Stage 5 with utterances such as 'mae nhw yn mynd yn ol i bye-byes'('they are going back to bye-byes') and 'tedi mynd i fana a doli mynd i bath' ('teddy goes there and dolly goes to the bath').

Gareth (MM)

Gareth had reached Stage 3 by the third recording with utterances such as 'fan bach wedi disgu' ('little van fell') and 'mam neud hwnna' ('mam do that'). He was using a few English words only. By the fifth session he had reached Stage 4 with at least four elements in his sentences: 'dwad i codi heina'n munud ia?'('come to pick those up in a minute yes?') and 'mae tractor bach yn mynd i fana rwan' ('the little tractor is going there now'). At the next session, when he was about 30 months old, he was using English syntax for some of his utterances, at about Stage 3 level. These included: 'I want a cup of tea'/ 'I don't know'/ 'that's my cwpan'(cup). Possibly Stage 3 is an underestimate, but as these examples suggest, it's not clear if phrases such as 'a cup of tea' are understood as separate words. At the last session he had reached Stage 4 for English with utterances such as 'it's the wrong way in there' and 'I put it in the trailer'. For Welsh he had reached Stage 5 with 'mae isio mynd ffor trwy fana ag i Llangefni'('[it] wants to go along through there and to Llangefni') and 'dod allan y tractor rhoid nhw yn y trailer'('come out of the tractor to put them in the trailer').

David (MM)

David's language was slow to develop, but by the fifth session he was using two word and occasionally more complex utterances ('I de (don't) like bridge'). This pattern continued. Despite occasional examples of higher stage functioning, most of David's recorded utterances were single words, even up to the seventh session when he was three years old. By then he was also producing Stage 4 sentences such as 'I put it in the bin' and 'me can't find the king' but generally he did not produce much spontaneous speech.

Nia (WF)

Examination of the scripts suggests that Nia was at Stage 3 by the third session at about age 21 months. Utterances included: 'I gonna take it'/ 'men go in it'/ 'Mummy make tan (fire)'/. By the fifth session she was using Stage 4 utterances such as: 'I did fell on the bike' and 'I had buy a ice cream'. By the eighth session she told her mother: 'Mom you're a naughty girl knocking that over' and 'I can knock them over with my hand', both examples of Stage 5 functioning.

Mathew (WF)

Mathew's language was slow to develop, but by the fourth session he was at Stage 2, using utterances such as 'horsey jump' and 'come on mam'. By the sixth session he had progressed to Stage 3 ('where's daddy gone' 'I want brechdan (sandwich)'). He continued to use occasional Welsh words and phrases and at the last session, when he was about three years old. He had then moved to Stage 4 with utterances such as 'I don't like him' and 'he doed his hair now'.

Llywela (EE)

Llywela's language developed rapidly, and her eagerness to express herself often outpaced her accuracy. Initially she was quite difficult to understand, even for her mother. However, by the fourth session when she was just over two years old she was using embedding such as 'I know where the jigsaw is'/ 'where's these bits of Tommy's go?' and 'I want to play with this purse' which is at least a Stage 4 skill. By the sixth session she was at Stage 6, with utterances with tags such as 'you won't do a silly one on this page will you?' and 'this house hasn't got round windows has it?' and by the last session was using conditionals and negative auxiliary verbs. Although there are still mistakes, her meaning is clear: 'all the glasses of wines aren't meaning to go into the house'/'he has something what he doesn't always want to do' and 'when I came back I would put him straight on the stairs.'

Michael (EE)

Initially Michael too had difficulty with pronunciation. He does not appear to have reached the second stage until the fourth session, but at that time, as well as many two-word utterances, some three-element utterances were recorded: 'where's frog gone' and 'dis frog do dis'. By the sixth recording, when he was 30 months old, he was at Stage 4, saying 'the dolly can't see them'/ 'her will go back to bed'/ 'there's a cup on her place'/ and by the seventh session (his last) he was using clauses freely and co-ordinating sentences as in 'I'd better get the teas for the party'/ 'we'd better put this on for her' and 'do this one and get the tea things', features of Stage 5.

Stages summarised

These results are summarised in Table 8.2. All 10 children were at Stage 1, one-element utterances, at 19 months old (session two), and had reached at least Stage 4, involving simple embedding, by three years old. An English-speaking child had progressed the most (to Stage 6), but at least one child from each kind of background had reached Stage 5. Therefore, there seems to be no link between stage of language development and the language being developed. Neither do there appear to be major differences in the pattern of progress between the Welsh and English speaking children.

Of especial interest are the three boys who gave evidence of learning two languages. Iwan (WW), Emyr (WM) and Gareth (MM) all reached Stage 5 in Welsh and at least Stage 3 in English by session eight. Table 8.2 shows that they reached at least Stage 4 in their first language before moving beyond single-word utterances in their second language (which was English in each case). Also, none of these three was slow to move beyond single utterances. Two further children, Nia (WF) and Becky (WM), developed their second language to at least Stage 3 in their fourth year, after the end of the detailed study, and it is possible that some of the remaining children would do so over the subsequent year.

Table 8.2 Stages reached by individual children by session according to according to criteria from Brown and Crystal, with MLU for each child

		I	II	III	IV	V	VI	VII	VIII
Nerys	Stg-W	1	1	1	2	2	2	4	4
WW	MLU	1.67	1.54	1.36	1.58	1.89	1.51	2.19	2.08
Iwan	Stg-W	1	1	2	3	4	5	5	5
WW	Stg-E	1	1	1	1	1	1	3	(3)
	MLU	1.90	1.88	2.37	2.89	2.65	3.00	2.76	4.53
Becky	Stg-W	1	1	1	2	3	3	4	4
WM	MLU	1.40	1.18	1.89	1.85	1.89	2.00	2.32	2.35
Emyr	Stg-W	1	1	2	2	3	4	5	5
WM	Stg-E	1	1	1	1	1	1	3	(3)
	MLU	1.30	1.21	1.60	2.16	2.46	2.76	2.32	2.43
Gareth	Stg-W	1	(1)	3	3	4	4	4	5
MM	Stg-E	1	(1)	1	1	1	3	3	4
	MLU	1.61	–	2.53	2.70	3.15	2.81	3.51	3.27
David	Stg-E	1	(1)	(1)	1	2	3	3	4
MM	MLU	1.88	–	–	1.82	1.94	1.79	1.99	2.42
Nia	Stg-E	1	1	3	3	4	4	4	5
WF	MLU	1.07	1.47	2.21	2.32	3.03	2.64	2.70	3.31
Mathew	Stg-E	1	1	1	2	2	3	3	4
WF	MLU	1.17	1.48	1.47	1.79	1.61	2.82	2.30	2.77
Llywela	Stg-E	1	1	3	4	5	6	(6)	6
EE	MLU	2.50	1.55	2.52	3.48	3.12	2.95	–	4.67
Michael	Stg-E	1	1	1	2	3	4	5	(5)
EE	MLU	2.18	1.05	1.72	2.01	2.61	2.70	3.15	–

Stg-E = Stages in English. Stg-W = Stages in Welsh.
Three children moved beyond Stage 1 in their second language: Iwan, Emyr and Gareth. Where a session was not recorded, the stage value for the previous session is assumed (in parenthesis).

Development in the Population

The families who replied to the second questionnaire reported on aspects of language development reached by age three in the larger population. Every child was given a score for every aspect of both languages, 18 scores in all. About two-thirds (66%) of the population had begun to use simple sentences in English according to their parents, probably a Stage 3 level at least, and about half were talking about yesterday and telling stories, a Stage 4 or 5 level. Also, just less than half of them (48%) were at about Stage 3 in Welsh, and between 34% and 43% were at Stage 4/5 in Welsh. As all parents were asked about the development of both Welsh and English, these results are influenced by monolingual speakers from both languages. An attempt to disentangle these groups is reported later in this chapter.

The small sample mirrors these results quite well, especially in the development of English. However, all the data were taken from questionnaires, including those for the small sample and there are discrepancies. Three of the mothers in the small sample seem to be unaware of the amount of English being used by their Welsh-speaking children (as shown in the recordings), and two of the mothers of English-speaking children appeared to have overstated their child's ability in Welsh. Parents of mostly Welsh-speaking children don't always notice how much English their children are using. They are surrounded with the English language, and do not always identify it as not-Welsh. This was the subjective impression given during recordings.

As regards to the English speaking children, they might have used much less Welsh during the recorded sessions than normally, but there were no indications of this in the informal discussions held with their mothers at the time. Both of the discrepant children were from WF families where the father was a Welsh speaker and mother spoke English. In these two families there was pressure on the children to use Welsh, a pressure most evident in the session with child and father alone. Possibly these mothers, having little or no Welsh themselves, were being over-optimistic about the use of that language by their children.

This nicely illustrates the dangers of self-report questionnaire data. Parents are not the most objective observers of their own children, and a degree of over-estimation is to be expected. This applies all to families and to both parents as there were no significant differences between the reports of either parent on the development of aspects of English or Welsh in their children.

A bilingual variable was created to identify those in the population who were learning to communicate in two languages. To do this, each child's score in Welsh was subtracted from that in English. As described in Chapter 6, those with scores approaching or near zero were termed 'bilingual'. This gives three groups, Welsh, bilingual and English children. Most of the group of children identified as bilingual could use simple sentences in either language by age three, probably Stage 3. The abilities of the three groups of children are presented in tabular form (Table 8.3) and in graphic form (Figure 8.1 for aspects of English, and Figure 8.2 for aspects of Welsh).

Table 8.3 Children's language development in the QII population: Language groups by aspects of Welsh and English

% using aspects	Welsh N = 41		Bilingual N = 57		English N = 79	
	in E	*in W*	*in E*	*in W*	*in E*	*in W*
Single words	7%	100%	81%	93%	99%	10%
Many words	0%	95%	75%	90%	100%	4%
Two words together	0%	100%	90%	91%	94%	4%
Allgone/ Wedimynd	18%	93%	81%	79%	95%	3%
Big-little/ Mawr-bach	5%	98%	72%	80%	89%	0%
Sentence	0%	95%	75%	79%	94%	1%
Colours	5%	90%	48%	68%	71%	9%
Yesterday	0%	83%	40%	43%	80%	0%
Stories	0%	93%	53%	67%	81%	0%

Percentages frequently achieving each aspect of language according to mother's reports, N = 177. Aspects above the dotted line are referred to as Simple Aspects, those below as Complex Aspects.
NB Only those children reported to use an aspect of Welsh or English 'often' are included above. 'Sometimes' and 'not yet' replies have been omitted.

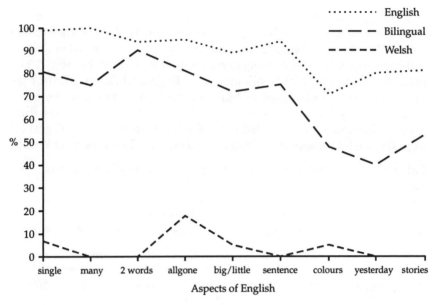

Figure 8.1 Use of aspects of English by children in the three language groups

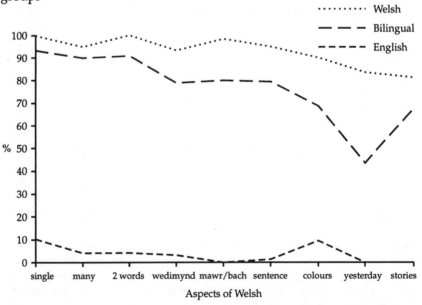

Figure 8.2 Use of aspects of Welsh by children in the three language groups

It is interesting to compare the bilingual group with both the Welsh and English groups, particularly with reference to the complex aspects of language use. When compared with the Welsh group, fewer of the bilingual group were using complex Welsh aspects, but more were using complex English aspects. Compared with the English group, fewer were using complex English aspects but more were using complex Welsh aspects. At least 40% of the bilingual group have reached about Stage 4 or Stage 5 in one language at least, and that percentage may be higher.

Most of the children assigned to the Welsh group in the population had no English and most of those assigned to the English group had no Welsh. Slightly fewer children in the bilingual group had mastered the simple aspects of Welsh or English than had the monolingual groups; about 50% used complex English and about 70% used complex Welsh aspects of language. As more children in this group had mastered the simpler and the complex aspects of Welsh than of English, it is arguable that the first language of bilingual children in this population is more likely to be Welsh.

In summary, these bilingual children had reached at least Stage 4 in their first language and Stage 3 in their second language by age three. Virtually all of the Welsh-speaking group had reached Stage 4/5 by age three, as had virtually all of the English speaking group. The seven monolingual children from the small sample were at least at that stage by the same age, and the bilingual children in the small sample were at similar stages to those of the larger group.

Summary

Clearly, as the children acquire more language their MLU increases. In the early sessions with the small sample, MLUs were around 1.5, or one and a half words per utterance. By the eighth session they had increased to around three. Some children progressed further and at a faster pace than others, but this did not appear to be related to one language rather than to another, or to the presence or absence of a second language. The child who had best mastered a second language by age three had a slightly above average MLU at the end.

MLU is a crude measure of language development, but stage models allow for more sophisticated classification of language development. Thus, each child was assigned to a stage, using the work of Brown (1973), Crystal (1976), and Ball (1987). It proved more difficult to assign levels to the Welsh-speaking children, and so these scores may be conservative. However, all the children were at Stage 1 at the start of recording and all had moved to at least Stage 4 by the last session. The three who showed evidence of developing their second language did not do so until their first language was at least at Stage 4, and then progressed to Stage 3 in their second language by age three.

The larger sample achieved comparable results. By separating them into three groups it is possible to see that most of the bilingual group achieved Stage 4 in one language and about Stage 3 in a second language. Most of the children in the monolingual groups were using all aspects of their first language and so they too had achieved Stage 4/5 by age three. There are indications that the first language of bilingual children is more likely to be Welsh than English.

9 How Do Young Children use Language and Do They Know What They are Doing?

Introduction

Pragmatics and language awareness

Learning language is not just learning words and what they mean: it is learning how to make use of language in context. It is not just learning to communicate information to other people: it is learning the shared conventions that allow you to make language the vehicle for a wide range of messages about thoughts and feelings, past and present, and in particular about social relationships. It is an extremely sophisticated process. Messages can be conveyed through choice of language, of code, of word, of intonation, of timing and in many other ways. One can choose the obscure adjective in Latin, can make questions sound like imperatives and can allow silence to speak for you. The use of language in such differing ways to perform many different functions is known as pragmatics, the practice of language. It is concerned not so much with the accuracy of syntax and pronunciation, but with the function of language and how language is employed to communicate, frequently at more than one level (Dore, 1975, 1979).

Although a subtler skill than word or even syntactic learning, normally children become skilled in pragmatics even before they acquire language. Babies learn timing at the breast (Kaye, 1977), and very young infants learn to share their mother's frame of reference through looking and touching, and later through specific gestures such as pointing, waving and holding their arms up (Bates *et al.*, 1979). These are later accompanied by demonstrative words such as 'da', 'der', 'yli', 'look', and so forth. It is possible that the function of many early words is simply to draw the attention of another person rather than to name the object (Atkinson, 1979; Tomasello, 1992).

Later both monolingual and bilingual children are taught what to say 'please' and 'thank you', how to say it (no shouting) and when to say it ('speak when you're spoken to and don't interrupt'). They learn to recognise social distance and relative power in relationships and respond accordingly. Young children have been shown to address requests to fathers less directly than to mothers, and to treat siblings less politely than strangers (Ervin-Tripp 1982).

Language awareness

In the process they can also become aware of language itself, of who speaks as they do and who does not, and of how different people say things differently. In Wales, they notice that people use differing languages before they can identify them as Welsh and English. It has been argued that this is the beginning of metalingual awareness. The latter part of this chapter looks to the small sample of children for indications of metalingual awareness, and talking about talking is the clearest evidence of this.

The functions of language

The first part of the chapter looks at the development of other pragmatic skills. Children from all backgrounds are able to use language both functionally and stylistically, and children from the small sample under discussion provide illustrations of this in all of the age groups studied. The examples identified are then examined for evidence of a functional sequence. There are no differences which can be associated with language background.

Is There a Functional Sequence?

Some suggestions

Many researchers have suggested that children learn to use the functions of language and communication in a developmental sequence (for example, Bates, 1976; Bruner, 1977; Sugerman-Bell, 1978; Halliday 1979; Ellis 1994). Elizabeth Bates (1976) described the development of children's use of language in context from demonstratives and locatives ('that over there') through reference to participants in a dialogue, and connecting terms ('I went there and John did that') to time references and performatives. Performatives entail an intention to ask, command, promise, etc. Her view was that the child actively constructs meaning and uses language to do so.

Bruner's (1977) view was that the child–parent dyad is important, and communication rather than language *per se* is the tool. He suggested that children learn modes of communication. Initially they *demand*; once an expectation is established, they learn to *request*, and then to *exchange* both concrete objects and communication. Thus, the child learns that language can be used to communicate and to make things happen. Halliday (1979) suggested a similar progression, namely that early communication begins as primarily instrumental, becomes regulatory, then inter-actional and later self-expressive. Control of the environment and of the people in it would seem to be primary functions, with shared dialogue and self-expression coming later.

In their book *Child Language and Cognition*, Rice and Kemper (1984) suggest that children develop communication skills and social awareness at the same time, the one process informing the other; and Macnamara (1982) proposed that children learn language just *because* they are already skilled at making sense of human interactions. On his reading, learning to ask rather than demand and to offer in the expectation of exchange indicates an understanding of the social context on which language learning is built. Tomasello (1992) explains language development as the growth of social-pragmatic skills. Young children learn language in the flow of social interaction. They learn their mother's intentions along with the words she uses.

Children come to understand the social world around them, to communicate with others and, in most cases, to use language. It is doubtful if these are separable. For some children, the social world is a bilingual one, their communication is with speakers of two languages (in North Wales, these are usually Welsh and English), and many will learn to use two languages. The model adopted here is similar to that of Rice and Kemper and of Tomasello, namely that children learn about their social context as they learn to communicate. Therefore, the sequence of language functions proposed by Halliday (instrumental, regulatory, inter-actional, self-expressive) is here extended to include clarification or maintenance of the social situation (societal) and understanding of experience (cognitive) in these early language users.

The examples to be discussed here were collected from a bilingual environment as described already. They are grouped under functional headings. By noting the session at which each event was recorded, the opportunity arises to comment on the absence or existence of a sequence of language functions. Finally, it will become clear that differences in the development of these functions between monolingual English, monolingual Welsh and bilingual children are not evident.

Functions

When the scripts from this small group of children were examined, only clear examples of marked pragmatic use were considered. There is little to be found in the early scripts (before about two years old) except single-word utterances used functionally either in reply to a maternal comment, as a demand or, later, as part of a naming game. Some of the more noticeable examples initially were those relating to word play, bilingual development or language awareness. These are discussed in more detail later in the chapter.

Instrumental

Children under two years of age can use language to achieve concrete ends. By the second and third sessions (age 18 and 21 months) the children are using language successfully to demand and obtain what they want. Often this is by repeating a single word such as 'diod', 'drink', 'book' and 'more'. There are no differences between the children that can be related to language background.

Regulatory

There are many examples in the scripts of children trying to regulate or control the behaviour of their mothers, as well as examples of mothers trying to regulate their children. From about two years of age there are indications that the children were using language to placate mothers. Typically, children engrossed in play would respond with 'yea', 'ia', 'okay', 'later', 'wedyn' while ignoring maternal requests for attention.

From about this time, all of the children are telling or asking their mothers what to do and getting compliance. Sometimes they ask for food, sometimes for an object, sometimes for action on the part of the mother. It is possible that the presence of an observer inhibited the mother's behaviour, but rarely did the child fail in a simple request.

By about 27 months (fifth session), some children had become even more skilled at controlling their mothers. Iwan's mother (WW) offered to sing. Iwan looked at her, and then said '/Just deryn bach canu/' (just little bird sings). At the same age, Gareth (MM) asked his mother to '/Deud a

Grandma dod yn car glas./' (Tell Grandma to come in the green car), and
the following dialogue took place between Nia (WM) and her mother. Her
mother tried to get Nia to talk about a donkey and she was clearly reluctant.

Mother:	/a donkey isn't it?/	
	/has she got a donkey?/	
Nia:	/I don't like it/	
	/it making a ... /	
	/it making ...a sme .../	
Mother:	/you didn't like it?/	
Nia:	/what's that?/	
Mother:	/what's what?/	
Nia:	/there/	[points to her bum]
Mother:	/where?/	[looking]
Nia:	/there/	[pointing again]
Mother:	/that's your bottom/	[Mother embarrassed]
Nia:	/what's that?/	[still pointing]
Mother:	/your bottom/	
Nia:	/no it's not/	
	/it's poo there/	
Mother:	/I don't think it is/	[looking]
	/no it's not/	[very embarrassed]
	/you've just got ... /	
	/it's a bit ... /	
	/you've been sitting on there with the cat hair all stuck on you/	
	/that's the trouble/	

With very few words, Nia successfully distracted her mother and the
donkey was forgotten. At about two and a half, Llywela was able to control
her mother's behaviour using language alone. In the following,

Llywela:	/you can do the house/
Mother:	/I can do the house can I/
Llywela:	/you're a big girl now/

Llywela is using a statement as a directive, and flattery to clinch the
argument.

By the later sessions, some of the children had become not only skilled in controlling the interaction between themselves and their mothers, but extremely persistent in their efforts. At the seventh session, before she was three, Nia (WF) used 23 utterances to match her mother's 22 in a discussion about whether she needed something to eat immediately rather than at lunchtime, and Becky's persistence lasted through 158 utterances altogether (WM). During that time, when Becky's mother was trying to persuade her to get dressed, she argued that;

> she was too warm,
> too hot,
> too cold,
> couldn't hear,
> needed a drink,
> wanted to see Nain,
> could do it herself,
> wanted her pyjamas,
> was going to draw a picture,
> was a dog,
> didn't want the teeshirt, and
> the teeshirt was wet.

Her mother won the day, but Becky demonstrated tremendous skill at playing the control game. Similar examples were recorded across the whole range of language backgrounds.

Interactional; narrating

Most language use is interactional at some level, and so to focus this section only narration is considered. Children enjoy recounting their experiences to their mothers. Although it could be argued that this narration also has a self-expressive, cognitive or even societal function, the interactive element is central. Children tell stories for the sake of an audience.

Children tell their mothers what they can see and what is happening from age two years onwards. Emyr commented '/ a lori mawr neis 'di tori/' (and the nice big lorry's broken); Llywela stated '/that's my drink/'; Gareth reported from the window '/wedi gorffan rwan/'(finished now).

They also give running commentaries on what they are doing at about the same age. At the fourth session Llywela said '/I can't find it/ I can now/ I can't it/ where's it gone?/ ...' during a game. Mathew, while playing at being a dog in the sixth session said '/doggie's in bed/ doggie's asleep/ doggie's is sleep/ and the feet the feet/ he's gone to sleep/ he's quiet/ he's gone to sleep/'; David described how to put a tape in a recorder at the sixth session as follows: '/it go in there/ like that/and put on/ and/and plug him off/ and make it go down/and round/ and it works/ and put .../ a way right/ yea/' (some parental interjections have been omitted).

There are examples of all 10 children using language to relate stories, to provide a commentary on their own activities, and to enrich their pretend play. By the fifth session (28 months) Gareth frequently became absorbed in his play, using language to confirm what he was doing and to remind himself about what he was going to do. Occasions on which children reported events in the past or unknown to their mothers were rare.

Self-expressive; the expression of feelings

The expression of attitudes, opinions or choices all require a level of development beyond the age of the small sample. However, children of this age are beginning to express their feelings. Unfortunately, apart from demands and negations, there was not a lot of evidence that this group of children were able to do so at an early age.

At about two years old Llywela used feelings as an excuse ('Weya's a bit tired now Mommy') and David as a threat ('I [will] cry'). Nia was able to remember her feelings. Her mother asked her why she had cried at the gym club (which she called the 'baby boing' club). She replied 'c(r)ied boing club/ shouldn't to clap/' meaning that the clapping had upset her. At the fifth session, David said he didn't like the bridge, referring to a ride through a railway tunnel that had scared him; and at the seventh session, Nerys reflected 'a dwi isio .../ be dwi isio rwan?/' (and I want .../ what do I want now?/).

The most interesting recorded example is one illustrating how difficult it can be to express feelings at this age, or to use language to escape from a difficult situation. Michael, at age 33 months had taken a book to his mother for her to read it.

Mother: /you know this story/
              /you can tell me this story can't you?/
Michael: /I can't/
Mother: /you can/
Michael: /I can't/
              /you read it to me/
Mother: /okay/
              /we'll both read it shall we?/
Michael: /yea/

Mother:	/once upon a .../	[pauses expectantly]
Michael:	/..time/ /there was a .../ /I can't/	
Mother:	/you../	
Michael:	/I can't/	
Mother:	/okay/ /there were three little .../	[pauses]
Michael:	/I can't/	
Mother:	/goats/	
Michael:	/no/ /three little pigs/ /you twit/	
Mother:	/you/ /don't call me a twit/	

The conversation proceeds like this for 14 more utterances during which Michael gets more agitated and his mother doesn't appear to notice. The dialogue continues (with the mother still reading and pausing).

Mother:	/but take care that the .../[pauses] /wolf doesn't.../	[pauses]
Michael:	/don't be horrible/	[agitated]
Mother:	/I'm not being horrible/	
Michael:	/don't be horrible/	
Mother:	/just watch it!/	
Michael:	/just watch it you/ /don't be horrible/	
Mother:	/right/ /well d'you want the rest of this story?/	
Michael:	/no/	
Mother:	/no/ /right/ /fine/	
Michael:	/I .../ /I want my dummy/	

Michael was aware that he was not getting what he'd asked for (the reading of a story) and that he was being pressured to do what he said he couldn't do (fill in the gaps), but he didn't know how to comment on the situation and ended by being rude.

Astington and Gopnik (1988) suggest that children can talk about their internal states from about age two, but do not indicate with what frequency this happens. The experimental method adopted here sampled rather than monitored the development of these children. Perhaps occasions known to engender anger or unhappiness in the children (and consequent expressions of anger or unhappiness) were carefully avoided by mothers in the presence of a visitor. But that doesn't explain why children didn't talk about their positive feelings more often.

Societal; pretence

By pretending, children are able to separate language from immediate experience, and so to use it as a tool for exploring and assimilating the environment. Through play with toys they can clarify and practise roles and relationships, and test what might happen if they break the rules they are learning.

At age 28 months Michael told a long, involved, make-believe story about an imaginary pond in the living room. He and his mother spent ages avoiding the water, capturing sandhoppers and rescuing frogs. At 28 months Llywela was pretending that her doll was real;

/ This wants watch the wheely bin lorries/
/ I think you will sit there and wait/ (to doll)
/ I think she will sit on the window/ (to Mum)

Emyr, Michael, Matthew, Gareth, Becky and Nia all pretended the doll and teddy were real at about 30 months, and Iwan even pretended he knew what she wanted. His mother wanted him to read a book. He replied;

/ doli 'misio/(to Mum)
/ doli isio jcb/
/ spia doli spia/(to doll)
/ spia jcb yn fana/
/ 'misio darllen llyfr i doli/(to Mum)

(/dolly doesn't want it/ dolly wants the jcb/ look dolly look/ look the jcb there/ don't want to read the book to dolly/)

Pretence is a first step towards the creative use of language. Lying too is a creative use of language, though perhaps it would be better to call it making false or pretence statements. There were a few examples in the scripts of children saying things that were not true. Nia at session six was embarrassed when she spilled her drink and said '/I spilled a lot/'(Mum said 'oh dear') /'I haven't spilled a lot/'. The societal function of her language is clearly evident. More interesting was Iwan's use of pretence to make a difficult situation better. In the course of the sixth session he broke a wooden doll's table. He went very quiet, looked at his mother. She asked him what he had done and he said he'd broken it, then that he'd fix it. He then propped it up and said it was fine. When his mother laughed, he added:

Iwan: /wedi neud bont bach/

Mum: /ti 'di neud bont bach ond dim pont bach di o fod/
/naci/ bwrdd 'di o fod ynte?/

Iwan: /pont bach bwrdd/
/pont y bwrdd di hwna/

(Iwan: /made a little bridge/

Mum: /you've made a little bridge but it's not a little bridge/ no/ it's a table isn't it?/

Iwan: /a table little bridge /
/a table bridge it is /)

Everyone then laughed and Iwan was relieved. Such creative use of language implies a decoupling of thought from reality.

Cognitive

The field of cognitive development is large and it is not appropriate to venture far in the present work. However, some examples of pragmatic language use illustrate the beginnings of logical argument, sequencing and perspective taking in this small sample.

Logical argument

At two years old Llywela was the youngest to be recorded trying to give reasons, but failing. She said she was a bit tired and would have a rest. When her mother suggested going to bed she countered with:

'/no/ it/ it's tired cos I have a rest/'

However, at 28 months Nia was very clear.

'/Aron hit me acos I on the bike./'

Llywela was especially adept at argument and when, at about 30 months old, her Mother didn't draw the house she wanted the following dialogue ensued;

Llywela: /that's a funny house anyway/

Mother:	/why is that a funny house?/
Llywela:	/cos this/ .../a round window/
Mother:	/a round window?/
	/can't a house have a round window?/
	/yes it can/
Llywela:	/look!/ [going to the window]
	/this house hasn't got round windows has it?/
Mother:	/no/

Mother drew another house without round windows. By this age (about 30 months), half of the group had recorded examples of good argument. With the others examples were recorded later.

Sequencing

Although both Gareth and Iwan were recorded talking of a sequence of intended actions, the clearest example recorded was from Llywela. At 28 months she said: '/When I've finished I'll put them back on the tray/', and at 31 months she said (whilst completing a jigsaw) '/and and I'll do one first and then you/ and then I gonna do this one before that one/'.

Perspective-taking

Michael, at 31 months, gave the only clear example of taking the perspective of another. In a tea-party game he hid the teapot and then the cups from the doll saying:

/ the doll can't see that/
/ I put the kettle out there/
/ I put the teapot there/
/ one up there and one up there/
/ and one up there/
/ the dolly can't see them/
/ okay/

Thus, it is possible for children to develop logical, perspective-taking or sequencing skills by about 31 months or possibly earlier.

Out of sequence

Apart from demands (instrumental function), there is no evidence of pragmatic language use, as the terms have been defined here, before the fourth session when the children were about two years old. The instrumental function was evident at around age 19 months (second session), and the regulatory at around age 28 months. However, the interactive function, supposedly the next in sequence, was evident earlier than that, at about two years old. For most children there were no recorded examples of expressive function until the sixth session (about 31 months), the same time as the societal function was evident. There were very few examples of cognitive functions of any sort, but those that were recorded were at around age 28 to 31 months. There are no obvious differences in the rate or number of skills used by children from monolingual compared with bilingual backgrounds.

Thus the evidence for a sequence is ambiguous. It does seem, however, that between the ages of 25 and 31 months, children begin to learn a number of pragmatic skills.

When Do Children Become Aware of Language *per se*?

What counts as language awareness?

We look next at those children who became aware of language itself at a very early age. There is a difference between using language and being aware that you are using language, much as there is a difference between walking and being aware that you are walking. Often the complexity of language use (or of walking) only becomes apparent when you fail in some way. When challenged to explain exactly what we mean by a casual remark, most of us would stumble trying to repair a misunderstanding.

Young children use language as a tool to get what they want, and it is not easy to see whether or not they know what they are doing. It is difficult to avoid imputing more knowledge and awareness than can be justified. Children may be skilled pragmatically (such as making requests in just those circumstances where parents find it hard to refuse) without knowing how they do this. It can be misleading to ask for an explanation. In so doing one is alerting the naive child to the possibility of alternative meanings and as such, promoting rather than describing language awareness.

Many terms have been employed to describe this phenomenon, and the terms 'language awareness' and 'metalingual awareness' appear to be used interchangeably. The term 'metalingual' has been used to mean anything from simple pragmatic language use to all forms of knowledge about language and pragmatics. Bialystock (1991b) has suggested defining metalinguistic ability by the operations needed to solve specific tasks, and identifies these operations as skills *and* awareness. This approach has been very fruitful, and her work will be discussed in more detail later in this chapter.

Here the simpler term 'language awareness', is used. The clearest evidence of language awareness in children is when they talk about talking. Metalingual ability is only used to include both language awareness and other skills entailed in knowing about language and linguistic systems.

Metapragmatics

There is sometimes confusion between the terms 'metalingual' and 'metapragmatic'. Metalingual knowledge is knowledge *about* language and linguistic rules. To use language appropriately according to circumstance is not necessarily evidence of awareness. It is only when children notice language and use of language and then begin to comment on it, that one can talk of the beginning of metalinguistic ability, the ability 'to think about language in addition to being able to think through language.' (Bialystock, 1992:504).

As described earlier in the chapter, pragmatics is using language for differing purposes according to context. The content of a sentence is not the same as its use. Metapragmatic knowledge is knowledge *about* achieving different goals using language. It is possible to describe some metalinguistic events as pragmatic, or even as metapragmatic, but the focus of the first is on language and the focus of the second is on context. For example, a student may ask a teacher to repeat a scientific term (such as 'foci'), knowing that is sounds like an English taboo word. The student's knowledge about language (metalingual ability) allows a use of language (pragmatics) to embarrass the teacher. If the student had started to shout the word, but then decided to use a polite question form for maximum effect, that would be evidence of metapragmatic ability as well.

Elizabeth Bates (1976) showed that, between the ages of 18 and 42 months, children referred to participants in a speech act, to its place and time and, by using connective terms, tied the speech act into a narrative. She used the term 'metapragmatics' to describe these events, and cited them as evidence of language awareness. Her arguments are persuasive, but she ended by acknowledging that talking about talking is the clearest evidence of 'metapragmatics'. The term 'language awareness' is preferred here, but talking about talking is still the clearest evidence for this phenomenon.

Code-switching needs a further comment, as this can indicate pragmatic skill or metalinguistic skill or both. In conversation people make choices constantly regarding the appropriate code to adopt. The most obvious choice of code is between formal and informal: 'hiya' to a friend and 'good morning' to the bank manager. As adults we all use a wealth of covert rules governing how we speak and in what circumstances. Grice (1968) outlined some of the features of this knowledge which is shared by members of a language community, and of particular interest here is the use of polite forms. To ask someone if you can have a loaf is the polite form of a demand and can also be an indirect request. Mostly adults use these forms appropriately according to factors in the environment and with little awareness that they have made a choice. They move from exercising these pragmatic skills to more metapragmatic (or metalinguistic) skills when they decide to use an informal code with their bank manager in an effort to shift the relationship on to a more intimate footing.

Children learn pragmatic skills when they learn language, as was shown in the first part of this chapter. Metalingual skills develop more variably. Although it used to be thought that children only became aware of language at about age seven, recent writers on Theory of Mind have suggested that they develop an awareness of representational states at age four or five. This 'metalanguage', as Olson (1988) terms it, allows them to think about and comment on their own and other people's beliefs as distinct from a given reality. (See Astington *et al.*, 1988; Wellman, 1988; Astington & Gopnik, 1991, for detailed discussion of the development of theories of mind). Language is a representation of reality, and children who can comment on the language of themselves and others provide evidence of some metalanguage skills at least.

These concepts are easily confused but Figure 9.1 may help. This shows development proceeding from the centre, with pragmatic ability growing

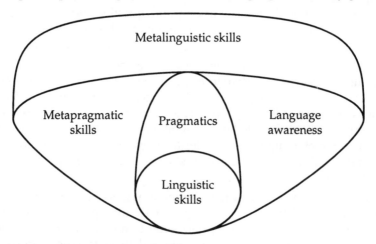

Figure 9.1 Metalinguistic abilities

from and with linguistic ability. From these two sets of skills language awareness and metapragmatic ability develop separately, and metalingual skills encompass all of these abilities.

Metalingual ability and bilingualism

Vygotsky (1962) was probably the first to suggest that, as bilingual children learn to see their first language as one system amongst many, so they become aware of linguistic usage. The question about the link between metalingual ability and bilingualism arose following a suggestion by Vihman and McLaughlin (1982) that metalingual awareness might be greater in people who were bilingual. Although no evidence supported the original suggestion, it made sense in Vygotskian terms. Arnberg and Arnberg (1985) commented that those children who became aware of both languages rarely mixed their languages. They suggested that metalingual awareness was often prompted by some dramatic event in the child's life, such as the first experience of a failure of communication. Vihman (1985) also suggested that differentiation of languages was associated with language awareness. At the time when her subject, Raivio, began to separate his languages, he also began to ask for translation and to comment on own speech acts. The boy was 25 months old when this was first noted. These two studies (Arnberg & Arnberg, 1985 and Vihman, 1985) suggest that some time after their second birthday, potentially bilingual children start to separate their languages and to become aware of language *per se.* More recently Bialystock (1991b, 1992) has summarised research in this area. She reports both her own work and that of others which show that bilingual children consistently perform better on a number of metalingual tasks, especially those requiring selective attention.

Consequently, the rest of this chapter looks first at indications of language awareness and general metalingual ability in the scripts of the small sample. It then turns to occurrences within the language development of those children who subsequently developed skills in both languages in an attempt to trace the beginnings of bilingualism. It will be interesting to see if there are connections between these two themes.

Language Awareness

Creativity and word play

In the recordings made with the small group of children, the first indications that they were becoming aware of language came through examples of word play. They appeared to notice the sounds of a word or phrase and similarity with other words or phrases during play. At about 28 months Iwan said 'no na not/' in reply to a question and laughed, looking at both the observer and his mother, and repeated the joke with delight. ('Na' is the colloquial Welsh 'no'). Nerys at 33 months seemed fascinated with repetition, listing:

the little boys with the puss,
the little boys with the baby chair,
the little boys with the motor bike,
the little boys with the skateboard,
the little boys with the ball, before she lost interest.

Mathew at 31 months old, when he was putting a teddy to bed in a dog's basket said: '/he's gone to basket/ he's gone to biscuit/ .../teddy's biscuit/ .../I get a biscuit/' and promptly charged off to the kitchen to do so. The 'basket' was substituted for the 'bed' implied in the game, and then replaced by 'biscuit', of which he was very fond.

Verbal jokes require an awareness of language and often of the mismatch between words, or between the ideas they represent. Whether the joke is created by the child or remembered and copied, the child needs to be aware of the words involved and their meanings. Nerys (seventh session, aged 33 months) described herself as 'colli balance/ .../wedi meddwi/' (lost balance/ drunk/). David at three years old (eighth session) told his mother he wanted sweetcorn for lunch. And snakes. He knew they were prawns not snakes and looked at his mother with a broad grin.

Iwan's creativity in the sixth session (30 months) has already been mentioned when he renamed the broken table 'pont y bwrdd'. The same table provided Gareth with ideas in the seventh session when he described it as. an elephant, indicating which was its head and which the legs. The final example of creative language use comes from Llywela in the last session. She used 'some glass of wine', 'the pizza', 'the bottle' and 'the coffee' as characters in a long story.

Sometimes it was not clear how knowing the child actually was. In the sixth session, Nia's mother had been discussing her pregnancy and the birth of a friend's baby. Nia asked (about the baby) 'has it comed out yet?/' and when her mother said yes, added 'to play?/'. Later in the conversation her mother asked Nia what the baby was bringing her and she answered 'a present/' and when asked what sort, added 'a baby one/'. In both instances the adults laughed at the ambiguity of the rider, but it wasn't clear whether Nia's response had been intentionally playful.

Intonation and pretend play

Children use pretend play from about age two onwards, and the children in the small sample were no exception. Nia was heard using 'a baby voice' shortly after the birth of her brother when she was about 28 months old, but that was probably pragmatic rather than language aware. Many small children adopt a more babyish style subsequent to the birth of a sibling. Pretend play was the usual context in which children were recorded choosing a different intonation from their normal speech. By age three Nia was able to use a baby voice only with her dolls in play. At the same age, Iwan was recorded using a special voice for the train in his play, as did Llywela in the story of the bottle.

Talking about talking

Llywela was recorded talking about talking in the fifth session (27 months). She told her mother 'she says that's a bath/' and during the sixth, repeating herself, she said 'I said I can't go/ these are broked/' (referring to stepping stones). At the same session (30 months) she confronted the observer with the statement 'I can speak properly/'. It transpired that she had asked her father about the purpose of the sessions and he had replied that they were to see how well she was speaking.

During the fifth session, Gareth also commented about talking, saying to his mother 'a deud a Grandma i dod yn car glas/' (and tell Grandma to come in the blue car). He, Iwan and Llywela were all heard to talk about what people said in their stories. During his session with his father Gareth said 'kangaroo yn deud wrth y dyn 'lle mae o?'/' (the kangaroo said to the man 'where is it?'). In the last session when he was three years old, Iwan wanted the people to tell the little children what time to come on the train (and needed a clock to help them). During the story of the bottle, Llywela said 'they said "why are you crying bottle?"/'.

A further group of examples illustrates children's awareness of language, in this case, of how things are said. All of the children had baby words for things early on, words such as doggie, gee-gee, and ta. As they grew older they adopted the conventional words instead, but only a few were recorded commenting on the process. As early as the sixth session, at about 31 months, Gareth said 'oen bach dim mee-mees di nhw/' (little lambs are not mee-mees), but it wasn't till the last session (with his father) that he said 'mae Taid yn deud mee-mees a defaid/ … /a defaid dwi'n deud/' (Grandad says mee-mees for sheep/ and I say sheep/). The earlier observation about language has become an observation about language use. He also commented that he says 'excuse me' in school ('"excuse me" dwi'n deud yn yr ysgol/'), a comment that is metapragmatic as well as language aware.

Code-switching and speech acts

In conversation people make choices constantly regarding the appropriate code to adopt. Children learn to do this too, but there are few examples in the scripts, and those which are evident came towards the end of the study. From an early age all the children in the study, Welsh and English, were taught that 'please' was the magic word for getting goodies. The following example from Nia's penultimate script demonstrates an ability to do more than parrot the key word. Nia re-forms her wish from a demand into a polite request;

	N: that drawing's in the way/
M: your drawings?/	**N:** yea/
	N: get it out of the way/
M: what d'you say?/	**N:** please can you put on the table?/

Llywela was adept at switching codes. In the last session she clearly shifted from fantasy to reality when she told her mother, who was holding a cat and looking at a book:

	L: I think he wants one of those words/
M: he wants one of those words?/ which one d'you think he wants?/	**L:** he wants all of them/
M: that says good food/	**L:** he can't eat them/ it's only on a picture/

Becky was good at switching codes. In the scene already quoted (when she used more than a dozen arguments to prevent her mother dressing her), she shifted from 'little girl lost' to 'assertive show-off' to 'sweet reasonableness' and back again to 'poor me'. All the examples of code switching have come from girls in the study, but from different language backgrounds.

Conclusion

Although the instances quoted above are clear examples of language awareness, they are few in number. Therefore it is difficult to decide whether children exposed to two languages in the home are more aware of language *per se* than are those in monolingual homes. Gareth (MM) was especially aware of language and language differences, and he was bilingual by age three. However, examples of language awareness of one sort or another were recorded from all the children, irrespective of language background. Thus, it is fair to assume that children of three are likely to be aware of language as well as able to use language (or languages).

Becoming Bilingual

It would be useful to describe in detail how young children become bilingual. So far, it is not possible to do so. As the results of the second questionnaire highlight, most parents on Anglesey want their children to be bilingual. Although many will rely on the education system to do that for them, it has been shown that the school environment is not sufficient to ensure that that happens (Baker, 1994).

What follows is an attempt to trace events in the language development of the children monitored which seem to have been associated with the development towards bilingualism. Some of the information is gleaned from data presented in previous sections and that will be referenced, and much more comes from the scripts from the recording sessions. However, in the early stages of language acquisition, children resist invitations and exhortations to demonstrate their skills, and so mothers' reports were solicited.

One meaning of code-switching has been described, but it is also used to mean switching between languages. Swain (1972) would argue that these two uses are the same in essence. Grosjean (1982) and Nelde (1989), for example, have detailed the circumstances in which bilinguals switch from one language to the other, the most frequent occasion being the arrival of a non-language speaker into a conversation. Some examples from both mothers and children were found in the scripts from the small sample. Also found were many examples of borrowing from one language, which appeared to be largely unnoticed by either party, and some examples of awareness of the difference between the two language systems noticed by the child.

The scripts examined were those of the three children who showed clear evidence of bilingual development by age three (Gareth, Iwan and Emyr), and from four who did so subsequently (Nia, Becky, Nerys and Mathew). It is notable that all of these families have at least one parent who is a first language Welsh speaker. Table 9.1 summarises the examples discussed below.

Table 9.1 Elements of bilingual language development

Name	Age (months)	Examples
Nerys (WW)	21	Has a few E words/plays with E friend/E TV/
	27	Created 'slipio'/
	30	E phrases such as 'go to sleep'/
	33	Upset if doesn't understand E children/
	36	Answers E questions in W/
Iwan (WW)	24	Some E words/plays with E friend/
	27	Uses W with E word in correct place/
	36	Answered E question in W/
		Laughed at mother addressing him in E/
Becky (WM)	30	Understands E from dad/ Won't accept E from mother/Parents use E together/
	33	Uses E intonation in 'pretend E' play/ Answered E question in W/
	36	Very upset if 'wrong' language used/ Asked dad questions in E/
Emyr (WM)	24	Parents use E together/
	27	Won't let mother use E with him/
	33	Replied in W to E questions/
	36	Asked questions of dad in E/
Gareth (MM)	27	Uses some E words and phrases/
	30	Speaks E by using W with E intonation/ Responds to E conversations/ Practises E/
	33	Speaks E to E speakers/ Seems to understand E/ Different intonation for W word if in E/ Follows mother's code-switch/
	36	Switches easily from W to E and back/ Aware that he does so/ Can speak for hours in E/ Spoke only W with dad/
Nia (WF)	24	Uses some W words/ Occasionally translates/ Mother uses W phrases/
	30	Dad speaks W to her/ Parents use E together/

Table 9.1 Elements of bilingual language development *(cont.)*

Nia		Doesn't like mother to use W/
(WF)	36	Using W at nursery/ Understands half of dad's W/
(cont.)		Asked dad questions in W/
Mathew	27	Picking up W words/ Mother uses some W words/
(WF)	30	Occasionally translates/
	36	Understands some of father's W/

W = Welsh and E = English
The children were seen at about three-month intervals from age 15 months to three years. Approximate ages are given, but children could be up to a month older than the age stated.

Single words; borrowing

Initially, single words are used from the second language, often unnoticed by the child or parent. Words included in the Dictionary of Common Words (Appendix III) will not be used in examples, as they have an unclear provenance. By two years the children whose first language was Welsh were using single words such as 'stuck', 'jumps', 'chips', and 'just' in their ordinary conversation, and phrases such as 'naughty girl', 'cup of coffee' and 'never mind' shortly thereafter. Some of the children acquiring English first also used Welsh words in speech. Nia and Mathew, both with a Welsh father, slipped words such as 'tan' (fire), 'coedan' (tree), 'brechdan' (sandwich) and 'pechod' (what a pity) into their conversations from about the same time.

Peers

Between the fourth and seventh sessions (ages about 24 to 34 months), children were reported to use their second language with peers for whom it is the first language. Whether this was actually so is unclear. There is stronger evidence that they had developed some understanding of the second language. Not only did mothers report this phenomenon, but the writer experienced Becky (WM), Iwan (WW), Nerys (WW) and Emyr (WM) accurately responding in Welsh to her comment in English.

Translations

At about the same time translations occurred, first by the parent (Nia's mother said 'make tan?/ yes that's right/ make fire/') and then by the child. At the fourth session Nia said 'it's a tree/', her mother queried her and she replied 'yea/ it's a coedan/'. At the sixth session Mathew said of his father 'he's gone to work/ he's gone to gwaith/'. Finally, at the sixth session (age 31 months), Gareth switched from Welsh to say 'want a cadair/ want a chair/'.

Intonation

Children notice intonation developmentally (Karniol, 1990). In this group, both Becky and Gareth were reported to speak 'pretend English' by using Welsh with English intonation, at 33 and 30 months respectively. Gareth was heard to play with the intonation of his English conversation, and to practise phrases until they were more correct. His mother noticed that he pronounced 'tren-train' appropriately according to context by the last session. Finally, by the time he was three years old, Mathew's intonation was decidedly Welsh some of the time, but it did not vary reliably.

The wrong language

A number of the children objected when parents used the 'wrong' language. At 31 months, although Becky (WM) would listen to her father talking to her in English, she made a big fuss if her mother spoke to her in English. Examples of this event were recorded at the sixth and eighth sessions. Emyr, the other WM child, was reported to object if his mother used English to him, and Nia (WF) refused to acknowledge that she understood her mother's Welsh in the sixth session:

M: what's this?/	N: dolly's hair/
M: yn Gymraig?/ (in Welsh?/)	N: what is it?/
M: gwallt/ (hair/)	N: no!/ what's that?/
M: that's hair/ gwallt/	N: it's not/ it's a hair/

She had translated single words to Welsh in the fourth session, and was reported to use Welsh as well as English in conversation with her father. She understood what her mother was offering her (an alternative name in a different language), but she was pretending that she did not.

Allied to this is the idea of the 'right' language. Although not on tape, Mathew's mother reported that he used 'thank you' to her and 'diolch' to her husband (they mean the same thing). Gareth was reported to differentiate between Welsh and English speakers by session seven, and Iwan's reaction was to laugh when his mother tried to talk to him in English. He looked at her and at the writer (whom he later addressed in

English) and simply laughed and refused to answer. This was in the final session when he was three.

Creativity

A number of the Welsh speakers use made-up words that are sometimes called 'Wenglish'. Adults may use 'swimio' (to swim) instead of nofio and pushio (to push) instead of gwthio for example, and so some of the made-up words recorded could have been copied. Others, however, may well have been creative inventions of the child. One created word was captured. During the fifth recording session Nerys repeated 'slipio', a word her mother did not understand at first, until she repeated it in the context of 'doli wedi slipio/' (the dolly has slipped).

As with other features of bilingual development, that there is only one clear example does not invalidate the observation. Recordings were made once every three months, and covered just over an hour of the child's conversation. It is possible that some of the commonplace Wenglish words were unique to the child heard using them and that many more instances of word creation occurred with most of the children, but unfortunately, not when the tape recorder was running. This illustrates why so much work in this area has been done by parents themselves, able to reach for the tape recorder when their child was in a talkative mood.

Distress

There were a few occasions when the presence of two language systems appeared to cause distress to these children. Nerys was said to become very upset when she did not understand the English used by children in the Nursery. More frequently, though, they became distressed when attempts to encourage them to use their second language were pressed too hard. Reference has already been made to Becky's distress when her mother tried to get her to reply in English. Once it ended in a tantrum. The two other examples on tape are when Welsh fathers tried to get Mathew and Nia to speak to them in Welsh only. Mathew changed the subject or ran out of the room when he did not understand, but Nia became quite upset when she did not understand more than about half of what her father was saying to her. On all three occasions the parent changed back to the language with which the child was more familiar.

Chunking

When children began to use their second language spontaneously, it often became evident with the use of chunks of the second language. These started with phrases that could almost be one word such as Nerys' 'go-to-sleep' at age 31 months and Mathew's 'ban-ti-ni' (off we go) at the same age. Later larger chunks were used. Becky, Nia and Emyr used questions such as 'where's it gone?/' 'be di hwnna?/' (what is it?) and 'where is picnic?/' at and around three years old. Nerys appeared to understand the chunks of the English story she repeated back to her mother, and at the same age, Emyr and Nia used simple sentences in their second language with their fathers. Gareth was using sentences in English at 31 months.

Bilingual before three

Finally, mention must be made of the one child in the group who appeared to be more or less a balanced bilingual by the time of his last session at three years old. Gareth had parents with a mixed language background and, although both his parents wanted his first language to be Welsh and used Welsh primarily, his mother preferred the English language and used it frequently. By 28 months he was using English intonation to pretend to be speaking English, using many English words, and his mother was using both languages with him. At 31 months he was using sentences in English with some Welsh words and sentences in Welsh with some English words, and by the seventh session he was following his mother's switch of code with no indication that he was aware of the change, but dropping back easily into Welsh if he could not find the right expression in English. This often happened mid-sentence.

By the last session Gareth was leading the code switch from one language to the other, and refusing to use Welsh (or English) at his mother's request if he did not feel so inclined;

M: ti am siarad Gymraeg rwan?/ G: na/

M: pam?/ G: yn Saesneg/

M: yn Saesneg?/ G: oh/ ah all this rubbish/

M: tyd ochr yma ta i siarad G: oh look all this rubbish/
efo fi/   cos this in my ways/

(M: are you going to speak G: No/
Welsh now?/

M: how?/ G: in English/

M: in English?/   G: oh/ ah all this rubbish/
M: come to the side here to   G: oh look all this rubbish/
    talk with me/   cos this in my ways/)

He was aware of the language code he was using, if only by recognition. The choice of Welsh–English could still have been automatic. In a recording made within a few weeks of this last session, he spoke no English at all with his Welsh-speaking father. This nicely illustrates the limitation of work in this area; had the language use of his two parents been reversed, it would not have been apparent that his second language was developing so strongly. Indeed, given the differing roles that parental language seems to play, his second language might not have developed so strongly (see next chapter).

Connections

There are three possible relationships between metalingual abilities and the development of bilingualism (that is excluding no relationship at all). Bilingual development could lead to enhanced metalingual awareness, metalingual awareness could lead to enhanced bilingual development, or the two might interact, enhancing (or delaying) the development of each other.

Gareth, the boy whose bilingual abilities were the most strongly developed, was aware of language from an early age, and of a number of aspects of language. On the other hand, Llywela, who was arguably the most able child metalinguistically, appeared to have made little or no progress bilingually. Their development supports the first proposition, namely that bilingualism enhances metalingual development. Furthermore, the children whose bilingualism developed later, Iwan (WW) and Emyr (WF), both gave evidence of some metalingual ability, and so no counter examples were recorded (that is, bilingual children who did not develop metalingually). However, the third proposition, that there exists a supportive interaction, could still be true, and might better describe all three cases. In young children where both abilities are developing, it is difficult to imagine how the interactive proposition could be invalidated. Possibly it could be tested with later developing bilinguals.

Llywela is clear evidence that metalingual ability is not dependent upon bilingualism.

Again it must be stressed that the recordings only sample the language of the target children; many of their metalinguistic skills may not be represented on tape. They may also have bilingual abilities which are not evident.

Summary

The beginning of this chapter looked at pragmatic development. Pragmatics is a difficult concept, and trying to identify the roots of pragmatic skills in the early development of children's language is not easy, especially if one wants to avoid linguistic definitions.

The scripts from the small sample provided examples of the ways in which this group of children were beginning to use language itself as a tool. They were ordered into six categories of language function; instrumental, regulatory, interactional, self-expressive, societal and cognitive. This enabled them to be compared and contrasted, although no differences could be ascribed to language background: being monolingual or bilingual does not seem to make a difference.

The functions of language described and used to categorise the examples do not seem to form a sequence. The instrumental function appears earlier than the rest, at about 19 to 22 months. The other functions all appear at between 24 and 30 months, or thereabouts, and it is not possible to suggest an order. However, children are able to use language pragmatically in some ways at least between two and two and a half years of age.

Children can also develop language awareness before age three. There is evidence of creativity with words and word play, and of the deliberate use of intonation differences. Children of this age are beginning to talk about talking. They notice what words other people use and what they themselves say. They are also beginning to code-switch.

Looking at factors associated with the development of bilingualism, children use words borrowed from a second language, try to understand peers using a second language, copy the intonation of a second language and also learn to translate. They may learn the second language in chunks, can use it creatively, but can be distressed by their inadequate understanding. Many have strong feelings of who should use which language; contextual correlates of learning are strong. The section ended with the story of a boy who became bilingual before he was three years old.

The connections between these last two themes are not easy to disentangle; a monolingual child developed good metalinguistic abilities compared with most of her bilingual peers. None the less it seems that children who develop bilingual skills early tend to develop metalingual skills early. Learning to translate infers an awareness of the existence of more than one language system, and metalingual skills can focus the attention of children in a way that makes it easier to learn a second language. However, the opportunities to use a second language (with a parent, for example) are probably at least as important as metalingual skills for those who want their children to become bilingual.

10 Which Parent Has More Influence on the Language of the Home?

Introduction

The mother tongue?

It is usually assumed that mothers have more influence than fathers on the language development of their children; the first language learned is often referred to as the 'mother tongue'. On the face of it this is a reasonable assumption as, in most cultures, mothers are the regular caretakers of children and so the idiosyncratic language used by the mother is the one most frequently heard by the child. However, some research has suggested that, compared with maternal language, the language of the father is influential in a different rather than lesser manner (Blank-Greif, 1980; McLaughlin *et al.*, 1983; Rondal, 1980; Tomasello *et al.*, 1990).

In the bilingual field there are indications that the father's language influences choice of home language in cross-language marriages (Harrison *et al.*, 1981; Lyon, 1991). It is to the question of language influence in the home that this chapter is addressed, that is the language environment in which the children in the base population and in the small sample are developing.

Cross-language marriages

The evidence of parental influence in cross-language marriages is examined using the 1988–89 survey of parents. Excluding single-parent families from this group leaves a total of 384 families, containing from one to six children. Approximately two-thirds of the group used a second language to some degree.

Data from the second questionnaire (QII) are then examined and maternal and paternal questionnaires compared. Excluding those families who returned only one QII, leaves 177 families. As well as examining the comparative influence of mothers and fathers, it is possible to look for changes in influence over time. Finally, some issues regarding cross-language marriages, gender and influence are considered.

Parental Influence in the 1988–89 Sample

Language heard at home

The first questionnaire asked about the language used by each parent in a number of situations. The replies were organised into five groups of couples to try to identify the influence of one partner on the language use of the other and on the language use in the home. It was assumed that the language learned by the child would be that or those heard within the child's home. As described previously, the groups were Welsh-speaking parents (WW), English-speaking parents (EE), families with a Welsh-speaking mother and a non-Welsh-speaking father (WM), families with a Welsh-speaking father and a non-Welsh-speaking mother (WF) and finally, a mixed group (MM). The phrase 'Welsh speaking' is used to mean someone whose first language is Welsh and who has been defined as a primary Welsh user on the basis of replies to the first questionnaire. It is rare in North Wales for a Welsh speaker to be unable to speak English. The phrase 'English speaking' is used for someone whose first language is English and who has been defined as using virtually no Welsh on the basis of replies to the first questionnaire. There are many people in North Wales who do not knowingly speak a word of Welsh.

Only with the Welsh-speaking couples (WW) is Welsh used regularly and frequently at home. Similarly, only the EE couples use English all the time with almost everyone at home. In other words, if both partners have the same first language, that language is the only language heard at home in virtually all of these homes. This is hardly surprising.

But what happens in cross-language partnerships or marriages, where one partner is a first language Welsh (or English) speaker and the other is not? In cross-language marriages just under half of the Welsh-speaking parents use Welsh all the time. Over half of the English-speaking parents use English all the time. That is, in these partnerships about half of the partners are not using their first language as much as they might in a monolingual home. The picture is less clear in families with mixed language backgrounds. There more than two-thirds of the parents use English all the time at home.

Which situations encourage or discourage the use of a parent's first language? About 70% of Welsh mothers in the WM group and 70% of Welsh fathers in the WF group use Welsh with their own parents and children, and a similar percentage of their English-speaking partners use English with their own parents. Their language use with their children is less predictable, some using their first language, some using their second and some a mixture of the two.

The families where two languages are available bear closer examination, and details for the cross-language groups can be seen in Table 10.1. The interesting comparisons are between the non-Welsh-speaking partners in cross-language marriages. Amongst the non-Welsh speaking women, 21% use mostly Welsh with the children, 20% do so with neighbours and 17% use Welsh with friends. In comparison, 17% of the non-Welsh-speaking men use Welsh with their children, 9% do so with neighbours and 12% of these men use Welsh with friends. In other words, more female partners of Welsh speakers use Welsh than do male partners.

Looking at the Welsh-speaking parents, there is less movement away from the first language. Amongst the women, although 20% use mostly English with neighbours, only 6% do so with friends or with the children. Of the men, only 11% use mainly English with neighbours, 2% with friends and 8% with the children. That is, cross-language marriage appears to increase the major use of Welsh marginally more than the major use of English in the 'other language' partners of either sex. However, there is a decline overall in the percentage of both men and women using their first language.

Language used for talking to one another

Table 10.2 looks at the language partners choose to use with one another and is somewhat complicated. In same-language marriages, virtually all couples use only their main language. In cross-language marriages there is a general decrease in the number of couples using one language mainly, and there are gender differences in the amount of the decrease.

The first comparison is between the women in the WM group and those in the WW group. Both sets of women are first language Welsh speakers, but the latter have partners who are primarily Welsh speaking whereas the former do not. Virtually all of the WW women use mainly Welsh with their partners, but only 19% of the WM group do so. Instead, 75% of them use mainly English.

Table 10.1 Language use by mothers (M) and fathers (F) from cross-language partnerships in different situations

		Almost always or mostly Welsh		Half and half		Almost always or mostly English	
		M (%)	F (%)	M (%)	F (%)	M (%)	F (%)
Parent	WM	97	8	3	6	0	86
	WF	11	64	11	12	78	5
Friend	WM	56	12	39	9	6	80
	WF	17	65	11	33	72	2
Neighbours	WM	47	0	31	9	20	83
	WF	20	62	13	27	67	11
Shops	WM	36	3	53	11	11	86
	WF	4	46	20	39	76	16
Work	WM	66	3	28	12	7	85
	WF	3	68	33	29	63	2
Church	WM	81	9	19	5	0	86
	WF	23	79	27	18	50	4
Children	WM	72	17	22	22	6	61
	WF	21	46	26	46	54	8

WM = Couples where the mother is Welsh-speaking and the father is not.
WF = Couples where the father is Welsh-speaking and the mother is not.

E.g. more Welsh-speaking mothers in WM (or WM-M) use Welsh always or almost always with their children (72%) than Welsh-speaking fathers in WF (WF-F = 46%), and more non-Welsh-speaking mothers in WF (WF-M) use Welsh always or almost always always in church or chapel (23%) than non-Welsh-speaking fathers in WM (WM-F = 9%).

Table 10.2 Present language use by couples by language background group (in percentages)

		Almost always or mostly Welsh	Half and half	Almost always or mostly English
Mother to father	WW	99.0	1.1	0.0
	WM	19.4	5.6	75.0
	WF	27.3	11.4	61.4
	EE	0.0	0.0	100.0
Father to mother	WW	99.0	1.0	0.0
	WM	16.7	2.8	80.6
	WF	29.5	13.6	56.8
	EE	0.0	0.0	100.0

Calculations based on Table 10.2	Welsh (%)	English (%)
(A) W Mothers to W fathers (WW)	99	0
W Mothers to E fathers (WM)	19	75
i.e. decrease in % using W =	80	—
and increase in % using E =		75
(B) W Fathers to W mothers (WW)	99	0
W Fathers to E mothers (WF)	30	57
i.e. decrease in % using W =	69	—
and increase in % using E =		57
(C) E mothers to E fathers (EE)	0	100
E mothers to W fathers (WF)	27	61
i.e. increase in % using W =	27	—
and decrease in % using E =		39
(D) E Fathers to E mothers (EE)	0	100
E fathers to W mothers (WM)	17	81
i.e. increase in % using W =	17	—
and decrease in % using E =		19

So from (A) and (B), if mother is W in the cross-language partnership, then fewer Welsh-speakers use mostly W, and more use mostly E (80% and 75%) than if father is W and mother is E (69% and 57%).

And from (C) and (D), if mother is E in the cross-language partnership, then fewer English-speakers use mostly E, and more use mostly W (39% and 27%) than if father is E and mother is W (19% and 17%).

Complementary groups are the Welsh-speaking men in the WW and WF groups. Again, virtually all of the men use mainly Welsh in the WW group but this drops to 30% in the WF group, 57% of whom use mostly English with their partners. That is, more Welsh-speaking men continue to use Welsh in cross-language marriages than do Welsh-speaking women, and fewer change to using English.

The next comparison is between the women who are not primarily Welsh speaking in the EE and WF groups. In the EE group they all use English with their partners. In the WF group only 61% do so and 27% use mostly Welsh. The men who are not primarily Welsh speaking all use English in the EE group. In the WM group, this drops to 81% using English and 17% of them use mostly Welsh. Again there is more change by the female partners: 20% fewer English-speaking women speak only English and 10% more speak mostly Welsh than do English-speaking male partners in cross-language marriages. As can be seen in calculations beneath Table 10.2, accommodation is to the English language and the male partner.

In the group of couples where each has a mixed language background, the gender effect is not evident. Nearly 90% of fathers spoke to their partner in English almost all of the time and almost 90% of mothers spoke to their partner in English most of the time.

Returning to Table 10.2, a comparison can be made between those who use at least half Welsh and those who use virtually only English. Looked at this way, 43% of Welsh-speaking men continue to use Welsh for a considerable part of communication in their cross-language partnership (and 38% of them are responded to in this way). Only 25% of Welsh-speaking women report using this amount of Welsh in these relationships, and only 20% get a similar response. That is, almost two-fifths of English-speaking women use a substantial amount of Welsh with their Welsh-speaking partners, whereas only one-fifth of English-speaking men communicate similarly in Welsh with their Welsh-speaking partners. As stated earlier, 81% of English-speaking men and 61% of English-speaking women continue to use almost entirely English in cross-language partnerships and are spoken to in English in 75% and 57% of cases respectively. The women who completed this questionnaire emerge as more likely to accommodate their partner's main language than he is to accommodate theirs.

It is possible that women are better at learning a second language than are men (Ellis, 1985). It is also possible that men retain a more powerful position in most families and so decide the medium of discourse.

Finally in this section, the main effect of the language itself should not be overlooked. Table 10.2 demonstrates clearly that whereas 75% of

Welsh-speaking women and 57% of Welsh-speaking men use mostly English with their partners in cross-language marriages, only 27% of primarily English-speaking women and 17% of the men use mostly Welsh. The language itself appears to have a greater influence than gender, especially on the language partners use together.

Differences in the opinions of parents

Is Welsh important?

The general opinions of parents were reported in Chapter 6. This section looks at differences between the opinions of mothers and fathers. When asked how important they thought the Welsh language was, 5% of all mothers and 6% of all fathers thought it was unimportant, and 46% of mothers and 49% of fathers thought it was important. There was similar proximity between parents in some groups, but not the two cross-language groups. In the Welsh mother (WM) group, 3% of non-Welsh-speaking fathers thought Welsh was unimportant whilst none of their wives held that opinion. Furthermore, only 72% of these men felt Welsh was important compared with 81% of the Welsh-speaking women in this group. In the other cross-language group (WF), 10% more of the Welsh-speaking men thought Welsh was important than did the women, but neither thought Welsh was unimportant.

Clearly in cross-language marriages, Welsh-speaking partners value their language more than do their partners. But there is also a gender effect here. Welsh-speaking women are more likely to value Welsh than are Welsh-speaking men and non-Welsh-speaking women are less likely to devalue Welsh than are non-Welsh-speaking men.

It is interesting to compare Welsh-speaking women and men who married Welsh speakers with those who did not. The Welsh-speaking women in the WW and WM groups responded very similarly. The Welsh-speaking men in the WW and WF groups did not. Although few devalued Welsh, those in cross-language partnerships were less likely to think Welsh was important (67% compared with 80%). It would seem that female Welsh speakers are less influenced by their partnership than are male Welsh-speakers.

There was less discrepancy between the female and male non-Welsh-speakers in cross-language partnerships. People of either gender who married Welsh speakers were more likely to think Welsh was important than those who married English speakers (72% of fathers in WM compared with 18% of fathers in EE and 57% of mothers in WF compared with 18% of mothers in EE). The results seem to indicate that the men are more influenced by their relationships than the women. However, as with all of the questions of opinion, the only significant effect was of language background, not gender.

Do you want your child to learn Welsh?

There was cross-gender agreement regarding the language parents wanted their children to learn: 62% or 64% wanted them to be fluent and 24% or 23% wanted them to learn Welsh at school. However, there were differences between parents when the results were analysed by group. More Welsh-speaking fathers (83%) and Welsh-speaking mothers (92%) wanted their children to be fluent in Welsh than their cross-language partners (76% and 86%) respectively. And 8% more fathers than mothers wanted their children to be fluent in the mixed (MM) group. The Welsh-speaking women in WM more nearly approximated those in WW than did the two groups of male Welsh-speakers, although the differences were less marked than for the Importance of Welsh.

More than 95% of all parents in the cross-language groups (and in WW) wanted their children to learn Welsh, either at school or fluently. A higher percentage of women in WF (20%) opted for 'school Welsh' rather than 'fluent' as compared to the men in WM (8%). Both groups are non-Welsh-speaking partners. Perhaps this reflects a perception on the part of the mothers that fluent language use is learned in the home.

The future of the Welsh language

Regarding the future of the Welsh language, there was a tendency for fathers to be more pessimistic than mothers. The exception appears to be fathers in the WF group. They were more likely to believe that Welsh would be used more in the future than were the mothers (22% compared with 13%) and less likely to believe that Welsh would be replaced by English (2% compared with 7%). In the other cross-language group (WM) a complementary trend is observable, with 37% of the non-Welsh-speaking fathers believing Welsh will be used less compared with 29% of the women.

Welsh-speaking women who marry non-Welsh speakers are less optimistic than their sisters; 15% fewer think the use of Welsh will increase and none think it will replace English. Welsh-speaking men who marry non-Welsh-speakers don't seem to differ from their brothers; although fewer think Welsh will replace English, more think its use will increase. Non-Welsh speakers in cross-language marriages responded similarly to other non-Welsh speakers. There was a slight trend for this group to be less optimistic about Welsh than people in the EE groups. It seems that the language factor is more significant than gender for this question.

Who do you want your child to marry?

The last question in this section asked who parents hoped their children would marry: a Welsh-speaker, a non-Welsh-speaker, or either? Again there was general agreement between the mothers and fathers with the great majority (85% or 86%) saying they could marry either. The one notable difference was in the WM group where 19% of the Welsh-speaking mothers would prefer their children to marry Welsh speakers. None of their partners made this choice.

Welsh speakers who married non-Welsh speakers appear to have been influenced away from their peers. Only 11% of men in cross-language marriages wanted their children to marry Welsh speakers compared with 42% in WW, and only 19% of women made a similar choice, compared with 42% of WW. Choices of non-Welsh speakers remain more similar to those made by women and men in EE. Thus again it seems that language background is a more influential factor than gender.

It seems therefore that the differences so far identified between the opinions and language use of fathers and mothers are subtle, and most in evidence in cross-language partnerships. In these relationships women seem to be more adaptable to the language of their partner. More Welsh-speaking men continue to speak Welsh and fewer English-speaking women continue to use only English than their counterparts. Is that the influence of the language, the gender of the speaker, or the partnership?

In 1991–1992, both parents were asked respond to QII independently. Consequently the data gathered (and reported below) is probably less contaminated than that already discussed. It is also possible to separate maternal and paternal free text opinions and so to compare their content.

Questionnaire Two

Three years later

Whereas 384 complete families returned the first questionnaire, 177 families returned the second. Of these, both parents completed separate questionnaires in 124 families. It is these 124 families that are used for comparisons in this section. Although about 82% of couples were categorised in the same language background group on both occasions, the greatest attrition was from the WF (Welsh-speaking father) group. Those so categorised on the first occasion tended to drift into the MM category. That is, Welsh-speaking fathers tended to use less Welsh on the second occasion than on the first.

When all of the QII replies were considered, more fathers of monolingual English-speaking children omitted to complete a questionnaire than did fathers from the other two groups. This was significant (χ-square = 7.905, p <0.05). It is not important in itself, and cannot bear too much weight, however, it adds to the picture of fathers as less involved in language issues and more accepting of the ubiquity of English than are mothers.

Maternal and paternal answers compared

Correlations and t-tests between parental reports (maternal/paternal) on questions from QII were examined closely for evidence of significant differences. These included:

'What Language does your Child hear from Siblings?'
'What Language does your Child hear from Peers?'
'What Language does your Child Use?'
'What Language does your Child Understand?'
'Which Language do you prefer for Reading?'
'Which Language do you prefer for Reading to your Child?'

All of these have a five-point scale from 1 (almost always Welsh) to 5 (almost always English). The 'Child Development' question ('Are you happy with your child's language development?') is binary, and the last question, on amount of Welsh learning chosen for their child, is on a four-point scale (1 = only English, to 4 = fluent Welsh).

Few significant differences between maternal and paternal reports were discernible. More mothers thought their children understood some Welsh than did fathers (p= 0.028). There were also marginally significant differences in the language chosen for personal reading (p = 0.044) and in the language chosen to read to their children (p = 0.047). Mothers chose less English than fathers when reading and when reading to their children.

This is supported by data abstracted from QI which shows that, compared with QII, maternal language choice for reading changes over time towards Welsh. It is possible that both of these differences are associated with the language used with a growing child. This is in accord with comments made by mothers in the small sample, and on the returned questionnaires. In other words, the child influences the language choice of the mother, at least in terms of her reading (and possibly viewing) material.

Next to be examined were parental responses to questions about the development of nine aspects of Welsh and nine aspects of English on a three-point scale (1 = not yet, to 3 = often). They were largely in agreement. The exceptions related to single-word use in Welsh (p = 0.023), many-word use in English (p = 0.034) and stories in English (p = 0.034). All significance levels were marginal, but mothers were more likely to say that their children used single words in Welsh, used many words in English, and tried to tell stories in English. Thus it seems that mothers tend to attribute more language skills to their offspring than do fathers.

Parental opinions about learning Welsh

As discussed earlier, there was a large measure of agreement between the parents when asked, at QI, about how much Welsh they wanted their children to learn when they were older. Almost all parents wanted their children to learn Welsh at school. This opinion did not change between the first and second questionnaire.

Parental opinions were examined in detail in Chapter 6, and the examination included an analysis of the comments made on the 1989 questionnaire (QI). At that time it was not possible to attribute the comments to mothers or fathers. In the second questionnaire, QII, that was possible, and Table 10.3 shows the overall results. As can be seen, fathers made about 13% fewer comments overall than did mothers, but their reasons for wanting their children to learn Welsh (or not) were remarkably similar. Mothers tended to give reasons associated with improved communication skills and job prospects and fathers tended to make comments emphasising the importance of both languages. This emphasis on the usefulness of both languages is a change between the two questionnaires in general.

The greatest difference between the opinions of fathers and mothers was in the WW group: 35% of the comments made by Welsh-speaking fathers in this group refer to the importance of learning English as well as Welsh, compared with only 22% of the comments from mothers. The other difference worth a mention is that between parents in the MM group: 10% more of the men's comments than those of the women related to the Welsh heritage or identity.

Are there major differences?

The evidence that one gender has more influence than the other over the language used at home is not great. Those who marry someone with a different first language will hear a second language spoken by someone special, whether they are male or female. Thus, the greatest differences are to be found in cross-language partnerships, and in the present research, the greatest influence was the language with all parents keen to speak Welsh with their children.

Table 10.3 Parental reasons for wanting (or not wanting) their children to learn Welsh. Results from QII, shortly after the children were three years old in 1992

	Mothers (%)	Fathers (%)	Both parents (%)
1. Both languages are important	15	19	17
2. It is an advantage	5	8	6
3. Better job prospects	8	5	7
4. Communication	8	6	8
5. Non-reason comments	24	22	23
6. Keep back the English	2	1	2
7. Irrelevant or unnecessary	11	12	11
8. Welsh identity and heritage	26	26	26
		100	100
Number of comments	155	135	290
Number of subjects	124	124	248

Figures given are the percentage of the comments for mothers, fathers and all parents.

However, against that background, women do adapt their language use more than do men. In comparison with the men, fewer Welsh-speaking women use Welsh and more use English with non-Welsh-speaking partners and more English-speaking women use Welsh and fewer use English with their Welsh-speaking partners. Table 10.2, which presents the evidence for this, bears close scrutiny. Is this influence? Are the majority of men deciding the language used at home? Or is it rather that many women are skilled at languages in general and are taking the opportunity to become bilingual?

A further difference noted was in the importance ascribed to the Welsh language. Both the Welsh-speaking and the English-speaking women in the cross-language partnerships put a higher value on Welsh than did their partners. They were also more optimistic about the future of Welsh. It must be remembered, however, that the fathers were mostly in full-time employment, in a world where Welsh does not yet have equal status to English. Seeing the ubiquity of the English language, these Welsh-speaking fathers are keener to encourage English (as well as Welsh) in their children than are any other group of either sex.

Gender and Influence

Those who marry across cultures

Early research on choice of marriage partners showed that people tend to choose those who are similar to themselves in cultural background, attractiveness and economic status (see Thibaut & Kelley, 1959; Bernstein, 1971). In choosing someone out of their own culture, potential partners must feel very committed to one another, and strong enough to resist social pressures (Shakespeare described the situation rather well!). Once the partnership is established, many things that could have been taken for granted by members who shared a common background will have to be negotiated. In cross-language partnerships, the language they use at home is arguably one of the most important.

There is little research on the effects of the language of one person on the language of another. If one or both partners have to learn a second language, then, according to research by Dulay et al. (1982), their chances of linguistic success are enhanced, that is if you assume a positive emotional state, empathy and strong motivation. Self-confidence is also associated with success in second language learning, and it seems reasonable to assume that those who marry out of their own culture are quite self-confident. This leads to the expectation that cross-language partners in general tend to become bilingual.

The situation is not so clear in North Wales. Although there are cultural differences between English and Welsh backgrounds, virtually all Welsh people speak English (although not all Welsh people speak Welsh, for historic reasons). Cross-language marriages in North Wales are not always cross-cultural marriages. Both partners are likely to speak English and one will also speak Welsh. Of interest here is whether these partnerships tend to produce bilingual speakers (that is increase the overall use of Welsh), or will people take the easy option and use the language they already share?

The data from the first questionnaire indicate that neither extreme situation occurs. Not all partners in cross-language marriages become bilingual, neither do they revert to using only English. Instead, most non-Welsh-speaking partners seem to make an effort to use some Welsh, and most primary Welsh speakers use less Welsh than their peers in all-Welsh partnerships. In other words, both parents (and both languages) have an influence in the home.

The only study that approaches the question of parental influence using a Welsh-speaking population is that by Harrison and his colleagues, who looked at the language used by of two- to seven-year-old children in Wales (Harrison *et al.*, 1981). In an attempt to discover why so many bilingual mothers in Wales raise their children monolingually, they found that monolingual English-speaking fathers have a great deal of influence on whether one or two languages were used in cross-language marriages. Where these fathers discouraged the use of Welsh, their children were all monolingual English speakers, but where they encouraged the use of Welsh, only 35% were monolingual English speakers. They did not look at the full spectrum of language backgrounds, but focused on what the present study has called WM and WW families, and interviewed only the mothers in their sample.

The role or the gender?

It is possible that the *role* rather than the gender of the parent is the important variable. The mother's role in her children's language development is honoured in the phrase 'mother-tongue'. Little attention was paid to the role of fathers until recently. Gleason and her colleagues have now shown that men do adapt their speech to young children, but that the quality of child–father communication is less smooth and more challenging than child–mother communication (Gleason, 1975; Gleason & Greif, 1983). This accords with the findings of this study. Fathers interrupted more, spoke more, gave more directions and generally dominated the conversations more than did mothers in the small sample. It could simply be that children spend more time with mothers, as they did in the present group, and that children perform with more confidence with a familiar partner. It would be interesting to find a group of male primary carers, and compare their child–father communications with those of female primary carers and both sets of partners.

The effects of gender on language use have been studied extensively, and an outline of the feminist position and a discussion of dominance can both be found in Chapter 1. However, mention must be made at this point of two sets of findings, the first which show that women are good at second language learning (e.g. Carroll & Sapon, 1959), and the second which show that women have a number of skills which facilitate communication with children (e.g. Henley & LaFrance, 1984). However, Newson (1979) has argued that these last are not inborn skills, but are those which the culture expects women to acquire. He comments that, if it were socially acceptable, many men could learn baby-minding skills and how to talk to young children.

The influence of the partner or partnership?

It was assumed at the start of this project that the joint language background of the parents, the environment into which a particular child had been born, would have a major influence on the subsequent language development of the child. That it does have an influence will be shown in the multiple regression analyses in the next chapter, but it is not the major influence. Both the language of the mother and the language of the father explained more of the variance. That is, the coupleness of the family is less influential than the parents separately.

But it is also clear that the parents do not have *equal* influence on the language of the home. As the calculations beneath Table 10.2 demonstrate, the father has more influence than the mother, whether his first language is English or Welsh. More Welsh is likely to be used in cross-language marriages when the Welsh speaker is a man than when it is a woman. However, when the Welsh speaker is a woman, more families expect their children will become fluent Welsh speakers than when it is the father who speaks Welsh. It seems that mothers influence the language of their children more than the language of their husbands.

Influence is hard to quantify. Welsh-speaking men in cross-language partnerships are less likely to think that Welsh is important than their peers who have a Welsh-speaking partner, whereas Welsh-speaking women are not influenced in this way. Less Welsh may be used in a cross-language partnership if the Welsh speaker is a woman, but Welsh will be considered more important in those circumstances than if the Welsh speaker were a man.

Fathers and English

In the first survey, there were fewer couples allocated to the two cross-language groups, WF (46, 12%) and WM (36, 9%). By the second questionnaire, all numbers were reduced, but the Welsh-speaking father group was reduced to just six families, 5% of the reduced sample, while the WM group only reduced to 16 (13%). The biggest attrition was from the WF group to the MM group. In other words, men who were primarily Welsh speakers in 1988 had increased their use of English so much that they were at least using the two languages equally across a number of their current activities. There is similar attrition from the MM group to the EE group. Here one can state that less Welsh is being used in the family, probably by both partners, but it could be less than little. To be a WF father a man had to be using a lot of Welsh widely in 1988.

Considering the parallel situations of fathers in WF in 1988 and in 1991, and mothers in WM in 1988 and 1991, what factors could account for the greater loss of Welsh usage in the first group compared with the latter? The most obvious is that the men went out to work and the women stayed at home with the new baby. Almost all the men in the second sample were in full employment, although no details are available about where they worked or what kind of work they did. Home provides many of the situations where Welsh is used frequently, with children, family and friends. These are factors which do not change greatly over time. In the domestic situation, a woman can also control the language used for reading and viewing, and can avoid using English at all if she has a mind to.

On the other hand, in the work situation English is probably unavoidable. Work is a factor that is more subject to change. Although most public employers now require people to speak Welsh, many private employers do not. More English than Welsh is heard in public places, and if a man's work colleagues happen to be English speaking, he is likely to adopt their language during the day out of natural courtesy.

There are indications that English-speaking men are the group least interested in language per se and in the Welsh language in particular. It was mostly the monolingual English-speaking fathers who did not return the second questionnaire. Just as the Welsh-speaking mother can avoid English in her everyday life, so the English-speaking father can avoid Welsh, both at work and at home.

As a counter to the drift away from Welsh by Welsh fathers, there is a small consolation. Six children coming from families designated as EE families at QI were found to be Welsh speaking or bilingual at age three. They represent 12% of the EE families that remained from 1988 to 1991 and as such are not statistically significant. They are interesting as they indicate that the language drift is not entirely towards English.

Thus, it seems that the father has greater influence than the mother on the language used in the home, although he may well be less interested in language. As will be demonstrated in the next chapter, the language background of the family has less influence on the subsequent language development of the child than had been expected.

Summary

Overall there is more similarity than difference between the genders on questions of language use and attitudes, both in the initial sample and in the 1991–1992 sample.

In the 1988–89 sample, differences were identified in the language use at home in the cross-language partnerships. English-speaking women used more Welsh with their children, with neighbours and with friends than did English-speaking men in these marriages. In other words, more female partners of Welsh speakers use Welsh than do male partners. There was more similarity between the Welsh-speaking men and Welsh-speaking women married to English speakers. Thus women are more likely to adapt their language use than are men in cross-language partnerships.

Differences were also discernible in the language used for talking to each other. More Welsh-speaking men continue to use Welsh in cross-language marriages than do Welsh-speaking women, and fewer change to using English. Fewer English-speaking women speak only English and more speak mostly Welsh than do English-speaking male partners. In other words, almost 40% of English-speaking women use Welsh with their Welsh-speaking partners, whereas only 20% of English-speaking men use Welsh with their Welsh-speaking partners.

Concerning the importance attributed to the Welsh language, comparisons were made between Welsh speakers who married fellow Welsh speakers and those who did not. There was little difference between the two groups of women, but the men were less likely to think Welsh was important. Non-Welsh speakers of either gender in cross-language partnerships were more likely to think Welsh was important than those who married English speakers. Although cross-language partnerships obviously influence the value placed on the Welsh language, Welsh-speaking women are less influenced by their partners than are men.

In general, two-thirds of all parents wanted their children to be fluent in Welsh, and a further quarter wanted them to learn Welsh at school. Again it was only in the cross-language marriages that differences could be discerned by gender. More Welsh-speaking mothers than Welsh-speaking fathers wanted their children to be fluent in Welsh, but there was no overall gender difference on this question. Again a significant difference was found according to language background.

Men were generally less optimistic than women about the future of the Welsh language, but Welsh-speaking women who marry non-Welsh speakers are more pessimistic than those who do not. There was no significant gender difference overall in these opinions, nor was there a significant interaction here between parent and language background.

Thus, although it seems that women *use* more of their partner's language in cross-language marriages, it's not clear if their *opinions* are as easily changed. Welsh-speaking women married to non-Welsh speakers still value Welsh, still want their children to be fluent in Welsh, but they do think Welsh will be used less in the future.

The last set of comparisons come from the second sample, those answering QII in 1991–1992. More women than men returned this questionnaire, and significantly more fathers of monolingual English children failed to do so.

Significantly more mothers than fathers thought their children understood some Welsh but there were no significant differences in their reports of language heard or language used, or in their satisfaction with their child's general language development. Mothers chose Welsh for personal reading and for reading with their children significantly more frequently than did fathers. This could be linked to the growing needs of the child.

Parents were largely in agreement about the development of specific aspects of Welsh and English. There was a tendency for mothers to attribute more language skills to their offspring than did fathers. They were again asked how much Welsh they wanted their children to learn, and again almost all parents wanted their children to learn Welsh at school. Although fathers made fewer comments overall, their reasons for wanting their children to learn Welsh (or not) were not very different. They were more likely to emphasise the need for both languages, and mothers were more likely to comment on job prospects and communication skills.

Overall, the differences between the genders were not found to be great, especially in the two questionnaire samples. In the small sample, although the differences are more marked, the data are selective and suggestive rather than conclusive. It is the data from cross-language partnerships that are most provocative. It would seem that in some ways the man does have more influence on the language used at home, but less influence on the opinions of his partner.

However, there are a number of unresolved issues entangled in the gender question. The differences identified applied to some but not all of the kinds of family background identified; the language itself has an influence as well as the sex of the speaker; the parental role may be more influential than whether the primary caretaker is male or female.

11 What Predicts a Child's Language?

Introduction

Looking forwards, looking backwards

Babies born on Anglesey in North Wales enter families which use a mixture of languages, mostly Welsh and English. Some become monolingual and some become bilingual. Few monolingual Welsh-speaking children remain by the time they enter secondary school, but children remain who are monolingual English speakers or use Welsh as little as possible. A third group seem to become bilingual early in life and to remain comfortable with both languages. Talking to such children, they can describe what they remember of the language situation at home when they were young, and it usually includes people with whom they spoke Welsh and people with whom they spoke English.

Such retrospective investigation is stimulating but selective and biased. Knowing themselves to be bilingual, people look for explanations and remember details that make sense. The trick would be to identify and measure key variables *before* children's language has developed and, once it has been established whether or not they are bilingual, to re-examine those variables and see which ones predicted subsequent language use.

Predictors

It was thought that predictors might be found in any of three areas, within the language backgrounds of the children, within the attitudes and opinions of the parents and within parental language use itself.

When the Anglesey Project was designed, it was hypothesised that the language background would play a significant role in the development of children's language. Having identified five different language backgrounds, they or factors within them, seemed the most likely predictors of the future language use of children. Those associations will be examined first.

Parental attitudes to language have already been shown to make a difference to the extent to which the language is used. Perhaps attitudes also influence the language learned by children. The range of data is narrower in this area, and an 'Aspirations for Welsh' factor did not provide any additional information.

Thirdly, the search turned to parental language itself. The previous chapter discussed the evidence that parents separately influence the language used at home, and found no significant differences between their answers on the questionnaires. The language of parents in the small sample is scrutinised here, and comparisons are made of the scripts from maternal and paternal sessions at age three from these children. Differences in aspects of language use such as parental mirroring (echoing a child's remark) and interrupting are also discussed, as are the activities chosen by each dyad.

Finally, data from the two questionnaires were subjected to a series of multiple regression analyses to identify the contribution that parental language use (separately and jointly), and opinions in 1988–89 made to the language of their offspring in 1991–92.

The Development of Language

Identifying bilingual children

Before looking for factors predicting language development, perhaps it would be useful to remember how language development was defined for the purposes of this study. Three-year-old children from the base population were described as Welsh speaking, English speaking or bilingual on the basis of parental reports in QII.

As described in chapter 4, parents were asked to say how much their children were using 18 aspects of language, nine in Welsh and the equivalent nine in English. A three-point scale was used as follows:

Not yet (Dim eto) = 1
Sometimes (Weithiau) = 2
Often (Yn aml) = 3

Thus, each child had two scores, one for each language, and they were subtracted one from the other, to highlight the language they used most frequently. On the basis of these answers, children were identified as 'Welsh' (N = 41) meaning that they spoke almost only Welsh, 'English' (N

= 79) meaning that they spoke almost only English, or 'bilingual' (N = 57) meaning that the development of their two languages was similar. This scoring allows both those children whose language is advanced and those whose language is slow to be included.

Language levels?

Had there been children whose language had not begun to develop at all, they too would have been included in the bilingual group by this method of scoring, and so questionnaires were scrutinised for such instances. Luckily all the children were reported to use some language, and virtually all parents reported that they were satisfied with their child's language development.

Furthermore, the levels of language used by the three groups of children were also checked. By counting only those reported to use aspects frequently ('Often' 'Yn aml') 71% of the English-speaking children were using all nine aspects of English and virtually no Welsh. Similarly, 83% of the Welsh-speaking children were using all nine aspects of Welsh and rarely using any English. (The exception was the use of 'allgone' which should probably have been counted as a Common word/phrase and not included in the list). A fairly balanced development of the two languages was shown by the bilingual children, with 43% using all aspects of Welsh and 40% using all aspects of English. About three-quarters of this group were using all of the simpler aspects of both Welsh and English, that is, had begun to use simple sentences in both languages. These results were detailed in Table 8.3 of Chapter 8.

Both languages are spoken widely on Ynys Mon. Why did not all the children develop bilingually? The rest of this section looks at possible reasons for the separation of children in this way.

Language Background as a Predictor

Where are the bilingual and monolingual children?

Originally, the five language background groups were identified from the first questionnaire. Families responding to the second questionnaire remained within the same groups as previously for the most part. Thus, given that language background remains stable, it was to be expected that children identified as mostly monolingual Welsh speaking at age three would have WW backgrounds, children identified as mostly monolingual English speaking would have EE backgrounds, and the bilingual children would have one of the other three backgrounds, namely WF, WM or

MM.This is largely the case. At the time of QII, 88% of the 'Welsh-mono-lingual' children were in the WW group, 73% of the 'English monolingual' children were in the EE group, and 84% of the bilingual children were in the other three groups. That is, 81% or 100 of the 124 children live in families whose language background is concordant with the language they are using.

The above is a description of a current situation. It does not address directly the question of prediction. For that, the question has to be turned round: into what kind of language background had these Welsh, English and bilingual children been born? A larger group (N = 166) is available for this question, as classifications were retrieved from families at QI, even for those whose fathers did not reply on the second occasion.

There is still a good degree of concordance between language background of origin and current language use: 82% of the monolingual Welsh speakers had been born into WW homes, 60% of monolingual English speakers had been born into EE families, and 68% of bilinguals had been born into WM (28%), WF (21%) and MM (19%) homes, making 112 of 166 children (67%) who had been brought up in the kind of family to be expected, given their language use. However, looked at this way, less of the children's current language use could have been predicted. Compared with their current language backgrounds, fewer of the Welsh children were born into WW families (82% compared with 88%), fewer of the English children into EE families (60% compared with 73%), and fewer of the bilingual children into WM, MM and WM families (68% compared with 84%).

What became of children from different backgrounds?

The data can be re-examined prospectively, looking at what became of the children from the original language backgrounds. As expected, the bulk of those from EE became monolingual English speakers (88%) and none of the children from WW did so. Those children became monolingual Welsh speakers mostly (73%), or else bilingual (27%). The MM group produced mostly English speakers (70%) and bilinguals (30%), and more than half of the children from WF and WM backgrounds became bilingual. A WF background seems more likely to produce monolingual English speakers than a WM background, but numbers are small in both of these groups, making generalisation hazardous.

However, when the mixed language background groups of QI are collapsed, it is possible to show that a WW background is significantly associated with the development of monolingual Welsh children and a EE background is significantly associated with the development of monolingual English children, not an unexpected finding! Conversely, significantly few children from EE backgrounds became Welsh speakers (or bilingual) and no children from WW backgrounds became monolingual English speakers.

The middle group, where families had a mixture of languages in their background, produced associations which are less easy to interpret. Half of the children from this group became bilingual, which is significantly higher than from any other group. However, nearly that many (42%) became English speakers. 27% of children from WW homes become bilingual, that is learn to use English as well as Welsh. In comparison, only 10% of children from EE homes learn Welsh as well as English, implying that the English language has the greater influence.

It seems that for two out of three children their language development at three years of age can be guessed from the language background into which they were born. WW backgrounds tend to lead to Welsh speaking, EE backgrounds to English speaking and the other three backgrounds produce either bilingual children or English speakers. However, a lot of the deviation from this generalisation is not explained.

Family features

The final part of this section puts aside language background and looks at all the answers to questions in QII describing features in the current environments of these children. Answers are available about how much Welsh and English parents use, children hear and children understand. These data are also compared with the children's language development.

Table 11.1 compares these selected features in the families of children classed as monolingual or bilingual. As can be seen, virtually all of the monolingual Welsh children are said to hear and to understand mostly Welsh and to have parents who almost only use Welsh. Virtually all of the monolingual English children understand almost only English, and most hear mostly English. However, 41% hear both English and Welsh, and 30% of their parents use both English and Welsh. The bilingual children appear to hear more Welsh than English and are more likely to have parents who use mostly Welsh. But 70% of them are said to understand both Welsh and English.

The picture for the monolingual Welsh-speaking children is clear; having parents who use mostly Welsh and hearing and understanding mostly Welsh is associated with becoming a Welsh speaker. The picture is less clear for the monolingual English-speaking children (let alone the bilinguals). At least 30% of these children have bilingual parents, parents who use both languages. So at least some bilingual parents produce English monolingual children.

Table 11.1   Features of the current background of children in QII

		Welsh (%)	Bilingual (%)	English (%)
Language parents use	Mostly W	95	53	0
	Both	2	32	30
	Mostly E	2	16	70
Language child hears	Mostly W	98	60	1
	Both	2	39	41
	Mostly E	0	2	58
Language child understands	Mostly W	93	26	1
	Both	5	70	5
	Mostly E	2	4	94

Percentages of children classed as Welsh-speaking, bilingual or English-speaking, according to parental language use, language heard, and language understood at home.

Parental Opinions

Current preferences

Current parental preferences for reading, thinking, talking and watching television, alone and with their children, are shown in Table 11.2 (overleaf). Information on current activities is used because there are no comparable data from the first questionnaire for activities with children. They were only babies at that time. As can be seen, virtually all of the parents of monolingual English children prefer to do everything in English. Most of the parents of monolingual Welsh children prefer to think and to do things with their children in Welsh, but less than half prefer to read or watch television in Welsh. The parents of bilingual children mostly prefer English for their own reading and viewing, and are more likely to talk to their children in Welsh.

Comparing activities with and without children, their presence does make a difference. More parents of Welsh children preferred to read to their children in Welsh than preferred to read for themselves in Welsh (88% as

Table 11.2 Parental language preferences at QII by children in the three groups

		Welsh (%)	Bilingual (%)	English (%)
Parental reading	Mostly W	39	5	1
	Both	24	22	1
	Mostly E	37	73	98
Reading to child	Mostly W	88	25	1
	Both	10	46	7
	Mostly E	2	29	92
Parental television viewing	Mostly W	44	4	1
	Both	46	41	9
	Mostly E	10	55	90
Viewing television with child	Mostly W	68	21	1
	Both	25	50	4
	Mostly E	7	29	95
Parental thinking	Mostly W	71	48	3
	Both	22	14	6
	Mostly E	7	38	91
Talking to child	Mostly W	98	64	1
	Both	0	18	7
	Mostly E	2	18	92

to 39%), and more of the same parents preferred to watch Welsh television with their children than chose it for themselves (68% as to 44%). A similar trend is evident amongst parents of bilingual children; they are less likely to read English (29% from 73%) and watch English television (29% from 55%) if they have their children with them than if they are alone. No differences are observed in the parents of monolingual English children.

Parents wanting Welsh

In both questionnaires, parents were asked to say how much Welsh they wanted their children to learn, and there was not a great deal of difference in their answers as reported already. It was thought possible that this choice might have a predictive value, and so responses by mothers, shortly after the birth of their babies, were compared with the subsequent language development of their children. Table 11.3 shows that 95% of the mothers of children who became monolingual Welsh speakers wanted their children to be fluent Welsh speakers. However, the majority of all the mothers (71% of the total) made that choice originally, and 47% of the mothers of monolingual English-speaking children had wanted them to be fluent in Welsh, as had 88% of those who became bilingual.

Table 11.3 Maternal choice of language for baby (at QI), by subsequent language of child (at QII)

Maternal choice	Children: Welsh monolingual	Bilingual	English monolingual	Totals (Maternal choices)
English only			5% [4]	2% [4]
Some Welsh		5% [3]	13% [10]	7% [13]
School Welsh	5% [2]	7% [4]	35% [28]	19% [34]
Fluent Welsh	95% [39]	88% [50]	47% [37]	71% [126]
Totals (children)	23% [41]	32% [57]	45% [79]	177

When parental language choices were bifurcated, χ-square = 9.16, p <0.05.

When the choices are collapsed into two categories, 'some or no Welsh' and 'school or fluent Welsh', significantly more mothers of all children wanted their children to learn Welsh than did not (χ square = 9.16, df 1, p <0.05). That is to say, the overwhelming majority of mothers on Anglesey want their children to learn Welsh, but this in no way predicts how successful they will be, at least before they go to school.

Opinion variables in the multiple regression analysis

Finally, in this section, the multiple regression analysis (to be discussed in more detail at the end), included four 'Aspiration for Welsh' variables from QI. These were all parental opinions, and again it was hypothesised that they might have a predictive value. Parental choice regarding the degree of Welsh fluency wanted for their children was var58; var60 was the importance ascribed to the Welsh language, var62 was the opinions held about the future of the Welsh language and var74 represented parental hopes regarding the language status of their child's future marriage partner.

They were entered as independent variables, but accounted for little of the variance (see Table 11.5). Variable 58 made a small contribution to the development of Welsh, and var62 to the development of Welsh *and* to the development of English. Hopes about future marriage account for a small amount of the variance in the development of English and bilingualism, but the major contribution comes from parental language and will be discussed at the end.

Thus, the evidence concerning parental opinion is confusing. It does make a difference, but not directly on the language the child uses. Instead there are indications that the child influences the language use of his or her parents. The presence of a young child increases maternal preference for reading and viewing through the medium of Welsh.

Parental Language

The small sample: background

As the language of children in the small sample developed, it was the *mother's* dialogue with her child which was recorded and analysed, with one exception. After the eighth session, when the child was about three years old, fathers were asked to record a session of play and conversation with their children. It is these sessions which can now be compared with the last mother–child session.

There are some differences between the two. Firstly, mothers and children had become familiar with the practicalities of the sessions and had largely lost any inhibitions. Fathers needed quite a lot of coaxing to participate. Consequently, although the observer was present for all the maternal sessions, the recorder was left with the father and he was instructed on how and what to record. Thus field notes could not be written to accompany the paternal scripts, restricting the number of comparisons that could be made. Thirdly, in maternal sessions recording was stopped if the child became silent, angry or distressed. In paternal sessions the recorder was left to run for the best part of 45 minutes. Fourthly, in the eighth maternal session, the Reynell test and part of the WPPSI (Weschler

Pre-school and Primary Scale of Intelligence) were administered before the dialogue for analysis was recorded. The fathers were able to talk and play with a child untired by previous effort. Finally, there was about a three-week gap between the last maternal session and the paternal session, and although that is a relatively short interval, language develops continually. However, this was the nearest approach to obtaining comparable data that could be devised, and as such provides some interesting contrasts.

Maternal/paternal differences

Table 11.4 (overleaf) summarises the language stage for each language and the MLU achieved by nine children at the last maternal session (eighth session) and the session with their fathers. (The tenth child moved away after the seventh session). In eight out of nine cases the MLU is shorter with fathers than with mothers, and with one child, Iwan, considerably shorter (3.30 compared with 4.53).

Six of the nine children demonstrated a lower stage of language use in their first language with fathers than with mothers, and the other three performed at the same level. In their second language (in the five children where a second language was evident), the two WF children achieved a higher stage with their father than with their mother. This is to be expected as for those two, Welsh was their second language and their father was the Welsh speaker in the marriage.

Comparisons of parent/child ratios for both lines and words were also made. (The dialogues become more even-handed as the ratios approach one). Most of the children produced differing ratios with each parent. In all cases except David, the father uttered more lines and more words than his child. For two (Iwan and Nia) the differences were slight. For Nerys and Llywela they were great. David's father was less overpowering than his mother, bringing their ratio close to the average for the group.

Percentage of language used

Comparisons were also made between the amount of Welsh, Common words and English used in these two sessions by the children and by each parent. There is little difference in the proportion of each language used by four of the children (Iwan, Becky, David and Llywela). Most surprising of those is Becky, one of the children from a cross-language partnership. However, the other three with parents from differing language backgrounds all changed their language use when conversing with their fathers. Emyr used Welsh only 59% of the time with his father, but 77% of the time with his mother. Nia used Welsh 22% of the time with her father and not

Table 11.4 Mothers and fathers compared: Session VIII and Session Dad

		VIII	*Dad*
Nerys*	Stage-W	4	3
WW	MLU	2.08	2.21
Iwan*	Stage-W	5	5
WW	Stage-E	(3)	(3)
	MLU	4.53	3.30
Becky*	Stage-W	4	3
WM	MLU	2.35	2.12
Emyr	Stage-W	5	6
WM	Stage-E	(3)	3
	MLU	2.43	2.26
Gareth	Stage-W	5	4
MM	Stage-E	4	(4)
	MLU	3.27	3.21
David	Stage-E	4	3
MM	MLU	2.42	2.40
Nia	Stage-E	5	4
WF	Stage-W	1	3
	MLU	3.31	2.92
Mathew	Stage-E	4	3
WF	Stage-W	1	2
	MLU	2.77	2.50
Llywela	Stage-E	6	6
EE	MLU	4.67	4.14

Stage-E and Stage-W are stages in the development of Welsh and English.
MLU = mean length of utterance.

Where scores appear in parenthesis, they were not recorded at that session, but had been achieved at a previous session. Four children showed no evidence of developing a second language. A fifth monolingual child had left the area before session VIII. Those children with an asterisk were reported to use a second language with peers.

at all with her mother; and Matthew used Welsh 11% of the time with his father and did not use Welsh at all with his mother.

Unexpectedly, Nerys used English 15% of the time and Welsh only 69% of the time with her father, compared with 5% for English and 83% for Welsh with her mother. Finally, Gareth, who used both languages about equally with his mother, used Welsh 85% of the time with his father.

Mostly the children's language reflected the language of their parents. This was so with Iwan, Emyr, David, Llywela, and Becky. It is also the case in the Nerys–mother, Gareth–father, Nia–mother and Mathew–mother dyads. Nerys used less Welsh and more English than her Welsh-speaking father, Gareth used more English and less Welsh than his bilingual mother, and, predictably, the two WF children used less Welsh and more English than their Welsh-speaking fathers.

From this it is clear that three out of four of the cross-language fathers were able to influence the language used by their children in their presence. The fourth child, Becky, had a father who was trying to increase his use of Welsh as a new job had given him Welsh workmates. Nerys appeared to react against her father's use of Welsh, but Gareth too appears to have been influenced by his father's greater use of Welsh.

Qualitative differences

The fathers found it more difficult to keep the conversation going with their children than did the mothers. There were more interruptions and directions and generally they were more awkward than the mothers. This has been difficult to quantify. Instances of mirroring were calculated, as were interruptions, reading and more formal game playing. However, apart from an increase in interruptions in the paternal–child dialogues, there were few measurable differences between the parents.

In about half of the families, mothers commented that it would be a novel experience for their husbands to play with and talk to their child for an extended period. Perhaps the awkwardness relates to lack of practice. On the other hand, all the mothers (with the possible exception of Nerys' mother) had become practised in keeping the child amused while attending to other matters such as a second child. The two WF fathers (of Nia and Matthew) were notable for the pressure they put on their children to converse in Welsh, each slipping back into English only in order to keep the dialogue going.

The large sample: multiple regression analyses

The evidence for the importance of parental language in the development of child language seemed clear, and so confirmation was sought from the large sample. Stepwise and full multiple regression analyses were performed, using the four 'Aspiration for Welsh' variables (described previously), and maternal, paternal and couple language as independent variables, all variables from the first questionnaire when the children were still babies. The first analysis used the development of Welsh as the dependent variables. In the first step, maternal language accounted for over 52% of the variance (adjusted R squared = 0.523, Beta = –0.725, p <0.0001), and subsequent steps showed Paternal Language accounting for a further 5% of variance, and Variable 58 (amount of Welsh learning chosen by mothers for their babies) accounting for a just over 1% more of the variance. It is remarkable to be able to account for so much of the variance. Subsequent analyses were similar, as Table 11.5 shows.

The next analysis had the development of English as the dependent variable. The first step had maternal language accounting for most of the variance (41%, p <0.0001), and paternal language for a further 12%. Couple language, or the language background within the family (categorised earlier as WW, WM, MM, WF, or EE) accounted for a further 7%. The third analysis used development of bilingualism as the dependent variable. This time, 58% of the variance was ascribed to maternal language (p <0.0001), with paternal and couple language adding about 10% and 3% respectively.

The language use of three-year-olds was the dependent variable in the next analysis, and again maternal language accounted for most of the variance, this time 64% (p <0.0001). Paternal language gave another 10%, and couple language almost another 2%. In the fifth and final analysis, language understanding of three-year-olds was the dependent variable, and here too maternal language was in the first step, accounting for 57% of the variance (p <0.0001). Again paternal language made a further contribution to the variance (of 14%).

These data are summarised in table 11.5, which illustrates that the largest contribution to all five dependent variables is maternal language. Paternal language has a further contribution to make to all three language development variables, and to the other dependent variables, child use and child understanding. Paternal language accounts for about 10% of the variance in all of these. Couple language is of less importance, adding only 1% to the variance in the development of bilingualism, and 8% to the development of English.

Table 11.5 Summary of multiple regression analysis, showing the amount of variance in the dependent variables accounted for by each of the independent variables

Dependent variables / Independent variables	Develop Welsh	Develop English	Develop bilingualism	Language child uses	Language child understands
Maternal language	52%	41%	58%	64%	57%
Paternal language	5%	12%	10%	10%	14%
Couple language	–	7%	3%	2%	–
Maternal wishes (var58)	1%	–	–	–	–
Maternal importance (var60)	–	–	–	–	2%
Maternal opinion (var62)	1%	3%	–	–	1%
Maternal marry (var74)	–	1%	1%	–	1%

Dependent variables (from QII).
Develop Welsh, develop English, develop bilingualism are the scores achieved by children on the nine aspects of English and of Welsh in the second questionnaire. Language child uses is the language the child used at age 3 years. Language child understands is the language the child understood at age 3 years

Independent variables (from QI).
Maternal and Paternal Language were calculated from QI. Couple Language refers to the language background of couples, namely EE, WW, MM, WM or WF. Var58, Maternal wishes, is maternal choice of Welsh learning. Var60, Maternal importance, is maternal importance ascribed to Welsh. Var62, Maternal opinion, is maternal opinion about the future of Welsh. Var74, Maternal marry, is maternal hopes regarding the marriage of their children.

However, in all five analyses, maternal language makes the first and by far the largest contribution to the variance observed in the development of Welsh, the development of English and the development of bilingualism in the child, and to the variance seen in the language use and language understanding of three-year-old children.

Conclusions

Language backgrounds

Children do largely conform to the language background expected by their current language use, but not reliably so. It is not enough to be born into a family where both languages are spoken to ensure that a baby is becoming bilingual at three years of age. Nor does a monolingual background ensure monolingual pre-school development; some children from EE and from WW homes were using both languages more or less equally by age three. Thus, language background in itself is not predictive. In the multiple regression analysis, only small independent contributions were made by the language used by the couple. It had been expected that the language background would be the major influence on the child, and families in the small sample were chosen for their coupleness. However, describing types of family, even just in terms of language use, is perilous as was illustrated by that small group. One of the MM families turned out to use only English and the other to be bilingual.

Opinions

Much of the second questionnaire was devoted to eliciting opinions and measuring the attitudes of parents towards the Welsh language. However, they do not predict the language their children will use. The vast majority of parents want their children to learn Welsh, but at age three, about 40% of children are monolingual English speakers. Variables associated with attitudes accounted for little of the variance in child language at three. Again what people do seems to be more predictive than what they think, or at least than what they say they think.

Maternal language

A mother's language is the most powerful predictor of her child's language development. As a language partner, she elicits more language from her child, at a higher level of language complexity and with a longer average length of utterance in comparison with the father. The evidence from the multiple regression analyses is overwhelming. In these analyses, her language use accounted for between 41% (the development of English) and 64% (child language use) of the variance in her child's language at age three.

The language of the father, while not the main contributor, did have a significant, independent contribution to the language children developed (between 5% and 14%), though least to the development of Welsh. *Fathers influence the language of the home, mothers influence the language of the child.*

Why is maternal language so important?

Perhaps it would be useful to look at some of the reasons why it seems so obvious that the language used by the mother should predict that used by her three-year-old child.

- Mothers are the ones who spend most time with small children.
- Women have styles of speech which are more appropriate to talking with children.
- Mothers engage in a greater range of activities with their children than anyone else.
- Women are the more socially acceptable caregivers of small children.

All of the above statements apply to the children in the small sample. All 10 fathers were in full-time employment and their wives stayed at home. Fathers were more dominant in conversation with their children than were mothers. Some fathers displayed a reluctance to play with their children, let alone share in caretaking roles, and all of the women felt it was right to stay at home while their children were little. As these assumptions are still shared by many in the local community, it would be difficult to test some of them without interference. The man who chooses to run the home while his partner earns a salary is still exceptional.

The majority of mothers in the large sample did not work outside of the home (although some worked part-time) and the majority of fathers worked full-time. No other information relevant to these issues was available from QII. It might be possible to recruit families where both parents of small children work full-time and children are cared for in other ways. The first reason, that amount of contact is what counts, could then be tested. Within that set, there may well be some families that include 'new men' as fathers, men who value the gentler side of maleness, and who are willing to share the family tasks. Thus could the 'range of activities' reason be assessed. Finally, Newson (1979) suggested that there is no reason why fathers should not attune their language skills to meet the needs of babies, and so we might look to a time when caring for a home and a child is a commonplace occupation for either sex. At such a time it will be reasonable to expect that a child's language would be best predicted by that of his or her caregiver, not necessarily of his or her mother. Although 'caregiver tongue' is unlikely to be the term adopted.

Summary

Initially the procedure for trifurcating children from the second questionnaire into language use categories was described, and thereafter the three language groups of children, 'Welsh', 'English' and 'Bilingual' were used as the basis for all of the large sample analyses.

The first comparison was with the language background groups, both past and present. On the whole, past and current language background groups to which these children belonged remained constant. Group membership was as expected; the majority of the Welsh monolingual children came from WW backgrounds, the majority of English monolinguals from EE backgrounds and the majority of the bilinguals from one of the mixed background groups. Looked at predictively, most of the children from a WW background became Welsh speakers, most from an EE background became English speakers, and most of those in the two cross-language groups, WM and WF became bilingual. However, 70% of those from a MM background became monolingual English speakers.

Current parental preferences were then examined in the light of children's current language. Welsh-speaking children heard and understood almost only Welsh and had parents who used almost only Welsh. Most of these parents used their Welsh for thinking and for all activities with their children. Most English-speaking children have parents who use virtually only English, and prefer it for almost all activities, whether alone or with their children. However, a large minority of English monolingual children have bilingual parents. More bilingual children hear and understand Welsh and have parents who use Welsh than hear and understand English and have mostly English-speaking parents. These parents tend to use English to read and watch television, but, like the parents of Welsh-speaking children, they are less likely to do so if they are with their children.

Finally, evidence that parental language predicted child language, was gathered, first from the small sample and then from the base population. Evidence from the small sample is based on the last maternal session and a paternal session when child was about three years old. All nine children performed at the same or a lower stage of language use in their first language with their fathers than with their mothers, and all but one had lower MLUs. In those children where a second language was evident, two demonstrated a higher stage with their father than with their mother.

The father/child ratios were mostly greater than the mother/child ratios. All but one of the fathers used more lines and more words than his child, that is, took a more dominant part in the dialogue. Turning to the amount of Welsh, Common and English used in these two sessions, there is little difference between them for four of the children. Three of those from cross-language backgrounds adapted their language to that of their father, as did one child from a mixed language background.

There were qualitative differences between the maternal and paternal sessions, with fathers using more directions and interrupting more. However, these were hard to quantify.

The stepwise multiple regression analyses make it clear that mother's language has the greatest influence on child language. Maternal language is responsible for the largest part of the variance in the development of Welsh, the development of English and the development of bilingualism, as well as for most of the variance in the language children understand and the language they use.

Finally, the reasons for this situation are discussed, and a future is envisaged wherein a father's language could have as great an influence on his child's language. At that time, the prediction would become 'the language use of the caretaker when a child is born best predicts that child's language at age three'. Until then, *Fathers influence the language of the home, mothers influence the language of the child.*

12 How Do Young Children Become Bilingual?

Introduction

An overview?

Having looked in detail at the evidence collected from the Anglesey Project, this last chapter tries to stand back and address some of the broader issues that throw light on the whole question of bilingual language acquisition. It would be exciting to say that there are substantive answers. Unfortunately this is not yet possible. At best, all that can be offered are hints and suggestions that fill in a little more of the jigsaw or suggest how the next pieces might be found.

This chapter will re-examine some of the unresolved theoretical issues that have dogged the research before moving on to theoretical issues which play such a crucial role in developing fruitful concepts about childhood bilingualism.

Methodological issues

Childhood bilingualism is an area of study that is not easily contained. It has links with many disciplines and encroaches upon many topics such as child language, second language learning, and developmental and bilingual work in general. Perhaps this is why so many of the methodological problems in the study of childhood bilingualism are still to be resolved. Some of these issues will be highlighted before trying to address the crucial question of this book; how do young children become bilingual?

One of the first issues to be addressed is the choice of children to study. Should one choose those who are already becoming bilingual and if so which children can be called bilingual? Should one choose those children who live in bilingual families and if so what counts as a bilingual family? Or should one choose, as was done here, a proband of children in a bilingual

bilingual area and see how they all develop? Do you choose one child and study him or her in depth (as has been done classically) or do you choose a group of children to allow comparisons. And is there any value in adopting specific strategies to foster bilingual development?

In order to make any sense of these questions, measures have to be decided about what is meant by bilingualism. How can it be counted? Some suggestions are made in this regard and these include the device termed 'Common Language'.

Theoretical issues

Turning to theoretical matters, the theories which have been expounded in this area are also re-examined; both the two theories which attempt to explain bilingual language development, and the Threshold Model. The Threshold Model attempts to explain the effects of early exposure to two languages on a child's cognitive development.

These are dependent on how terms such as 'Language Separation' and 'Language Mixing' are interpreted. Partly this is involves reification and selective attention. If you call a phenomenon 'Language Mixing', that implies the speaker is muddled; whereas if you call it 'Borrowing', that implies a choice; and if you take either stance, you are likely to pay more attention to those instances which support your position and to ignore those that weaken it. A further term has been suggested as a heuristic, namely 'Common Language'. This is defined and then its occurrence explored. It has associations with motherese and babytalk which are not straightforward, but it does not appear to be a form of language mixing.

Finally, a third theory is suggested, the sequential theory of bilingual language development. Evidence for this theory is described, and it is discussed in connection with earlier studies. This theory leads to the suggestion of an expanded version of the Threshold Model. This would include the bilingual language development of younger children, not previously accommodated in the original model.

Which Children?

It matters how you do it

There seem to be an inordinate number of methodological tangles associated with bilingual language development. Perhaps this is because it spans so many areas of research within psychology, such as child language, developmental psychology, psycholinguistics, social psychology, second language learning, and cognitive psychology. Furthermore, bilingualism is a topic claimed by linguistics, sociology and even geography as well as psychology. Perhaps it should not be surprising that methods by which to explore the field have yet to be disentangled.

It matters which children are chosen for study, where they are studied, and with whom they are communicating. The social context within which children learn their language is of central importance. Amazingly, almost all children do acquire language, whatever the circumstances. However, as shown in Chapter 1, early acquisition can be facilitated and enriched by their communicative environment. It is especially necessary to take account of the interactive nature of communication and in order to do this the child's environment must be accurately described and, where possible, measured. It is not uncommon to find studies in which the language of the child's partner (usually the mother) is not specified in any detail. Such an oversight robs the data of the full richness of early child language.

And what of the language use of the researcher? Is it important that researchers of bilingualism are bilingual? Or multilingual? And do they have to be expert bilinguals? After all, they are part of the communicative context. It would be sad to think that only polyglots could study this fascinating area; but researchers would find it difficult to study a bilingual scene with no knowledge (or practice) in one of the two languages.

How do you choose your subject/s?

Single case studies have an honourable history in psychological research, and the field of language development owes a great debt to the single case work of Leopold (1945ab, 1954); Piaget (1952, 1959); and Brown (1973) to name only those most quoted in the present research. Moving to bilingual studies specifically, most have been not only single case studies, but have been related-subject studies (such as Imedadze, 1967; Saunders, 1982; Taeschner, 1983; Fantini, 1985). These children are special, if only because they have parents who are particularly interested in bilingual language acquisition, and the resources to attend closely to the minutiae of the process.

This study solicited data from *all* families of a proband of babies in a given area. It did not concentrate only on children who were or were becoming bilingual, but upon children from a range of backgrounds within a bilingual culture. Neither did it focus on parents who adopted formal strategies to assist their children's language development.

While acknowledging that the small group who agreed to take part in the recording sessions expressed an interest in their children's language (which cannot be taken for granted), these families were in no way exceptional, and arguably more representative of families in general than those with linguists, psychologists or psycholinguists as parents or friends. On the one hand, this means that parents were naive about language development and haphazard in the way they related linguistically to their children. On the other hand, they were not constrained by theory, and the recordings comprised spontaneous, unplanned discourse.

By choosing to record five types of family, those who later became bilingual can be described within the context of other possible language development paths. If only monolingual Welsh-speaking families had been studied, Iwan's early bilingualism could only have been discussed within the context of Welsh speaking, and all the rich variety of cross-language families would have been ignored. Because the total population of same age children were contacted, some generality can be assumed from the two questionnaires.

There are disadvantages in this approach. The language of individual subjects was not recorded with anything like the frequency of single case studies, and so data were lost. Although tapping more ordinary families, even these were selected to some extent, and were influenced by their inclusion in the project. The larger population was only contacted by mail and so the data received could not be expanded (or verified). This is an even more pertinent criticism when the population in question is bilingual. Translation is a notoriously thorny issue, and opportunities for misinterpretation abound. It cannot even be taken for granted that parents can say whether a word spoken to or by their child is English or not.

One person-one language?

It has been suggested that if parents do make the effort to be conscious of the language they use with their children that this can foster bilingual language acquisition. The most well-known suggestion is that first practised by Ronjat in 1913, namely that one person (usually a parent) should use one language only with the child, and the second person should use only the other. Thus the child would have two clear models from whom to learn two languages. This strategy has been widely reported since, but almost always with related subjects.

It has been pointed out that there is little research to indicate that this strategy has advantages over any other (see Redlinger, 1979 and Romaine, 1995). They have both listed alternative strategies, and these were discussed in Chapter 3. Given that this approach is the most widely known, if it is also widely practised a useful research project could be devised to solve some of the problems associated with single, related subject studies. A group of parents could be identified who were planning to adopt a one person-one language approach with their children, and a second group of bilingual parents who simply wanted their children to learn both languages. By adopting a similar recording procedure as described here it should be possible to identify differences between the language development of the two sets of children. This could begin to answer questions about the efficacy of the one person-one language strategy. The objectivity of the researcher would go some way towards answering questions about the subjectivity of related subject research.

More recently, Susanne Dopke (1992ab) began to investigate the language development of a small group of two-year-olds whose parents have endeavoured to use a one person-one language strategy. In a wide-ranging study she concludes that the separation of the languages is less important than the interaction between parent and child. Structural rules about language are acquired later than rules about social discourse.

It is not clear from the present study (or from Dopke's work) whether or not the 'one person-one language' strategy is the best way to encourage bilingual language development. As stated in Chapter 7, on the data available from the large sample, only five families appear to have adopted this strategy, all producing bilingual children at age three. However, it is not known if this was a deliberate strategy or a natural language choice by the parents. These families represent only 11% of all of the children who became bilingual.

In the small sample, only one of the families set out to use that approach rigorously – Mathew's parents. The second WF family seemed to adopt an approximate version naturally. Neither Nia nor Mathew used Welsh with their mothers, but managed most of the conversation recorded with their fathers in Welsh. Becky (WM) would not use English with her mother, but was reported to do so interchanging it with Welsh when talking to her father. Gareth (MM) used no English with his father, but used both languages equally with his mother. He was the child whose language was most clearly bilingual by age three, and who acquired his languages sequentially. Of the other two who followed the same pattern, Iwan's parents both preferred to use Welsh (WW), and Emyr (WM) had a father who was learning Welsh, and liked to use Welsh with his son. Thus, the three young bilinguals whose languages were acquired sequentially came from three very different language backgrounds.

In the classical studies (Ronjat, 1913; Leopold, 1939, 1949ab) time and effort were spent trying to ensure relatively equal exposure to the two languages for the children concerned. In a less leisurely age, it is not always clear how much time the working parent can and does spend attending to their child's developing bilingualism. In this study, the one person-one language strategy was not commonly adopted, and so parents planning to use this method could be difficult to find.

Being Bilingual

What does 'bilingual' mean?

It is easy to misinterpret the term 'bilingual'. It is a common experience to be told by someone you have heard using two languages that they are not *really* bilingual. As Grosjean reported, people are more aware of the limits of their two language use than of their skills (Grosjean, 1982). The notion of the 'balanced bilingual' has proved largely unworkable and not useful, but there needs to be some way of constraining the use of the term bilingual, at least as far as research is concerned, for it to have any meaning.

The problem is more acute when children are the subjects. How can you define a child as bilingual when his or her language is still only rudimentary? Many studies do so without further explanation. Is that because they assume that the children of parents knowing two languages are inevitably developing two languages? The dangers are clear. Attention needs to be paid not only to the child's language, but also to the child's language environment, which may not (or may) be what it seems.

Dodson's term 'developing bilingual' has proved useful (Dodson, 1983). Developing bilinguals were defined here as those children who were using two languages beyond Stage 1, however simply or inaccurately. That works with a young population, but the situation gets complicated once the two languages used by the child (or adult) are at grossly different levels. One can optimistically term an adult second language learner a 'developing bilingual' but, as that implies a process, a dynamic learning situation, the term is not appropriate for an adult (or child) who has settled for the odd phrase in a second language and has stopped trying to become more adept.

Perhaps with adults 'bilingual' should be used as a self-description by people who feel they can communicate in two languages. In everyday life that is probably what happens. However, that is not helpful for research purposes. When people were asked if they would describe themselves as bilingual or not in QI, the answers were very hard to interpret. Many people who had indicated that they rarely used Welsh still answered 'Yes', whereas some who had indicated that they used Welsh almost all the time but English in some circumstances said 'No'.

Thus, for research purposes some sort of measurement of bilingualism needs to be adopted. It is beyond the scope of this book to consider in detail how this might be done; but for the research reported here, measurement of language use rather than knowledge of a language was the principle adopted. Consequently, when children are referred to as bilingual in this study, it is solely on the basis of recorded language use or else of reported use of aspects of both languages.

Measures: you may know it, but do you use it?

Much has been written about how you can measure a person's bilingualism (see especially Baker, 1994). How can you measure a young child's bilingualism? How can you measure a young child's language, anyway? If the child will not speak, how can you measure language use; and if the child will not answer questions, how can you measure knowledge of the language? In practical terms, the most reliable data is actual language use, hard as it is to come by. However, there also exists a rich seam of stories available from parents about their children responding to language in ways that strongly suggest knowledge of language. This needs to be treated with more discretion, but cannot be totally ignored.

The language of the mother/parent also needs to be measured. Because of the diversity of speakers calling themselves bilingual at QI, parents were not asked to label themselves, but asked to say what they did. Those who said they used a mixture of the two languages in question could reasonably have been called bilinguals.

Using 'language use' rather than 'language ability' to define parents, families and children,can lead to apparent anomalies. If the language use of two parents is almost entirely English across a number of situations, these parents were said to belong to an English-speaking (EE) family. They may have had Welsh as their first language, but if they ceased to use it in childhood and use it rarely as an adult, they count as a non-Welsh-speaking family. Such a family may be prompted to revive its Welsh for the sake of a child, much as the general population of mothers increased its use of Welsh for reading and viewing with children.

Quite apart from arriving at a measure of an individual's bilingualism, the measurement of language is necessary to describe any communicative encounter. To make statements about the discourse that is unfolding between two people the language(s) they are using need to be specified. But how exactly? By the number of words, utterances or initiated topics of each party? By the ratio of utterances between them? By the type of response made by each person to every statement/utterance? There are good reasons for choosing any of these measures and more; but to use all of them would probably be beyond the resources of most researchers. The importance lies in clarifying and defending the measure/s chosen.

However, this raises an important issue. In order to make the measurements described above, all words and sentences have to be classified (or discounted). How do you define what can be included in a given language?

'Hi Jon, beer?' could belong to a number of European languages if it was heard rather than read. How do you decide what can be discarded? 'Eh?' is not a word in any language, but has communicative value.

Language that doesn't fit

In the current project, the solution to the last question was the creation of 'Common language'. As described earlier, Common language was defined as that part of language used in a Welsh/English bilingual culture which could not be claimed exclusively by either language. This includes five types of word: Proper names; Baby words; Foreign/technical words; words that sound and mean the same in Welsh and English; and 'Wenglish' words (words taken from English but used in Welsh form).

Sentences or utterances were termed Common language either when they contained only Common words and not enough structure to decide if the syntax was English or Welsh, or if they contained about the same number of Welsh and English words. Common language utterances were much rarer than Common language words, as might be expected. Many utterances had a basic English or Welsh structure and one or two second language words inserted. There were very few half Welsh half English utterances.

Common language provides a helpful way of conceptualising a part of language use, both bilingual and monolingual; but it is not yet clear if it serves another purpose. As adults use Common language, even when their children have progressed beyond the Stage 5 level, does it have any useful function in their speech? Is it simply a measure of their name dropping and foreign word usage, or do adults vary in the frequency with which they use words common to Welsh and English (like car and tren/train) and if so why?

As the last part of this chapter will show, there are problems with creating a category such as Common language. It has proved a very useful device for handling the data that did not fit the other two categories (Welsh or English), but it could be accused of functioning as a dustbin. The care taken to describe its contents and to list the complete Common Dictionary enables it to avoid that accusation, but it raises a further question. What happens to these ambiguous bits of data in other research? Are they ignored? Their presence is rarely acknowledged.

Doubtless Common language(s) are not the only way to solve this particular problem of measurement; but to avoid addressing the issue is surely to devalue subsequent findings.

About Theories

Issues

As described in the last section, one of the greatest problems in this as in much research is objective observation and reporting. Even naming can be theory laden. One time-honoured solution is to state clearly the theory which guides the researcher's investigations. That at least allows the reader to weight one report against another and to compare how awkward phenomena (and there always seem to be data that don't quite fit) are explained within the various accounts.

Theories to explain the acquisition of two languages by young children must account for how they learn to separate their languages and, almost invariably, choose the language appropriate to the environment. This can be achieved by three years of age. But is this language separation deliberate, or a response to an environmental stimulus?

Language mixing has been cited as evidence that this separation comes only gradually (for example, Volterra & Taeschner, 1978). Other workers (such as Poplack *et al.*, 1989) have suggested that to call the use of single words and phrases from another language 'language mixing' is to give it too much significance. Instead, laying much less emphasis on the event, they call it 'borrowing'.

Language mixing and borrowing play a central part in the two theories of bilingual language acquisition already described, and in the third theory to be expounded below. But first, what is meant by language separation?

Language separation

Arnberg and Arnberg (1992) use a Vygotskian model to account for the language separation of the bilingual child. Elementary mental functions account for learning a word or phrase in response to contextual attributes. Thus, at this level a child in a bilingual environment might respond with 'doggie' to an English television programme, and with 'ci bach' to the neighbour's puppy. It is not clear whether they think that this type of learning can also account for levels beyond Stage 1, that is single-word utterances. Higher mental functions are invoked to explain those instances when the child notices that two language systems are being used, when they can comment on this, and when they can, eventually, control their own use of the two languages. In the present study five children were either recorded or reported knowing which was the 'right' language for a speaker. The first three (Nia (WF), Becky (WM), and Emyr (WM)) did so by 31 months, and the other two (Gareth (MM), and Iwan (WW)) before three years old. Could they be described as functioning at a higher level, as aware of the existence of two systems, or were they reacting to a (wrong) stimulus? All were using two language systems by four years old. Earlier they had used only single words in their second language and, apart from this, little language mixing was heard or reported.

Referring to the one system/two system debate, DeHouwer (1990) suggested that to address someone in 'the wrong language' was indicative of pragmatic incompetence. Obversely, the child who is able to differentiate 'right language'/'wrong language' has achieved a measure of pragmatic awareness when he or she objects to being addressed incorrectly. So to use the 'right' language with someone and to react to the 'wrong' one, is more properly seen as pragmatic awareness than metalingual awareness. In the present study, the evidence for pragmatic awareness was also sketchy and suggestive. It did seem evident that children develop pragmatic skills as they develop lexical, syntactic and discursive skills, whether or not they are becoming bilingual.

A major difficulty with language separation is that it is not always conscious. Adult bilingual speakers do not always know which language they have been using unless they search for environmental clues; at a wedding party, a grandmother could not say whether she had spoken to the guests in Welsh or English as they were a mixed group linguistically. Presumably adult bilingual speakers can become aware of their language separation, even though they often function automatically. Are young bilinguals similarly aware of two systems? This difficulty also raises an uncomfortable question about the research study itself. If parents, and especially bilingual parents, are not always aware of the language they are using, how reliable are their reports of the language/s used by their children and reported in QII? English is such a pervasive language that Welsh parents are not always aware of what is 'not-Welsh'.

Theoretical implications of language mixing

Long before they separate their languages, children learn to communicate in whatever language is around. They start with looks and gestures, follow with largely unintelligible utterances and slowly begin to make sense to their mothers. Even before that they are keeping their place in what Bateson (1979) has called 'proto-conversations', grunting in the pauses, following gaze, pointing in response to a question and so on, learning about relations as well as about things.

Great interest has been focused on what happens once the child in a bilingual environment begins to acquire a lexicon. A major question still unresolved is whether or not such a child learns to differentiate the two languages from the beginning, or whether they learn one mixed set of words and phrases initially, picked arbitrarily from both languages which they differentiate later. This argument, outlined by Arnberg and Arnberg in 1985, is referred to as the one-system, two-system debate. In an earlier chapter it was referred to as the Gradual Differentiation and Separate Development Theories.

Almost all researchers see language mixing as the key issue, and they have either welcomed evidence of its existence as support for their theoretical position, or marginalised its significance and found alternative explanations to account for the phenomenon. Early language mixing has been reported in many studies, particularly in single case studies such as Leopold (1939, 1949ab) and Imedadze (1967). The argument is whether this early mixing represents a lack of discrimination and possible confusion, or whether it is largely insignificant.

The Gradual Differentiation Theory suggests that this mixing is important. An early mixed language lexicon develops a syntactic system with features mixed from both languages, and only slowly develops into two distinct systems (Volterra & Taeschner, 1978). Thus, evidence of early mixing, lexically and syntactically, is to be expected, as one system separates into two.

The Separate Development Theory postulates separation of two languages from the start, or from early on. Mixing can more appropriately be explained by other factors such as the lack of lexical alternatives, and is a phenomenon which can occur in as little as 2% of a child's total utterances (see Lindholm & Padilla, 1978). It can also be seen as immature pragmatic skills (Meisel, 1989) or else a reflection of unacknowledged parental language mixing (Genesee, 1989). Evidence of little mixing supports this position.

Common Language

Definition

Thus, in the current research project, it was necessary to find a way of deciding which language a child (or mother) was using at any particular part of the recorded session that did not presuppose a theoretical standpoint. Because of the geographical proximity of Welsh and English, they share many words which cannot fairly be claimed by one in preference to the other. Therefore, as described earlier, the term Common language was adopted as a device to allow analysis without prejudice to either language. However, the percentage of Common language decreased as the children's language developed, whether the developing language was Welsh or English. It is therefore worthwhile to look at Common language again to see whether it is simply language mixing, whether it is a variant of motherese, or whether it has some other function or explanation.

To restate the original definition, Common language includes five types of word, Proper names, Baby words, Foreign / technical words, words that sound and mean the same in Welsh and English, and 'Wenglish' words (words taken from English but used in Welsh form). Utterances were defined as Common either when they contained only Common words and not enough structure to decide if the syntax was English or Welsh, or if they comprised equal parts of Welsh and English. Half Welsh half English utterances occurred rarely.

Before considering whether Common language is a form of language mixing, it will be examined as potentially a kind of motherese or babytalk.

Common language as motherese or babytalk?

The language of mothers is different when talking with babies than when talking with older children or with adults, and this language is called 'motherese' (e.g. Snow & Ferguson, 1977; Furrow et al., 1979). Motherese has been described as short, correct, clearly enunciated utterances about things and happenings in the immediate environment (Gleitman et al., 1984). There is dissension about how facilitative and how necessary this is to the baby's acquisition of language, a debate not central to this study. What is important is that motherese has been so clearly described, and so Common language can be examined as a variant of motherese. By babytalk is meant simple language, and baby words and sounds for common objects and events. As such, it is so clearly a precursor of language proper as to be relatively uncontentious.

Of the types of word assigned to Common language, the childish, onomatopoeic words for things such as 'wow-wow', 'gee-gee', 'cwac-cwac/quack-quack' and 'bei-bei/bye-bye' are all part of babytalk, by definition. It was their common occurrence across the two languages that led to them being so assigned, and they were used by both mothers and children. Proper names were well represented – in the early sessions at least. Mothers talked to children about who they had seen, frequently used family photographs to encourage speech, and had many children's books featuring well-known characters such as Super Ted and Postman Pat. The children would often respond to a picture simply with a proper name, and mothers would accept that as sufficient. There was little evidence of Wenglish (Welsh–English creations), by mothers or children, and few foreign or technical words (apart from 'video' and 'okay'.

The bulk of Common language comprised words that are common in meaning and sound to both languages, words such as 'dad', 'doli/dolly' and 'lori/lorry'. They could be words that are generally acquired early and/or are used more frequently by all young language learners. They did refer to things in their immediate surroundings, and the games played and the topics of conversation changed little from dyad to dyad. Therefore it is possible that three of the five types of Common words could be expected to occur more frequently with this age group than with older children, thus associating it with motherese and with babytalk. However, further research is necessary to clarify this issue.

Common language as language mixing?

Language mixing and borrowing are sometimes confused. When two languages are in close contact, as are English and Welsh, borrowing inevitably occurs (see Poplack *et al.*, 1989). Elements from one language are used in the other, with nouns and verbs the elements most often and most easily transferring (Baetens-Beardsmore, 1982). In adults this borrowing occurs most often from English to Welsh in sentences such as 'Be 'di number yr engineer yn Ysbyty Gwynedd?' ('What's the engineer's number in Gwynedd Hospital?'). 'Rhif' is number, and 'pieriannydd' is engineer, but colloquially the English words are used in Welsh syntactic form. According to the definition of Common language above, such a sentence is Welsh. However, children's language is simpler in the beginning, with fewer and less reliable clues to an underlying syntax.

The study by Redlinger and Park (1980) found evidence of language mixing which decreased with the child's increasing language competence. Their study is similar to the present one in that a small number of subjects (four), were studied over a relatively short time (a year), and their development reported in stage of language development and mean length of utterance (following Brown, 1973). They pointed out that many of the early studies did not report stages or MLU when reporting language mixing, nor did they relate its incidence to total speech output. In their study, they excluded 'yeah' and 'ya' as too difficult to assign to either language. In the present study, such words were counted as Common language. Redlinger and Park (1980) report that, at Stage 1, levels of language mixing were between 20% and 30%, but dropped to between 2% and 6% by Stage 5. This, they say, supports the Gradual Differentiation Theory. They do not report whether the children had reached that stage in both languages, or only in their first language. Their subjects were four two-year-old children learning two languages from parents using a one person-one language strategy, and so the mixed input explanation is not possible.

Comparison with the present study is not straightforward. The three children who showed evidence of becoming bilingual (Iwan WW, Emyr WM and Gareth MM) had progressed to Stages 3, 2 and 4 respectively in their first language at about two years old, but were only at Stage 1 in their second language. By age three they were at Stage 5 in their first and at least Stage 3 in their second language. The frequency of Common language for these three children ranged from 23% at Stage 2-W (Welsh)/Stage 1-E (English), through 15% at Stage 4-W/Stage 1-E, to 5-18% at Stage 5-W/Stage 3-E. Thus, even though it contains more than language that is normally termed 'mixed', Common language decreases proportionately with increasing language proficiency in the two languages. So far the gradual differentiation theory is supported.

However, Common language decreased for monolingual children too, from 13-34% at Stage 2-E, through 12-20% at Stage 3-E, to 5-6% at Stage 5-E. (This refers to David MM, Llywela EE and Michael EE from age two to three years old.) Furthermore, maternal frequency of Common language dropped in line with that of their children, from 9-10% for the bilingual mothers when their sons were about two years old to 4-14% when they were three, and, for the mothers of monolingual children, from 5-15% at age two to 1-4% at age three. Arnberg and Arnberg (1985) noted the importance of the language model that children were exposed to. The children in the present study were exposed to mothers who used Common language as well as Welsh and/or English. So Common language cannot be equated with 'language mixing' as used in the literature currently, although Wenglish and utterances using both languages were included. And the Common language input from parents provides an alternative explanation which discredits the gradual differentiation theory, though it adds nothing to the separate development theory.

Borrowing, that is where a single word or phrase from one language is woven into an utterance in the other language, was not computed. Poplack *et al.* (1989), have already suggested that there needs to be a distinction between borrowing and code-switching. Speakers of English do not notice that 'bungalow', for example, is a borrowed word, and so a borrowed word in an utterance did not change its status. When single words occur in the context of another language system, it is not necessarily 'language mixing' either. Children label things and events in context, and, in the early stages, to use a Welsh rather than an English word for 'dog' is no more significant than labelling it 'wow-wow' or 'Fido'. When a single word was the whole of the utterance, the 'Common language' device allowed a classification for 'wow-wow' and 'Fido' that did not make them Welsh or English or even mixed language.

Without further work, no conclusions can be drawn about the function of Common language, apart from its heuristic function. Part of it maps on to motherese, and part on to language mixing, but proper names remain uncovered. Arguably it is more useful to handle the phenomenon of words and utterances that do not belong solely to one language by calling them 'common' than by calling them 'language mixes'.

A Third Theory

A further suggestion?

In the three children who were developing two languages by the end of the study, there is clear evidence that one of their languages developed first, and only when that had reached about Stage 4 or 5 did the development of their second language move beyond the one-word stage. Iwan WW, and Emyr WM, were 33 months old before their recorded English moved from Stage 1 to Stage 3, and Gareth made a similar move at about 31 months. As there was a three-month gap between recordings, these children could have moved through Stage 2 unrecorded, or else they needed a period of listening before they could use English. This phenomenon has been reported elsewhere (Karniol, 1990). The table of stages from Chapter 8 is repeated here for ease of reference (Table 12.1).

Schlyter (1987:46), reporting on three children who only learned to separate their languages by Stage 3, commented: 'when these children develop language-specific grammatical patterns, they should also be able to separate their languages lexically, i.e. should not mix.' Two of her three

Table 12.1 Simplified description of language development

Stage	Features	MLU	Approx. age
1	Naming/mostly one-word utterances	1.75	By 18 months
2	Using two words together	2.25	18–24 months
3	Three-element utterances	2.75	24–30 months
4	Simple sentences/four elements	3.50	By 36 months
5	Joining phrases with 'and' and 'but'/embedding	4.00	About 42 months
6	More complex utterances, pronouns, auxiliary verbs	Not useful	About 48 months onwards

subjects reached Stage 4 in one of their languages but not the second by about 39 months old. However, there are insufficient details reported to allow close comparison with the present study. She counted single-word borrowing as 'language mixing' and gave no data on the children's normal language models.

When the aspects of Welsh and English achieved by children in the large sample are examined, a trend can be observed that supports the development observed in the three bilingual children. Most of the children classified as bilingual had reached Stage 2 at least in both languages, and Stage 4 or 5 in one language. Caution must be exercised in attributing stageness at a distance, and based only on maternal reports of use of specified aspects of language. However, these results do not contradict those of the small sample.

The sequential model of bilingual language acquisition

Figure 12.1 (overleaf) compares models of bilingual language acquisition. (It is an extension of Figure 3.1, Chapter 3.) The first two, the Gradual Differentiation (one store) Model and the Separate Development (two store) Model have been discussed already, in Chapter 3. A third model, the Sequential Model, is suggested as a result of the development observed in three children in the small sample and not contradicted by the results from the survey. Like the first model but unlike the second, it allows for children

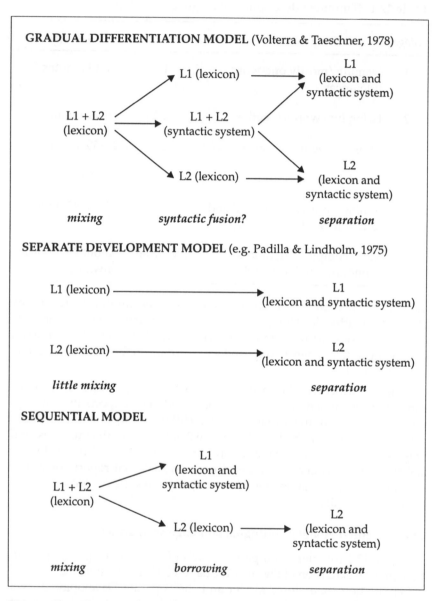

Figure 12.1 Three models of bilingual language acquisition

who do *not* become bilingual despite a few L2 words. Like the second model but not the first, it has the children acquiring L1 and L2 syntactic systems (however rudimentary) from the start. As it stands, it could also be a model for second language learning. When applied to a child learning language for the first time, the interval between the acquisition of a L1 syntactic system and a L2 syntactic system may be very brief, possibly no more than a few months.

Chapter 9 discussed features in the development of the three children which were reported by mothers during the sessions or else were noted by the observer. From having cross-language playmates, they moved to occasional translations and Wenglish creations, through awareness of intonation and of the right/wrong language according to speaker until, at least for one child, they could comment on their own language use. This pattern fits the general idea that, for some children at least, a level of competence in one language is necessary before children can begin to explore and develop their second language as well, even when both languages have been available from birth. That level seems to approximate to Stage 4 according to definitions by both Brown (1973) and Crystal (1976).

The sequential model in the context of early studies

In the classical studies (Ronjat, 1913; Leopold, 1939; 1949ab) time and effort were spent trying to ensure relatively equal exposure to the two languages for the children concerned. In a less leisurely age, it is not always clear how much time the working parent can and does spend with the object of their one person-one language strategy. In this study, the mother was the speaker who spent most time with the child. All of the fathers worked full-time and spoke with their children only after work and during holidays and weekends. Without equal input from both languages, it would not be reasonable to expect *balanced* bilingual language acquisition, unless the primary carer also balanced her languages in the child's presence. The argument is rather that, in the commonplace bilingual world, children establish themselves as competent to about Stage 4 or 5 (simple sentences and embedding) in one language first, before they develop their second language beyond Stage 1 (single words and phrases).

This is not what is usually meant by successive language acquisition, and although McLaughlin has arbitrarily called it simultaneous language acquisition 'if the child is introduced to the second language before that age [3 years].' (McLaughlin, 1984:101), it isn't really simultaneous either. Further, as has been said previously, the exposure to two languages simultaneously has no necessary connection with the acquisition of two languages simultaneously.

The children appear to learn one way of communicating before they try another as well. This process was seen (but not analysed) for a further two children during their fourth year, and the process did not differ superficially at least, from that observed in the first three children who reached that level by age three. The two later children were from WF and WM backgrounds, thus children from four of the five language backgrounds defined, followed the same pattern of bilingual language acquisition. The exception was the EE group. From that position, both languages are presumed to continue their developmental paths, although nothing can be said about whether competence in the second language reaches that of the first sooner, later or at all.

An expanded version of the threshold model

The sequential model has features of a model suggested for later bilingual development by Skutnabb-Kangas and Toukomaa (1976), and expanded by Cummins (1976, 1978a, 1980, 1984, 1991). They were especially interested in the relationship between bilingualism and cognitive abilities, and the phenomenon whereby some studies reported bilinguals to have a cognitive advantage over their monolingual peers, while others reported that bilingualism was associated with poor cognitive performance. The Threshold Model sought to explain these findings. It proposes that there are two thresholds (see Figure 3.2, in Chapter 3). Although the evidence from the present study is not overwhelming, what data there is could also fit into an expanded version of this framework as indicated in Figure 12.2.

In the expanded version of the Threshold Model, the higher threshold remains that above which the child has achieved age appropriate levels of competence in both languages (and is likely to reap the cognitive benefit of bilingualism). The neutral zone, between the higher and lower thresholds, is here called 'Developing Bilingualism' rather than 'Partial Bilingualism'. At this level, one language is developing at age-appropriate levels, probably beyond Stage 5, but the second language has still to catch up.

The area beneath the second threshold, called 'Limited Bilingualism' in the original, is called 'Potential Bilingualism' in this developmental version, as it is argued that children cannot be called bilingual on the basis of single words and phrases. At this point the child is usually somewhere between three and four years of age and only one syntactic system has been

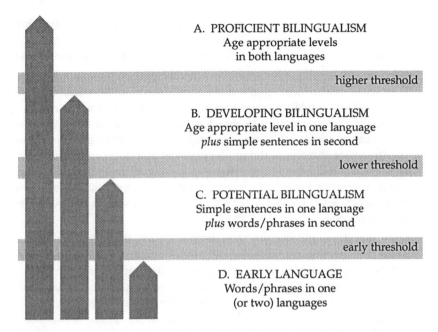

Figure 12.2   Developmental Threshold Model: level of bilingualism attained

discovered (about Stage 3–4). Simple sentences are used which is age-appropriate.

The earlier zone has been added. This is where the child first acquires language in the form of a lexicon comprising words and phrases from whatever language is heard. In the developmental model, children cross the early threshold when language begins to take off, when they move beyond simple words and phrases to simple sentences. Bilingual language acquisition is seen as a sequential process, and so the early threshold is crossed by one language initially. Failure to move on across the lower threshold in the first language could be compounded by the development of an L2 beyond the single-word threshold. This could result in a negative cognitive effect, as the child with two primitive syntactic systems could be at greater risk of interference.

It should be emphasised that this is a model to explain the normal development of bilingual children. Terms such as 'simple use', 'more complex use' and 'native-like level' are descriptors of the natural developmental sequence, and in no way derogatory. It is suggested that young children who are becoming bilingual as they acquire language, cross these thresholds naturally, first with one language and then with the next. Only when circumstances interfere with the process does the child become stuck at an early level for a shorter or longer period. This suggestion *extends* rather than amends the original Threshold Model.

This model needs to be tested. If the early threshold is crossed at about age three, when one language develops to the level of simple sentences (Stage 4), it will be necessary to look for children of about three who can produce simple sentences in two languages, to evaluate that hypothesis. Above the lower threshold, the model predicts that developing bilinguals will have reached different stages in their two languages, their first-learned language probably taking the lead. To find balanced bilinguals at this developmental level (possibly before school entry) would disprove that part of the model.

The lower threshold has not been defined clearly in the original model. By using the Developmental Threshold Model, and analysing the language of a large sample of potentially bilingual children at around the time of school entry, it might be possible to clarify the linguistic features necessary to ensure a child crosses the lower threshold, thereby avoiding the negative cognitive correlates of underdeveloped bilingualism. These are tentative ideas which need to be explored further and tested.

Summary

Methodological issues are particularly complex in this area. Suggestions were made concerning subject selection, and the range of subjects selected. The focus of measures of bilingualism was on the practice of languages rather than knowledge of them, although the difficulties involved with measuring the language of young children were acknowledged. The one person-one language strategy received little support, but remains popular.

Next, key theoretical ideas were explored. Language separation by young children was identified as the phenomenon which needed an explanation, and the significance of 'language mixing' was discussed. Common language, words and phrases shared by both English and Welsh, play an important part in clarifying what is implied by both language mixing and by borrowing. These concepts also play important parts in the Separate Development and Gradual Differentiation theories of bilingual acquisition.

Children can learn to separate two languages, if they are becoming bilingual, at a very young age. (They may be able to separate more than two, but that remains to be explored.) Although the mechanisms by which they do this are not understood fully, neither the Gradual Differentiation

Theory nor the Separate Development Theory completely accounts for the evidence. Children acquire a mixed lexicon, but their subsequent use of language is not best described as language mixing. They frequently use words and phrases here termed 'Common language', but Common language has more affinity to motherese than to language mixing and is not conterminous with either concept.

The Sequential Model of Bilingual Language Acquisition provides a better explanation for the data collected in this project. This model suggests that children need to reach an optimal level in one language (probably Stage 3) before they begin to acquire the second. Thence the two languages progress, with one usually remaining a little ahead of the other. As a *developmental* model, this can be used to extend and expand Cummins' Threshold Model, providing creative suggestions for the encouragement of bilingual language development.

Conclusions

- There appear to be *few differences* in the ways in which children learn to communicate and to use language, whether they are acquiring one language or two.
- It is *possible for metalingual awareness to emerge* in bilingual children before age three. Its significance and relationship with cognition and with bilingualism have yet to be explored fully.
- *Men appear to have greater influence on the language used in the home than women.* In cross-language partnerships, both languages are used, but there is more adaptation on the part of the women than by the men.
- *The mother's language is the best predictor of a child's language at age three.* Although fathers had some influence in their children's subsequent language use, by far the greatest predictor of future language use by children of three was their mother's language when they were born.
- *Common language* is a useful device to allow the description of *all* the language used by small children and their caregivers.
- Children who are becoming bilingual do not appear to learn one, mixed language code and then differentiate two codes, nor do they appear to develop two languages from the start. Instead, they develop one language to about Stage 4, the stage of embedding and complex sentences, before learning to use their second language for more than just single words and phrases. It is suggested that the potentially bilingual child develops his or her first language to a simple syntactic stage before beginning to develop a second language. This has been called the *Sequential Model of Language Acquisition*. The child's early

lexicon may well contain words or phrases from more than one language. Borrowing is not equated with language mixing.

- It is suggested that the Threshold Model can be extended. The extended version, the *Developmental Threshold Model* accounts for the language development of younger children than does the original model.

Thus, some suggestions have been made concerning how children become bilingual, and maternal language has been shown to be the most significant predictor of childhood bilingualism at age three. The Sequential Model of Language Acquisition is suggested as the best available account of how children become bilingual.

Bibliography

Andersen, E.S. (1990) *Speaking with Style: The Sociolinguistic Skills of Children*. London: Routledge.

Anisfeld, M. (1984) *Language Development from Birth to Three*. Hillsdale, NJ: LEA.

Arnberg, L.N. and Arnberg, P.W. (1985) The relation between code differentiation and language mixing in bilingual three to four year old children. *The Bilingual Review* 12, 20–32.

— (1992) Language awareness and language separation in the young bilingual child. In R.J. Harris (ed.) *Cognitive Processing in Bilinguals*. Amsterdam: North-Holland.

Astington, J., Harris, P. and Olson, D. (1988) (eds) *Developing Theories of Mind*. Cambridge: Cambridge University Press.

— and Gopnik, J. (1988) The development of children's understanding of the seeing-knowing dimension. In J. Astington, P. Harris, and D. Olson (eds) *Developing Theories of Mind*. Cambridge: Cambridge University Press.

— and Gopnik, A. (1991) Theoretical explanations of children's understanding of the mind. *British J. of Developmental Psychology* 9 (1), 7–33.

Atkinson, M. (1979) Prerequisites for reference. In E. Ochs and B. Schieffelin (eds) *Developmental Pragmatics*. New York: Academic Press.

Baetens-Beardsmore, H. (1982) *Bilingualism: Basic Principles*. Clevedon: Multilingual Matters.

Baker, C. (1985) *Aspects of Bilingualism in Wales*. Clevedon: Multilingual Matters.

— (1988a) Normative testing and bilingual populations. *J. of Multilingual and Multicultural Development* 9, 399–409.

— (1988b) *Key Issues in Bilingualism and Bilingual Education*. Clevedon: Multilingual Matters.

— (1991) *Bilingualism: Definitions, Distinctions and Measurement*. Clevedon: Multilingual Matters.

— (1992) *Attitudes and Languages*. Clevedon: Multilingual Matters.

— (1993) *Foundations of Bilingual Education and Bilingualism*. Clevedon: Multilingual Matters.

— (1994) Bilingual education in Wales. In H. Baetens-Beardsmore (ed.) *European Models of Bilingual Education*. Clevedon: Multilingual Matters.

— and Hinde, J. (1984) Language background classification. *J. of Multilingual and Multicultural Development* 5, 43–56.

Ball, M. (1987) *LARSP to LLARSP: A Design of a Grammatical Profile for Welsh*. Cardiff: School of Speech Therapy, South Glamorgan Institute of Higher Education.

— (ed.) (1988) *The Use of Welsh: A Contribution to Sociolinguistics*. Clevedon: Multilingual Matters.

Barbara, A. (1989) *Marriage Across Frontiers*. Clevedon: Multilingual Matters

Barrett, M. (1985) Issues in the study of single word speech: An overview of the book. In M. Barrett (ed.) *Children's Single Word Speech*. Chichester: Wiley.
— (1987) Early language development. In A. Slater and G. Bremner (eds) *Infant Development*. London: LEA.
Bates, E. (ed.) (1976) *Language and Context: The Acquisition of Pragmatics*. New York: Academic Press.
Bates, E., Camaioni, L. and Volterra, V. (1979) The acquisition of performatives prior to speech. In E. Ochs and B. Schieffelin (eds) *Developmental Pragmatics*. New York: Academic Press.
Bateson, M.C. (1979) The epigenesis of conversational interaction: A personal account of research development. In M. Bullowa (ed.) *Before Speech*. Cambridge: Cambridge University Press.
Beail, N. and McGuire, J. (1982) *Fathers: Psychological Perspectives*. London: Junction Books.
Bellin, W. (1984) Welsh phonology in acquisition. In M.J. Ball and G.E. Jones (eds) *Welsh Phonology: Selected Readings*. Cardiff: University of Wales Press.
Bernstein, B. (ed.) (1971) *Theories of Attraction and Love*. New York: Wiley.
Bever, T.G. (1982) Some implications of the non-specific bases of language. In E. Wanner and L. Gleitman (eds) *Language Acquisition: The State of the Art*. Cambridge: Cambridge University Press.
Bialystock, E. (1988) Levels of bilingualism and levels of linguistic awareness. *Developmental Psychology* 24 (4), 560–7.
— (ed.) (1991a) *Language Processing in Bilingual Children*. Cambridge: Cambridge University Press.
— (1991b) Metalinguistic dimensions of bilingual language proficiency. In E. Bialystock (ed.) *Language Processing in Bilingual Children*. Cambridge: Cambridge University Press.
— (1992) Selective attention in cognitive processing: The bilingual edge. In R.J. Harris (ed.) *Cognitive Processing in Bilinguals: Advances in Psychology*, 83. Amsterdam: North-Holland.
Bialystock, E. and Ryan, E.B. (1985) Metacognitive framework for the development of first and second language skills. In D.L. Pressley, G.E. Mackinnon and T.G. Walker (eds) *Metacognition, Cognition and Human Performance*. New York: Academic Press.
Blank-Greif, E. (1980) Sex differences in parent–child conversation. *Women's Studies International Quarterly* 3, 253–8.
Bloom, L. (1973) *One Word at a Time: The Use of Single Word Utterance Before Syntax*. The Hague: Mouton.
Bloomfield, L. (1933) *Language*. London: Allen & Unwin.
Bowerman, M. (1985) What shapes children's grammars? In D. Slobin (ed.) *The Cross-Linguistic Study of Language Acquisition* (Vol. 2). London: LEA.
Brown, R. (1973) *A First Language: The Early Stages*. Cambridge, MA: Harvard University Press.
Bruner, J.S. (1977) Early social interaction and language acquisition. In H.R. Schaffer (ed.) *Studies in Mother–Infant Interaction*. London: Academic Press.
— (1978a) The role of dialogue in language acquisition. In A. Sinclair, R. Jarvella and W. Levelt (eds) *The Child's Conception of Language*. Berlin: Springer-Verlag.
— (1978b) From communication to language. In I. Markova (ed.) *The Social Context of Language*. New York: Wiley.

— (1983) *Child's Talk: Learning to Use Language*. Oxford: Oxford University Press

Bullowa, M. (ed.) (1979) *Before Speech: The Beginning of Interpersonal Communication*. Cambridge: Cambridge University Press.

Burling, R. (1959) Language development of a Garo and English-speaking child. *Word* 15, 45–68. Reprinted in E. Hatch (ed.) *Second Language Acquisition: A Book of Readings*. Rowley, MA: Newbury House.

Carroll, J.B. and Sapon, S.M. (1959) *Manual for Modern Language Aptitude Test*. New York: Psychological Corporation.

Chomsky, N. (1959) A review of *Verbal Behavior*, by B.F. Skinner. *Language* 35, 26–58.

— (1965) *Aspects of the Theory of Syntax*. Cambridge, MA: MIT Press.

— (1968) *Language and Mind*. New York: Harcourt Brace Jovanovich.

Christie, P. and Wimpory, D. (1986) Recent research into the development of communicative competence and implications for the teaching of autistic children. *Communication* 10 (1), 8–12.

Clarke, A. and Clarke, A.D.B. (1976) *Early Experience: Myth and Evidence*. London: Open Books.

Clyne, M. (1982) *Multilingual Australia*. Melbourne: River Seine.

Condon, W.S. (1979) Neonatal entrainment and enculturation. In M. Bullowa (ed.) *Before Speech: The Beginning of Interpersonal Communication*. Cambridge: Cambridge University Press.

Conti-Ramsden, G. and Friel-Patti, C. (1986) Mother–child dialogues; Considerations of cognitive complexity for young language learning children. *Br. J. Disorders of Communication* 21, 245–55.

Crystal, D. (1976) *Child Language: Learning and Linguistics*. London: Arnold.

Crystal, D., Fletcher, P. and Garmon, M. (1976) *The Grammatical Analysis of Language Disability: A Procedure for Assessment and Remediation*. London: Arnold.

Cummins, J. (1976) The influence of bilingualism on cognitive growth: A synthesis of research findings and explanatory hypotheses. *Working Papers on Bilingualism* 9, 1–43.

— (1978a) The cognitive development of children in immersion programs. *Canadian Modern Language Review* 34, 855–83.

— (1978b) Bilingualism and the development of metalingual awareness. *J. of Cross Cultural Psychology* 9, 131–49.

— (1980) The construct of language proficiency in bilingual education. In J. Alatis (ed.) *Georgetown University Round Table on Languages and Linguistics, 1980*. Washington, DC: Georgetown University Press .

— (1984) *Bilingualism in Special Education: Issues in Assessment and Pedagogy*. Clevedon: Multilingual Matters.

— (1987) Bilingualism, language proficiency and metalinguistic development. In P. Homel, M. Palij and D. Aaronson (eds) *Childhood Bilingualism: Aspects of Linguistic, Cognitive and Social Development*. Hillsdale NJ: LEA.

— (1991) Interdependence of first- and second-language proficiency in bilingual children. In E. Bialystock (ed.) *Language Processing in Bilingual Children*. Cambridge: Cambridge University Press.

Dehouwer, A. (1990) *The Acquisition of Two Languages from Birth: A Case Study*. Cambridge: Cambridge University Press.

— (1995) Bilingual language acquisition. In P. Fletcher and B. Macwhinney (eds) *The Handbook of Child Language*. Oxford: Blackwell.

Dewart, H. and Summers, S. (1988) *The Pragmatics Profile*. London: NFER-Nelson.

Dodson, C.J. (1967) *Language Teaching and the Bilingual Method*. London: Pitman.
— (1983) Living with two languages. *J. of Multilingual and Multicultural Development* 4, 401–14.
— (ed.) (1985) *Bilingual Education: Evaluation, Assessment and Methodology*. Cardiff: University of Wales Press.
Dodson, C.J. and Jones, G.G. (1984) A Welsh medium TV channel for Wales: Development, controversies, problems, implications. *Int. Journal of Sociology of Language* 48, 11–32.
Dodson, C.J. and Price, E. (1978) *Bilingual Education in Wales, 5–11*. London: Evans/Methuen.
Donaldson, M. (1978) *Children's Minds*. Glasgow: Collins/Fontana.
Dopke, S. (1992a) *One Parent–One Language: An Interactional Approach*. Amsterdam: John Benjamins.
— (1992b) A bilingual child's struggle to comply with the 'One parent–one language' rule. *Journal of Multilingual and Multicultural Development* 13 (6), 467–85
Dore, J. (1974) A pragmatic description of early language development. *J. of Psycholinguistic Research* 3, 343–50.
— (1975) Holophrases, speech acts and language universals. *J. Child Language* 2, 21–40.
— (1979) Conversational acts and the acquisition of language. In E. Ochs and B. Schiefflin (eds) *Developmental Pragmatics*. New York: Academic Press.
Dulay, H. and Burt, M. (1974) Natural sequences in child second language acquisition. *Language Learning* 24, 37–53.
— (1978) Natural sequences in child second language acquisition. In E.M. Hatch (ed.) *Second Language Acquisition: A Book of Readings*. Rowley, MA: Newbury House.
Dulay, H., Burt, M. and Krashen, C. (1982) *Language Two*. Oxford: Oxford University Press.
Duncan, S.E. and DeAvila, E.A. (1979) Bilingualism and cognition: Some recent findings. *NABE Journal* 4, 15–50.
Elliot, A. (1981) *Child Language*. Cambridge: Cambridge University Press.
Ellis, R. (1985) *Understanding Second Language Acquisition*. Oxford: Oxford University Press.
— (1994) *The Study of Second Language Acquisition*. Oxford: Oxford University Press.
Elwert, W. (1959) *Das Zweisprachige Individuum: Ein Selbstzeugnis*. Mainz: Verlag der Akademie der Wissenschaften und Literatur.
Engle, M. (1980) Family influence on the language development of young children. *Women's Studies International Quarterly* 3, 259–66.
Ervin-Tripp, S. (1968) An analysis of the interaction of language, topic and listener. In J. Fishman (ed.) *Readings in the Sociology of Language*. The Hague: Mouton.
— (1982) 'Ask and it shall be given to you': Children's requests. In H. Byres (ed.) *Georgetown Round Table in Language and Linguistics*. Washington, DC: Georgetown University Press
Evans, M. (1987) Linguistic accommodation in a bilingual family: One perspective on the language acquisition of a bilingual child being raised in a monolingual community. *J. of Multilingual and Multicultural Development* 8, 231–5.
Fantini, A. (1985) *Language Acquisition of a Bilingual Child: A Socio-linguistic Perspective*. Clevedon: Multilingual Matters.

Fantz, R.L. (1961) A method for studying depth perception in infants. *Psychological Record* 11, 21–32.

Farris, C.S. (1992) Chinese preschool codeswitching: Mandarin babytalk and the voice of authority. *J. of Multilingual and Multicultural Development* 13, 187–213.

Ferguson, C. (1977) Baby talk as a simplified register. In C. Snow and C.A. Ferguson *Talking to Children*. Cambridge: Cambridge University Press.

Fillmore, L.W. (1991) Second language learning in children: A model of language learning in context. In E. Bialystock (ed.) *Language Processing in Bilingual Children*. Cambridge: Cambridge University Press.

Fishman, J.A. (1965) Who speaks what language to whom and when? *La Linguistique*, 67–68.

— (1980) Bilingualism and biculturalism as individual and as social phenomena. *J. Multilingual and Multicultural Development* 1, 3–15

— (1991) *Reversing Language Shift*. Clevedon: Multilingual Matters.

Foster, S. (1986) Learning discourse topic management in the preschool years. *J. of Child Language* 13, 231–51.

Frasure-Smith, N.E., Lambert, W.E. and Taylor, D.M. (1974) Choosing the language of instruction for one's children: A Quebec study. *J. of Cross Cultural Research* 6 (2), 131–55.

Freed, L. (1961) Personal Communication.

Furrow, D., Nelson, K. and Benedict, H. (1979) Mother's speech to children and syntactic development: Some simple relationships. *J. of Child Language* 11, 43–79.

Furrow, D. and Nelson, K. (1986) A further look at the motherese hypothesis: A reply to Gleitman, Newport and Gleitman. *J. of Child Language* 13, 163–76.

Gardner, R.C. (1985) *Social Psychology and Second Language Learning: The Role of Attitudes and Motivation*. London: Arnold.

— (1991) Attitudes and motivation in second language learning. In A. Reynolds (ed.) *Bilingualism, Multiculturalism and Second Language Learning: The McGill Conference in Honour of Wallace E. Lambert*. Hillsdale, NJ: LEA.

Gardner, R.C. and Lambert W.E. (1972) *Attitudes and Motivation in Second Language Learning*. Rowley, MA: Newbury House.

Genesee, F. (1989) Early bilingual development: One language or two? *J. of Child Language* 16 (1), 161–79.

— (ed.) (1994) *Educating Second Language Children*.Cambridge: Cambridge University Press.

Genesee, F., Tucker, G. and Lambert, W. (1976) Communication skills of bilingual children. *Child Development* 46 (4), 1010–14.

Giattino, J. and Hogan, J. (1975) Analysis of a father's speech to his language learning child. *J. Speech & Hearing Disorders* 40, 524–38.

Giles, H., Bouris, R. and Taylor, D. (1977) Towards a theory of language in ethnic group relations. In H. Giles (ed.) *Language, Ethnicity and Intergroup Relations*. London: Academic Press.

Givon, T. (1985) Function, structure and language acquisition. In D. Slobin (ed.) *The Cross-Linguistic Study of Language Acquisition* (Vol 2: Theoretical Issues). Hillsdale, NJ: LEA.

Gleason, B.J. (1975) Fathers and other strangers: Men's speech to young children. In D. Dato (ed.) *Developmental Psycholinguistics: Theory and Applications*. Washington, DC: Georgetown University Roundtable in Languages and Linguistics.

Gleason, B.J. and Grief, E.M. (1983) Men's speech to young children. In B. Thorne, C. Kramarae and N. Henley (eds) *Language, Gender and Society*. Rowley, MA: Newbury House.

Gleitman, L.R., Newport, E.L. and Gleitman, H. (1984) The current status of the motherese hypothesis. *J. Child Language* 11, 43–79.

Gonz, L. and Kodzopeljic, J. (1991) Exposure to two languages in the preschool period: Metalinguistic development in the acquisition of reading. *Journal of Multilingual and Multicultural Development* 12 (3), 137–63.

Goodz, N. (1994) Interactions between parents and children in bilingual families. In F. Genesee (ed.) *Educating Second Language Children*. Cambridge: Cambridge University Press.

Grice, H.P. (1968) Utterance meaning, sentence meaning and word meaning. *Foundations of Language*, 225–42.

Grosjean, F. (1982) *Life with Two Languages*. Cambridge, MA: Harvard University Press

Gutfreund, M.K., Harrison, M. and Wells, G. (1989) *Bristol Language Development Scales*. Windsor: NFER-Nelson.

Halliday, M. (1975) *Learning How to Mean*. London: Arnold.

— (1979) One child's proto-language. In M. Bullowa (ed.) *Before Speech: The Beginning of Interpersonal Communication*. Cambridge: Cambridge University Press.

Halliday, S. and Leslie, J. (1986) A longitudinal cross-section of the development of mother–child interaction. *Br. J. Developmental Psychology* 4, 211–22.

Harding, E. and Riley, P. (1986) *The Bilingual Family: A Handbook for Parents*. Cambridge: Cambridge University Press.

Harres, A. (1989) Being a good German: A case study analysis of language retention and loss among German migrants in New Queensland. *J. Multilingual and Multicultural Development* 10 (5), 383–99.

Harris, R. J. (ed.) (1992) *Cognitive Processing in Bilinguals: Advances in Psychology* 83. Amsterdam: North-Holland .

Harrison, G., Bellin, W. and Piette, B. (1981) *Bilingual Mothers in Wales and the Language of their Children*. Cardiff: University of Wales.

Harrison, G. and Piette, A.B. (1980) Young bilingual children's language selection. *J. of Multilingual and Multicultural Development* 3, 217–30.

Harrison, G. and Thomas, C. (1975) *The Acquisition of Bilingual Speech by Infants*. Cardiff: Welsh Language Research Unit (Final Report on SSRC Grant HR2104/1).

Hatch, E. (1978) (ed.) *Second Language Acquisition: A Book of Readings*. Rowley, MA: Newbury House.

Haugen, E. (1969) *The Norwegian Language in America: A Study in Bilingual Behaviour*. Bloomington: Indiana University Press.

Heller, M. (ed.) (1988) *'Code Switching': Anthropological and Sociological Perspectives*. Berlin: Mouton de Gruyter.

Helot, C. (1988) Bringing up Children in English, French and Irish: Two Case Studies. *Language, Culture and Curriculum* 1 (3), 281–7.

Henley, N.M. and Lafrance, M. (1984) Gender as culture: Difference and dominance in non-verbal behavior. In A. Wolfgang (ed.) *Non Verbal Behavior: Perspectives, Applications, Inter-cultural Insights*. New York: C.J. Hogrefe Inc.

Hickey, T. (1991) Mean length of utterance and the acquisition of Irish. *J. of Child Language* 18, 553–69.

Higgins, E.T. (1988) *Learning to Talk.* Leicester: The British Psychological Society.

Hoffmann, C. (1985) Language acquisition in two trilingual children. *J. of Multilingual and Multicultural Development* 6 (6), 479–95.

Homel, P., Palij, M., and Aaronson, D. (eds) (1987) *Childhood Bilingualism.* Hillsdale, NJ: LEA.

Hood, L., Fliess, K. and Aron, J. (1982) Growing up explained: Vygotskyians look at the language of causality. In C.J. Brainerd and M. Pressley (eds) *Verbal Processes in Children: Progress and Cognitive Development Research.* New York: Springer-Verlag.

Huntley, M. (1986) Experimental Welsh Version of the Reynell Developmental Language Scales. (See Reynell, 1987). The Wolfson Centre, London: Unpublished.

Hyltenstan, K. and Obler, L. (eds) (1989) *Bilingualism Across the Lifespan.* Cambridge: Cambridge University Press.

Imedadze, N. (1967) On the psychological nature of child speech formation under the condition of exposure to two languages. *Int. J. of Psychology* 2 (2), 129–32. Reprinted in E. Hatch (ed.) (1978) *Second Language Acquisition.* Rowley, MA: Newbury House.

Inhelder, B. and Piaget, J. (1964) *The Early Growth of Logic in the Child.* London: Routledge and Kegan Paul.

Itoh, H. and Hatch, E. (1978) Second language acquisition: A case study. In E.M. Hatch (ed.) *Second Language Acquisition: A Book of Readings.* Rowley, MA: Newbury House.

Kamhi, A.G. (1986) The first elusive word: The importance of naming insight for the development of referential speech. *J. Child Language* 13, 155–61.

Karniol, R. (1990) Second language acquisition via immersion in daycare. *J. of Child Language* 17, 147–70.

Kaye, K. (1977) Towards the origin of dialogue. In H.R. Schaffer (ed.) *Studies in Mother-Infant Interactions.* London: Academic Press.

Klein, W. (1986) *Second Language Acquisition.* Cambridge: Cambridge University Press.

Kohlberg, L. (1976) Moral stages and moralization: The cognitive developmental approach. In T. Lickona (ed.) *Moral Development and Behavior.* New York: Rinehart, Holt & Winston.

Krashen, S. (1981) *Second Language Acquisition and Second Language Learning.* Oxford: Pergamon Press.

— (1982) *Principles and Practice in Second Language Acquisition.* Oxford: Pergamon Press.

— (1985) *The Input Hypothesis: Issues and Implications.* London: Longmans.

Lambert, W.E. (1974) Culture and language as factors in learning and education. In F.E. Aboud and R.D. Meade (eds) *Cultural Factors in Learning and Education.* Bellingham, WA: Fifth Western Washington Symposium on Learning.

Lambert, W.E. and Tucker, G.R. (1972) *Bilingual Education of Children: The St. Lambert Experiment.* Rowley, MA: Newbury House.

Lanza, E. (1992) Can bilingual two-year-olds code-switch? *J. of Child Language* 19, 633–58.

Lenneberg, E.H. (1967) *The Biological Foundations of Language.* New York: Wiley.

Leopold, W. (1949a) *Speech Development of a Bilingual Child: A Linguist's Record. (Vol. 3: Grammar and General Problems in the First Two Years)*. Evanston, IL: North Western University Press.
— (1949b) *Speech Development of a Bilingual Child: A Linguist's Record. (Vol. 4: Diary from Age Two)*. Evanston, IL: North Western University Press.
— (1954 (1939)) *Speech Development of a Bilingual Child: A Linguist's Record. (Vol. 1: Vocabulary Growth in the First Two Years)*. Evanston, IL: North Western University Press.
Lewis, E.G. (1975) Attitude to language among bilingual children and adults in Wales. *International J. of the Sociology of Language* 4, 103–25
Lindholm, K. and Padilla, A. (1978) Language mixing in bilingual children. *J. of Child Language* 5 (2), 327–35.
Lindsay, A. and Norman, C. (1977) *Human Information Processing: An Introduction to Psychology*. New York: Academic Press.
Lyon, J. (1991) Patterns of parental language use in Wales. *J. of Multilingual and Multicultural Development* 12 (3), 165–83.
— (1993) The development of children's language in a bilingual culture. Unpublished PhD thesis. Bangor: University of Wales.
Lyon, J. and Ellis, N. (1991) Parental attitudes towards the Welsh Language. *J. of Multilingual and Multicultural Development* 12 (4), 239–52.
Lyons, J. (1968) *Introduction to Theoretical Linguistics*. Cambridge: Cambridge University Press.
Mackey, W. (1988) Geolinguistics: Its scope and principles. In C. Williams (ed.) *Language in Geographic Context*. Clevedon: Multilingual Matters.
Macnamara, A. (1982) *Names for Things: A Study of Human Learning*. Cambridge, MA: MIT Press.
McConkey, R. and O'Connor, M. (1981) *Putting Two Words Together*. Dublin: St. Michael's House.
McLaughlin, B. (1978) *Second-Language Acquisition in Childhood*. Hillsdale, NJ: LEA.
— (1984) *Second-Language Acquisition in Childhood (Vol. 1): Preschool Children*. Hillsdale, NJ: LEA
— (1987) *Theories of Second Language Learning*. London: Arnold.
McLaughlin, B. ,White, D., McDevitt, T. and Raskin, R. (1983) Mothers' and fathers' speech to their young children: Similar or different? *J. Child Language* 10, 245–52.
Meisel, J. (1989) Early differentiation of languages in bilingual children. In L.Obler and K. Hyltenstam (eds) *Bilingualism across the Lifespan*. Cambridge: Cambridge University Press.
Menn, L. (1982) Child language as a source of constraints for linguistic theory. In L. Obler and L.Menn (eds) *Exceptional Language and Linguistics*. New York: Academic Press.
Menyuk, P. (1969) *Sentences Children Use*. Cambridge, MA: MIT Press.
Mittler, P. (ed.) (1974) *The Psychological Assessment of Mental and Physical Handicap*. London: Methuen.
Mogford, K. and Gregory, S. (1980) Achieving understanding: A study of communication between mothers and their young deaf children. *Conference Paper to BPS Developmental Section*. Edinburgh: BPS.
Murray, L. and Trevarthen, C. (1986) The infant's role in mother-infant communication. *J. Child Language* 13, 15–29.

Myers-Scotton, C. (1988) Codeswitching as indexical of social negotiation. In M.
Heller (ed.) *Codeswitching: Anthropological and Sociolinguistic Perspectives.* Berlin:
Mouton de Gruyter.
— (1992) Comparing codeswitching and borrowing. *J. of Multilingual and Multicul-
tural Development* 13, 19–39.
— (1993) *Social Motivations for Codeswitching.* New York: Oxford University Press.
Nelde, P. (1989) Ecological aspects of language contact or how to investigate
linguistic minorities. *J. Multilingual and Multicultural Development* 10, 73–86.
Newport, E., Gleitman, H. and Gleitman, L. (1977) Mother, I'd rather do it myself:
Some effects and non-effects of maternal speech style. In C.E. Snow and C.A.
Ferguson (eds.) *Talking to Children: Language Input and Acquisition.* New York:
Cambridge University Press.
Newson, J. (1974) Towards a theory of infant understanding. *Bulletin of Br.
Psychological Society* 27, 251–7.
— (1977) An intersubjective approach to the systematic description of mother-
infant interaction. In H.R. Schaffer (ed.) *Studies in Mother-Infant Interaction:
Proceedings of the Loch Lomond Symposium.* New York: Academic Press.
— (1979) The growth of shared understanding. In M. Bullowa (ed.) *Before Speech:
The Beginning of Interpersonal Communication.* Cambridge: Cambridge University
Press.
Ochs, E. and Schieffelin, B. (eds) (1979) *Developmental Pragmatics.* New York:
Academic Press.
Office of Population Census and Surveys (1983) *Census 1981: The Welsh Language in
Wales.* London: HMSO.
— (1992) *Census 1991: Great Britain and County Monitors.* London: OPCS.
Oliverio, A. and Zappella, M. (eds) (1983) *The Behaviour of Human Infants.* London:
Plenum Press.
Olson, D. (1988) On the origins of beliefs and other intentional states. In J. Astington,
P. Harris and D. Olson (eds) *Developing Theories of Mind.* Cambridge, Cambridge
University Press.
Oppenheim, A.N. (1966) *Questionnaire Design and Attitude Measurement.* London:
Heinemann.
Padilla, A.M. and Liebman, E. (1975) Language acquisition in the bilingual child.
Bilingual Review, 34–55.
Palij, M. and Homel, P. (1987) The relationship of bilingualism to cognitive
behavior. In P. Homel, M. Palij and D. Aaronson (eds) *Childhood Bilingualism.*
Hillsdale, NJ: LEA.
Peal, E. and Lambert,W.E. (1962) The relation of bilingualism to intelligence.
Psychological Monographs 76, 1–23.
Piaget, J. (1959 (1926)) *The Language and Thought of the Child.* London: Routledge and
Kegan Paul.
— (1952 (1936)) *The Origins of Intelligence in Children.* New York: International
University Press.
Poplack, S., Wheeler, S., and Westwood, A. (1989) Distinguishing language contact
phenomena: Evidence from English-Finnish bilingualism. In K. Hyltenstan and
L. Obler (eds) *Bilingualism across the Lifespan.* Cambridge: Cambridge University
Press.

Price-Jones, E. (1982) A study of some of the factors which determine the degree of bilingualism of a Welsh child between 10 and 13 years of age. Unpublished PhD thesis. Bangor: University of Wales.

Redlinger, W. (1979) Early developmental bilingualism. *Bilingual Review* 6 (1), 11–30.

Redlinger, W. and Park, T.Z. (1980) Language mixing in young bilinguals. *J of Child Language* 7, 337–62.

Reynell, J.K. (1987) *Reynell Developmental Language Scales* (second revision). Windsor: Nfer-Nelson.

Rice, M.L. and Kemper, S. (1984) *Child Language and Cognition*. Baltimore: University Park Press.

Romaine, S. (1995) *Bilingualism* (Second Edition). Oxford: Blackwell.

Rondal, J.A. (1980) Fathers' and mothers' speech in early language development. *J. of Child Language* 7, 353–69.

Ronjat, J. (1913) *Le Development de Langage Observé Chez un Enfant Bilingue*. Paris: Champion.

Ross, J.A. (1979) Language and the mobilization of ethnic identity. In H. Giles and B. Saint-Jacques (eds) *Language and Ethnic Relations*. Oxford: Pergamon Press.

Saunders, G. (1982) *Bilingual Children: Guidance for Families*. Clevedon: Multilingual Matters.

Saussure, F. (1916) *Cours de Linguistique Generale*. Paris: Payot.

Schaffer, H.R. (ed.) (1977) *Studies in Mother-Infant Interaction: Proceedings of the Loch Lomond Symposium*. New York: Academic Press.

Schlyter, S. (1987) Language mixing and linguistic level in three bilingual children. *Scandinavian Working Papers in Bilingualism* 7, 29–48.

Schmidt-Mackey, I. (1971) Bilingual strategies of bilingual families. In W. Mackey and T. Andersson (eds.) *Bilingualism in Early Childhood*. Rowley, MA: Newbury House.

Schumann, J. (1978) The acculturation model of second language acquisition. In R. Gingras (ed.) *Second Language Acquisition and Foreign Language Teaching*. Washington: Centre for Applied Linguistics.

— (1986) Research on the acculturation model for second language acquisition. *J. of Multilingual and Multicultural Development* 7, 379–91.

Selinker, L. (1972) Interlanguage. *International Review of Applied Linguistics* 10, 209–31.

Selman, R. (1980) *The Growth of Interpersonal Understanding: Developmental and Clinical Analyses*. New York: Academic Press.

Sharp, D., Thomas, B., Price, E., Francis, G. and Davis, I. (1973) *Attitudes to Welsh and English in the Schools of Wales*. London: Macmillan.

Shatz, M. and O'Reilly, A.W. (1990) Conversational or communicative skill? A re-assessment of two-year-olds' behaviour in miscommunication episodes. *J. Child Language* 17, 131–46.

Shotter, J. (1979) The cultural context of communication studies: Theoretical and methodological issues. In A. Lock (ed.) *Action, Gesture and Symbol: The Emergence of Language*. New York: Academic Press.

Skinner, B.F. (1957) *Verbal Behavior*. New York: Appleton-Century-Crofts.

Skutnabb-Kangas, T. (1981) *Bilingualism or Not: The Education of Minorities*. Clevedon: Multilingual Matters.

Skutnabb-Kangas, T. and Toukomaa, P. (1976) *Teaching Migrant Children's Mother Tongue and Learning the Language of the Host Country in the Context of the Socio-Cultural Situation of the Migrant Family.* (UNESCO Research Report 15.) Tampere, Finland: University of Tampere.

Slobin, D. (1974) *Psycholinguistics.* Glenview, IL: Scott Foresman.

— (1982) Universal and particular in the acquisition of language. In E. Wanner and L. Gleitman (eds) *Language Acquisition: The State of the Art.* Cambridge: Cambridge University Press.

— (ed.) (1985) *The Cross-Linguistic Study of Language Acquisition,* Vol. 2: *Theoretical Issues.* Hillsdale, NJ: LEA.

Snow, C. (1977a) The development of conversation between mothers and babies. *J. Child Language* 4, 1–22.

— (1977b) Mother's speech research: From input to interaction. In C. Snow and C.A. Ferguson (eds) *Talking to Children.* Cambridge: Cambridge University Press.

Snow, C. and Ferguson, C.A. (eds) (1977) *Talking to Children: Language Input and Acquisition.* New York: Cambridge University Press.

Soh, K.C. (1987) Language use: A missing link? *J. of Multilingual and Multicultural Development* 8, 443–9.

Stubbs, M. (1981) Scratching the surface: Linguistic data in educational research. In C. Adelman (ed.) *Uttering, Muttering.* Edinburgh: Grant-McIntyre.

Sugarman-Bell, S. (1978) Some organisational aspects of pre-verbal communication. In I. Markova (ed.) *The Social Context of Language.* New York: Wiley.

Swain, M. (1971) Bilingualism, monoligualism and code acquisition. In W. Mackey and T. Andersson (eds) *Bilingualism in Early Childhood.* Rowley, MA: Newbury House.

— (1972) Bilingualism as a first language. Unpublished PhD thesis, University of California.

Swain, M. and Wesche, M. (1975) Linguistic interaction: Case study of a bilingual child. *Language Sciences* 37, 17–22.

Swain, M. and Lapkin, S. (1982) *Evaluating Bilingual Education: A Canadian Case Study.* Clevedon: Multilingual Matters.

Taeschner, T. (1983) *The Sun is Feminine: A Study on Language Acquisition in Bilingual Children.* Berlin: Springer-Verlag.

Taylor, D. and Giles, H. (1979) At the crossroads of research into language and ethnic relations. In H. Giles and B. Saint-Jacques (eds) *Language and Ethnic Relations.* Oxford: Pergamon Press.

Thibaut, J. and Kelley, H. (1959) *The Social Psychology of Groups.* New York: Wiley.

Tomasello, M. (1992) *First Verbs: A Case Study of Early Grammatical Development.* Cambridge: Cambridge University Press.

Tomasello, M., Conti-Ramsden, G. and Ewert, B. (1990) Young children's conversations with their mothers and fathers: Differences in breakdown and repair. *J. Child Language* 17, 115–30.

Toukomaa, P. and Skutnabb-Kangas, T. (1977) *The Intensive Teaching of the Mother Tongue to Migrant Children of Preschool age and Children in the Lower Level of Comprehensive School.* Helsinki: The Finnish National Commision for UNESCO.

Trevarthen, C. (1979) Communication and co-operation in early infancy: A description of primary intersubjectivity. In M. Bullowa (ed.) *Before Speech: The Beginning of Interpersonal Communication.* Cambridge: Cambridge University Press.

— (1983) Interpersonal abilities of infants as generators for transmission of language and culture. In A. Oliverio and M. Zappella (eds) *The Behaviour of Human Infants*. London: Plenum Press.

Van Kleeck, A. (1982) The emergence of linguistic awareness: A cognitive framework. *Merril Palmer Quarterly* 28 (2), 237–65.

Vedder, P. (ed.) (1995) *Multicultural Child Care*. Clevedon: Multilingual Matters.

Vihman, M.M. (1985) Language differentiation by the bilingual infant. *J. of Child Language* 12, 297–324.

Vihman, M. and McLaughlin, B. (1982) Bilingualism and second language acquisition in preschool children. In C. Brainerd and M. Pressley (eds) *Verbal Processes in Children*. New York: Springer-Verlag.

Volterra, V. and Taeschner, T. (1978) The acquisition and development of language by bilingual children. *J. of Child Language* 5 (2), 311–26.

Vygotsky, L. (1986 (1962)) A. Kozulin (ed.) *Thought and Language*. Cambridge, MA: MIT Press.

Wanner, E. and Gleitman, L. (eds) (1986) *Language Acquisition: The State of the Art*. Cambridge: Cambridge University Press.

Wellman, H.M. (1988) Children's understanding of perceptibility. In J.W. Astington, P.L. Harris and D.R. Olson (eds) *Developing Theories of Mind*. Cambridge: Cambridge University Press.

Wells, G. (1981) Describing children's linguistic development at home and at school. In C. Adelman (ed.) *Uttering, Muttering*. Edinburgh: Grant-McIntyre.

— (1985) *Language Learning and Education*. Windsor: NFER-Nelson.

Weschler, D. (1991) *Weschler Preschool and Primary Scale of Intelligence* (Revised UK edition). Sidcup: The Psychological Corporation Ltd., Harcourt Brace Jovanovich.

Williams, C.H. (1979) An ecological and behavioural analysis of ethnolinguistic change in Wales. In H. Giles and B. Saint-Jacques *Language and Ethnic Relations*. Oxford: Pergamon Press.

Williams, C. (1987) Location and context in Welsh language reproduction: A geographic interpretation. *Int. J. of Sociology of Language* 66, 61–83.

Y Geiriadur Mawr (1986) *The Complete Welsh-English English-Welsh Dictionary*. Llandysul: Swasg Gomer.

Y Geiriadur Lliwgar (1979) *Welsh Children's Picture Dictionary*. Caerdydd: Usborne Publishing Ltd.

Youngman. M. (1979) *Analysing Social and Educational Research Data*. London: McGraw-Hill/Washington, DC: Georgetown University Press.

Appendix I: Language Background Questionnaire (QI)

(a) English Version

(b) Welsh Version

LANGUAGE BACKGROUND QUESTIONNAIRE (Q.I)

If you have a partner living with you, please will you tick the answers that apply to him, as well as the answers that apply to you.

QUESTION 1   SELF   PARTNER

At present, which language
do you use :

with the baby ?

with other children ?

with close friends ?

with neighbours ?

with your parents ?

with shopkeepers ?

with people at work ?

at church or chapel ?

with one another ?

QUESTION 2

Which language do you prefer

for reading ?

for thinking ?

for watching television ?

QUESTION 3

How would you describe

your first School ?

your last School ?

QUESTION 4

Would you say you
are bilingual ? | YES | | NO | | YES | | NO |

Language Background Questionnaire

If you have a partner living with you, please will you tick the answers that apply to him as well as the answers that apply to you.

QUESTION 5   SELF   PARTNER

When you were a child in primary School, what language did you use

at home ?

with your Mother ?

with your Father ?

with your Brothers ?

with your Sisters ?

with your favourite Grandparent ?
with your best friend ?

at School ?

QUESTION 6

Are there other children living at home ?   YES   NO

if YES, what language does

the eldest use at home ?

the eldest use at School ?

the eldest use with friends?

Is there more than one child at home   YES   NO

(if NO, go to Question 7)

if YES, what language does

the youngest use at home ?

the youngest use at School ?

the youngest use with friends?

Language Background Questionnaire

If you have a partner living with you, please tick the answers that apply to him, as well as the answers that apply to you.

QUESTION 7

Do you speak Welsh ?   **SELF**   **PARTNER**

    No, not yet

    A few words and phrases

    Taking a Welsh course

    Can join in simple conversation

    Speak local Welsh with friends

    Fluent Welsh speaker

    I'd rather describe myself as   ————————   ————————

QUESTION 8

Do you want your baby

    to speak only English

    to pick up some Welsh

    to learn Welsh at School

    to speak Welsh fluently

    other (please specify)

    don't know

Please give reasons for your answer   ————————   ————————

    ————————   ————————

QUESTION 9

How important or unimportant do you think it is for children to learn Welsh?

SELF

UN-IMPORT.	NOT VERY IMPORT.	QUITE IMPORT.	VERY IMPORT.

PARTNER

UN-IMPORT.	NOT VERY IMPORT.	QUITE IMPORT.	VERY IMPORT.

Don't know

Language Background Questionnaire

If you have a partner living with you, please tick the answers that apply to him, as well as that apply to you.

QUESTION 10

Which is closest to your opinion ?
Do you think that, in your children's lifetime

	SELF	PARTNER
Welsh will replace English in this part of Wales	☐	☐
Welsh will be used more than it is now	☐	☐
Welsh will be used the same as it is now	☐	☐
Welsh will be used less than it is now	☐	☐
English will replace Welsh in this part of Wales	☐	☐

QUESTION 11

When your baby grows up, do you hope
that he/she will

	SELF	PARTNER
live on Ynys Mon ?	☐	☐
live in North Wales ?	☐	☐
live in Wales ?	☐	☐
live in Britain ?	☐	☐
live abroad ?	☐	☐

QUESTION 12

When your baby grows up, do you hope
that he/she will

marry a Welsh speaking person ?	☐	☐
marry a non Welsh speaking person ?	☐	☐
not mind either way ?	☐	☐

Language Background Questionnaire

To help me classify your answers, I'd like to ask you a few questions about yourself and your family.

QUESTION 13

What is your full name : _____

Your address   : _____

                         _____

                         _____

Your baby's name   : _____

Your baby's date of birth : _____

About how old are you ?

20 or younger
21 to 39
40 or older

How would you describe yourself ?

WORKING CLASS	LOWER MIDDLE CLASS	UPPER MIDDLE CLASS	UPPER CLASS		NOT SURE

QUESTION 14

Do you have a husband/boyfriend ?   YES   NO

                                           If NO, go to Question 15

If YES, about how old is he

20 or younger
21 to 39
40 or older

Does he have a job that regularly takes   YES   NO
him away from home ?

How do you think he would describe himself ?

WORKING CLASS	LOWER MIDDLE CLASS	UPPER MIDDLE CLASS	UPPER CLASS		NOT SURE

Language Background Questionnaire

If you have a partner living with you, please tick the answers that apply to him, as well as the answers that apply to you.

QUESTION 15

Are there other children at home | YES | | NO |
besides the baby ?

If NO, go on to Question 16

If YES, please tell me their NAMES and AGES

_____ _____

_____ _____

_____ _____

_____ _____

_____ _____

QUESTION 16

	SELF		**PARTNER**	
Have you always lived in this area ?	YES	NO	YES	NO

If NO, when did you first
move to Ynys Mon ?   _____   _____

QUESTION 17

Are either of your parents still alive ?	YES	NO	YES	NO

If YES, where do they live

    with you ?

    a few minutes walk away ?

    a short journey away ?

    some distance, but not too far away ?

    a long way away ?

QUESTION 18

Please add any comments about your language background, or about this questionnaire, which you think might be important.

_____

_____

_____

Thank you very much for your help.

Will you please check that you have answered everything and then send it back in the envelope provided.

HOLIADUR CEFNDIR IAITH (Q.I)

Os oes gennych bartner yn byw gyda chi, ticiwch yr atebion sy'n berthnasol
iddo ef, yn ogystal a'r atebion sy'n berthnasol i chi.

CWESTIWN 1   EICH HUN   PARTNER

Ar hyn o bryd, pa iaith
'rydych yn ei siarad:

        gyda'r babi ?

        gyda phlant eraill ?

        gyda ffrindiau agos ?

        gyda chymdogion ?

        gyda'ch rhieni ?

        gyda siopwyr ?

        gyda phobl yn y gwaith ?

        yn yr eglwys neu'r capel ?

        gyda'ch gilydd ?

CWESTIWN 2

Pa iaith sydd orau gennych ar gyfer

        darllen ?

        meddwl ?

        gwylio'r teledu ?

CWESTIWN 3

Sut y byddach yn disgrifio

        eich ysgol cyntaf ?

        eich ysgol olaf ?

CWESTIWN 4

A fyddech yn dweud eich | BUASWN | NA FUASWN | | BUASWN | NA FUASWN |
bod yn ddwyieithog ?

Holiadur Cefndir Iaith

Os oes gennych bartner yn byw gyda chi, ticiwch yr atebion sy'n berthnasol iddo ef, yn ogystal a'r atebion sy'n berthnasol i chi.

CWESTIWN 5

	EICH HUN					PARTNER			

Pan oeddech yn blentyn yn yr Ysgol Gynradd, pa iaith oeddech yn ei ddefnyddio

gartref ?

gyda'ch Mam ?

gyda'ch Tad ?

gyda'ch Brodyr ?

gyda'ch Chwiorydd ?

gyda'ch hoff Nain neu Daid ?

gyda'ch ffrind gorau ?

yn yr Ysgol ?

CWESTIWN 6

Oes plant eraill yn byw gartref ?   OES   NAGOES

os OES,   pa iaith ydi'r hynaf yn siarad

   yn y cartref ?

   yn yr ysgol ?

   gyda ffrindiau ?

Oes na mwy na un plentyn yn byw gartref   OES   NAGOES

Os NAGOES ewch ymlaen i
Cwestiwn 7

os OES,   pa iaith ydi'r ieuengaf yn siarad

   yn y cartref ?

   yn yr ysgol ?

   gyda ffrindiau ?

Holiadur Cefndir Iaith

Os oes gennych bartner yn byw gyda chi, ticiwch yr atebion sy'n berthnasol
iddo ef, yn ogystal a'r atebion sy'n berthnasol i chi.

CWESTIWN 7

Ydych chi'n siarad Cymraeg   EICH HUN   PARTNER

    na, dim eto

    ychydig o eiriau ac ymadroddion

    dilyn cwrs Cymraeg

    gallu ymuno mewn sgyrsiau syml

    siarad Cymraeg lleol gyda ffrindiau

    siarad Cymraeg yn rhugl

    Buasa'n well gen i fy nisgrifio
    fy hun fel   _____   _____

CWESTIWN 8

Ydach chi eisiau i'ch babi

    siarad Saesneg yn unig ?

    ddod i fedru rhywfaint o Gymraeg ?

    ddysgu Cymraeg yn yr ysgol ?

    siarad Cymraeg yn rhugl ?

    arall (nodwch)

    ddim yn gwybod ?

Rhowch y rhesymau dros eich ateb   _____   _____

                      _____   _____

CWESTIWN 9

Yn eich barn chi pa mor bwysig neu pa mor ddibwys ydi hi i'ch plant ddysgu
Cymraeg ?

EICH HUN

DIBWYS	DDIM YN BWYSIG IAWN	GWEDDOL BWYSIG	PWYSIG IAWN

PARTNER

DIBWYS	DDIM YN BWYSIG IAWN	GWEDDOL BWYSIG	PWYSIG IAWN

Ddim yn gwybod

Holiadur Cefndir Iaith

Os oes gennych bartner yn byw gyda chi, ticiwch yr atebion sy'n berthnasol iddo ef, yn ogystal a'r atebion sy'n berthnasol i chi.

CWESTIWN 10

P'run ydi'r agosaf at eich barn chi ?
Yn oes eich plant eich hun, ydych chi'n credu y bydd

	HUN	PARTNER
Y Gymraeg yn dod yn lle'r Saesneg yn y rhan hon o Gymru ?		
Y Gymraeg yn cael ei defnyddio fwy nag y mae yn awr ?		
Y Gymraeg yn cael ei defnyddio tua'r un faint ag y mae yn awr ?		
Y Gymraeg yn cael ei defnyddio llai nag y mae yn awr ?		
Y Saesneg yn dod yn lle'r Gymraeg yn y rhan hon o Gymru ?		

CWESTIWN 11

Pan fydd eich babi wedy tyfu ydych chi'n gobeithio y bydd ef/hi

	HUN	PARTNER
yn byw ar Ynys Mon ?		
yn byw yng Ngogledd Cymru ?		
yn byw yng Nghymru ?		
yn byw yn Prydain ?		
yn byw dramor ?		

CWESTIWN 12

Pan fydd ef/hi wedi tyfu, ydych chi'n gobeithio y bydd ef/hi

yn priodi person sy'n siarad Cymraeg ?		
yn priodi person sydd ddim yn siarad Cymraeg ? 'does dim gwahaniaeth y naill ffordd neu'r llall		

TUDALEN 5   J LYON

Holiadur Cefndir Iaith

Er mwyn helpu i ddosbarthu eich atebion, hoffwn ofyn ychydig o gwestiynau amdanoch chi a'ch teulu.

CWESTIWN 13

Beth yw eich henw yn llawn: _____

Eich cyfeiriad   :   _____

                              _____

                              _____

Enw eich babi   :   _____

Dyddiad geni eich babi :   _____

Faint ydi eich oed ?

                20 neu iau

                21 i 39

                40 neu hyn

Sut y byddech yn eich disgrifio eich hun ?

DOSBARTH GWEITHIOL	DOSBARTH CANOL IS	DOSBARTH CANOL UWCH	DOSBARTH UWCH		DDIM YN SIWR

CWESTIWN 14

Oes gennych chi wr/cariad ?   OES   NAGOES

os OES, tua faint ydi ei oed ?

                20 neu iau

                21 i 39

                40 neu hyn

Oes ganddo waith sy'n mynd ag ef oddi   OES   NAGOES
cartref yn aml ?

Sud ydach chi yn meddwl byddai ef yn ei ddisgrifio ei hun ?

DOSBARTH GWEITHIOL	DOSBARTH CANOL IS	DOSBARTH CANOL UWCH	DOSBARTH UWCH		DDIM YN SIWR

<u>TUDALEN 6</u>   <u>J LYON</u>

Holiadur Cefndir Iaith

Os oes partner yn byw gyda chi, ticiwch yr atebion sy'n berthnasol iddo ef yn ogystal a'r atebion sy'n berthnasol i chi.

CWESTIWN 15

Oes unrhyw blant eraill gartref heblaw'r babi ? | OES | | NAGOES |

Os NAGOES, ewch ymlaen i Cwestiwn 16

os OES, rhowch eu henwau a'u hoed

_____   _____

_____   _____

_____   _____

_____   _____

_____   _____

CWESTIWN 16

	EICH HYN		PARTNER	
Ydych chi wedi byw yn yr ardal hon erioed ?	DO	NADDO	DO	NADDO

os NADDO, pryd wnaethoch chi symud i Ynys Mon gyntaf ?

_____   _____

CWESTIWN 17

	YDI	NACYDI	YDI	NACYDI
Ydi eich Mam neu Tad yn dal yn fyw ?	YDI	NACYDI	YDI	NACYDI

os YDI/YDYNT ble mae'n nhw'n byw?

gyda chi ?

yn ymyl (gwaith ychydyg o funudau o gerdded) ?
taith fer i ffwrdd ?

tipyn o ffordd, ond nid yn rhy bell i ffwrdd ?
ymhell i ffwrdd ?

CWESTIWN 18

Ychwanegwch unrhyw sylwadau am eich cefndir iaith, neu am yr holiadur hwn, a allai fod yn bwysig yn eich barn chi.

_____

_____

_____

Diolch yn fawr i chi am eich help.

Gwnewch yn siwr, os gwelwch yn dda, eich bod wedi ateb popeth ac yn anfonwch ef yn ol yn yr amlen a ddaeth gyda ef.

Appendix II: Language Development Questionnaire (QII)

(a) Welsh Version

(b) English Version

HOLIADUR DATBLYGIAD IAITH (Q.II)

MAE'R HOLIADUR HWN AM EICH PLENTYN SYDD BRON YN DAIR OED

Ysgrifennwch M os mai chi yw ei fam/mam

neu T os mai chi yw ei dad/thad

CWESTIWN 1

Ar hyn o bryd pa iaith a ddefnyddiwch:	CYMRAEG BRON O HYD	CYMRAEG GAN AMLAF	TUA HANNER/ HANNER	SAESNEG GAN AMLAF	SAESNEG BRON O HYD
gyda'ch plentyn tair oed					
gyda phlant hyn					
gyda phlant iau					
gyda ffrindiau agos					
gyda'ch cymdogion					
gyda'ch rhieni					
gyda siopwyr					
gyda phobl yn y gwaith					
gyda phobl yn yr Eglwys neu'r Capel					
gyda'ch cymar					

QUESTION 2

Pa iaith sydd well gennych:					
ar gyfer darllen					
ar gyfer meddwl					
ar gyfer gwylio'r teledu					
ar gyfer darllen i'ch plentyn					
ar gyfer siarad gyda'ch plentyn					
ar gyfer gwylio'r teledu gyda'ch plentyn					

HOLIADUR DATBLYGIAD IAITH (Q.II)

CWESTIWN 3

Pa iaith mae eich plentyn
yn ei chlywed ?

	CYMRAEG BRON O HYD	CYMRAEG GAN AMLAF	TUA HANNER HANNER	SAESNEG GAN AMLAF	SAESNEG BRON O HYD
gennych chi					
gan ei riant/rhiant arall					
gan ei ffrindiau					
gan eich rhieni CHI					
gan ei daid/thaid a nain arall					
gan frodyr a chwiorydd					

CWESTIWN 4

Pa iaith (ieithoedd)
mae eich plentyn yn ei :

	CYMRAEG YN UNIG	CYMRAEG A RHAI GEIRIAU SAESNEG	HANNER CYMRAEG HANNER SAESNEG	SAESNEG A RHAI GEIRIAU CYMRAEG	SAESNEG YN UNIG
defnyddio					
deall					

CWESTIWN 5

A ydych yn hapus gyda'r modd y mae iaith eich plentyn   YDWYF___ NAC YDWYF___
                      yn datblygu?

Os YDYCH, beth yn eich tyb chi sydd wedi ei helpu hi neu o ?_____

_____

_____

_____

Os NAD YDYCH beth yn eich tyb chi sydd wedi ei rhwystro hi/rwystro o ?

_____

_____

_____

HOLIADUR DATBLYGIAD IAITH

CWESTIWN 6

A yw eich plentyn yn :

A yw eich plentyn yn :	DIM ETO	WEITHIAU	YN AML
defnyddio ychydig o eiriau unigol yn Saesneg			
defnyddio ychydig o eiriau unigol yn Gymraeg			
defnyddio llawer o eiriau unigol yn Saesneg			
defnyddio llawer o eiriau unigol yn Gymraeg			
rhoi dau air gyda'i gilydd yn Saesneg			
rhoi dau air gyda'i gilydd yn Gymraeg			
defnyddio 'all gone'			
defnyddio 'wedi mynd'			
dweud bod pethau yn 'big' or 'little'			
dweud bod pethau yn 'mawr' neu 'bach'			
gwybod lliwiau yn Saesneg			
gwybod lliwiau yn Gymraeg			
ffurfio brawddegau syml yn Saesneg			
ffurfio brawddegau syml yn Gymraeg			
siarad am ddoe yn Saesneg			
siarad am ddoe yn Gymraeg			
ceisio dweud storiau wrthych yn Saesneg			
ceisio dweud storiau wrthych yn Gymraeg			

CWESTIWN 7

A ydych chi eisiau i'ch plentyn :

siarad Cymraeg yn rhugl	
ddysgu Cymraeg yn yr Ysgol	
godi rhywfaint o Gymraeg	
siarad Saesneg yn unig	
arall (dynoder os gwelwch yn dda)	

RHODDWCH RESYMAU DROS EICH ATEB OS GWELWCH YN DDA :

_____

_____

HOLIADUR DATBLYGIAD IAITH

ER MWYN FY HELPU I DDOSBARTHU EICH ATEBION, CEIR YCHYDIG GWESTIYNAU AM EICH TEULU A'CH PLENTYN TAIR OED.

Beth yw ei enw/henw ?   _____

Beth yw ei ddyddiad/dyddiad geni ?   _____

Ai chi yw ei fam/mam ?   _____

    neu ei dad/thad ?   _____

A yw eich plentyn yn byw gyda chi ?   YDYW _____   NAC YDYW _____

A yw ei riant/rhiant arall yn byw gyda chi?   YDYW _____   NAC YDYW _____

A oes yna blant iau yn awr yn eich ty ?   YDYW _____   NAC YDYW _____

A yw eich plentyn yn mynd i :

Grwp Mam a Phlentyn   YDYW _____   NAC YDYW _____   PA MOR AML _____

Ysgol Feithrin neu   YDYW _____   NAC YDYW _____   PA MOR AML _____
    Feithrinfa
Gwarchodwr Plant   YDYW _____   NAC YDYW _____   PA MOR AML _____

Unrhyw un arall sy'n   YDYW _____   NAC YDYW _____   PA MOR AML _____
    gofalu amdano/amdani

Pa iaith a ddefnyddir ganddynt ?

	CYMRAEG GAN AMLAF	HANNER CYMRAEG HANNER SAESNEG	SAESNEG GAN FWYAF
Grwp Mam a Phlentyn ?			
Ysgol Feithrin neu Feithrinfa ?			
Gwarchodwr Plant ?			
Unrhyw un arall sy'n gofalu amdano/amdani			

A ydych chi'n gweithio amser llawn?   YDWYF _____   NAC YDWYF _____

           rhan amser ?   YDWYF _____   NAC YDWYF _____

YCHWANEGWCH UNRHYW SYLWADAU A ALLAI FOD O DDIDDORDEB YN EICH TYB CHI. DIOLCH YN FAWR IAWN AM EICH CYMORTH.

_____

_____

_____

LANGUAGE DEVELOPMENT QUESTIONNAIRE (Q.II)

THIS QUESTIONNAIRE IS ABOUT YOUR CHILD WHO IS NEARLY THREE

Please write M if you are his/her Mother

or F if you are his/her Father

QUESTION 1

At present which language do you use :	ALMOST ALWAYS WELSH	MOSTLY WELSH	ABOUT HALF & HALF	MOSTLY ENGLISH	ALWAYS ENGLISH
with your three year old					
with older children					
with younger children					
with close friends					
with neighbours					
with your parents					
with shopkeepers					
with people at work					
with people in church or chapel					
with your partner					

QUESTION 2

Which language do you prefer:

for reading					
for thinking					
for watching television					
for reading to your child					
for talking to your child					
for watching TV with your child					

LANGUAGE DEVELOPMENT QUESTIONNAIRE

QUESTION 3

Which language does your child hear :	ALMOST ALWAYS WELSH	MOSTLY WELSH	ABOUT HALF & HALF	MOSTLY ENGLISH	ALMOST ALWAYS ENGLISH
from you					
from his/her other Parent					
from his/her playmates					
from YOUR Parents					
from his/her other Grandparents					
from Brothers and Sisters					

QUESTION 4

What language(s) does your child :	ONLY ENGLISH	WELSH & SOME ENGLISH WORDS	HALF WELSH & HALF ENGLISH	ENGLISH & SOME WELSH WORDS	ONLY ENGLISH
use					
understand					

QUESTION 5

Are you happy with the way your child's language is developing? YES___ NO__

If YES, what do you think has helped him or her? _____

_____

_____

If NO, what do you think has hindered him or her? _____

_____

_____

LANGUAGE DEVELOPMENT QUESTIONNAIRE

QUESTION 6

Does your child :	NOT YET	SOMETIMES	OFTEN
use a few single words in English			
use a few single words in Welsh			
use many single words in English			
use many single words in Welsh			
put two words together in English			
put two words together in Welsh			
use 'all gone'			
use 'wedi mynd'			
say things are 'big' or 'little'			
say things are 'mawr' or 'bach'			
know colours in English			
know colours in Welsh			
make simple sentences in English			
make simple sentences in Welsh			
talk about yesterday in English			
talk about yesterday in Welsh			
try to tell you stories in English			
try to tell you stories in Welsh			

QUESTION 7

Do you want your child : to speak Welsh fluently

to learn Welsh at School

to pick up some Welsh

to speak only English

other (please specify)

PLEASE GIVE REASONS FOR YOUR ANSWER:

<u>LANGUAGE DEVELOPMENT QUESTIONNAIRE</u>

TO HELP ME CLASSIFY YOUR ANSWERS, THERE ARE A FEW QUESTIONS ABOUT YOUR FAMILY
AND YOUR THREE YEAR OLD.

What is his/her name?   _____

What is his/her date of birth?   _____

Are you his/her Mother?   _____

    or his/her Father?   _____

Does your child live with you?   YES _____   NO _____

Does his/her other parent live with you?   YES _____   NO _____

Are there now younger children in your house?   YES _____   NO _____

Does your child go to :

a Mother and Toddler Group?   YES _____   NO _____   HOW OFTEN _____

a Playgroup or a Nursery ?   YES _____   NO _____   HOW OFTEN _____

a Childminder?   YES _____   NO _____   HOW OFTEN _____

anyone else who looks after   YES _____   NO _____   HOW OFTEN _____
               him/her?

What language do they use?

	MOSTLY WELSH	HALF WELSH & HALF ENGLISH	MOSTLY ENGLISH
Mother & Toddler Group?			
Playgroup or Nursery?			
Childminder?			
Anyone else who looks after him/her?			

Do you work full time?   YES _____   NO _____

           part time?   YES _____   NO _____

PLEASE ADD ANY COMMENTS YOU THINK MIGHT BE INTERESTING.
THANK YOU VERY MUCH FOR YOUR HELP.

_____

_____

_____

Appendix III: Dictionary of Common Words

(as identified in corpus research from ten children)

English	*Welsh*
AUNTIE	ANTI
BAG	BAG
BALLOON	BALWN
BANANA	BANANA
BANK	BANC
BAR	BAR
BAT	BAT
BATH	BATH
BIKE	BEIC
BISCUIT	BISGET
BLOCK	BLOC
BOTTLE	BOTEL
BLOUSE	BLOWS
BOX	BOCS
BROWN	BROWN
BUCKET	BWCED
BUNNY	BWNI
BUGGY	BUGGY
BUS	BWS
BYE	BEI
CAP	CAP
CAR	CAR
CARAVAN	CARAFAN
CARPET	CARPED
CHOCOLATE	SIOCLED
CLAY	CLAI
CLEAR	CLIR

CLIP	CLIP
CLOCK	CLOC
CLOWN	CLOWN
CLUB	CLWB
COFFEE	COFFI
COMIC	COMIC
COT	COT
COVER	CYFER
CRAYON	CRAEON
CUSTARD	CWSTARD
DAD	DAD
DADDY	DADI
DANCE	DAWNS
DESK	DESG
DOLL	DOL
DOLLY	DOLI
DRILL	DRIL
DRAWER	DROR
ELEPHANT	ELIFFANT
ENGINE	INJAN
FARMER	FFARMWR
FENCE	FFENS
FLASK	FFLASG
FLAT	FFLAT
FORK	FFORC
FROCK	FFROG
GARAGE	GAREJ
GUITAR	GITAR
HAT	HET
HELLO	HELO
HURRAY	HWRE
JAM	JAM
JEANS	JINS
JELLY	JELI
JIG-SAW	JIG-SO
LABEL	LABEL
LAMP	LAMP
LIFT	LIFFT
LOT	LOT
LORRY	LORI
MAM	MAM
MAP	MAP
MARMALADE	MARMALED

MAT	MAT
MATTER	MATAR
MINUTE	MUNUD
MONKEY	MWNCI
MOO	MW
MOTOR	MODUR
NECKLACE	NECLIS
NICE	NEIS
OKAY	OKAY
OOPS	OOPS
PAINT	PAENT
PARCEL	PARSIL
PARK	PARC
PARTY	PARTI
PEAS	PYS
PEDAL	PEDAL
PEE	PI
PEEP	PIP
PENCIL	PENCIL
PETROL	PETROL
PHONE	FFON
PIANO	PIANO
PICNIC	PICNIC
PILLS	PILS
PINK	PINC
PLATFORM	PLATFFORM
POCKET	POCED
POO	PW
POSTMAN PAT	POSTMAN PAT
POT	POT
POWDER	POWDR
PRAM	PRAM
PUDDING	PWDIN
PUSS	PWS
PYJAMAS	PYJAMAS
QUACK	CWAC
QUARTER	CHWARTER
QUESTION	CWESTIWN
RECORD	RECORD
RIGHT	REIT
ROCKET	ROCED
ROUND	ROWND
SAM TAN	SAM TAN

SANDAL	SANDAL
SAUCER	SOSER
SCARF	SGARFF
SCREW	SCRIW
SHED	SIED
SHOP	SIOP
SKIRT	SGERT
SIGNAL	SIGNAL
SINK	SINC
SLIPPERS	SLIPERS
SPAGHETTI	SBAGETI
SPANNER	SBANER
SPLASH	SBLAS
SQUARE	SGWAR
STAND	STAND
STATION	STESION
STOP	STOP
STORY	STORI
SUGAR	SIWGR
SURE	SIWR
TA	TA
TANKER	TANCWR
TAP	TAP
TEDDY	TEDI
TELEPHONE	TELEFFON
THOMAS TANK	TOMAS TANC
TIP	TIP
TOAST	TOST
TOILET	TOILED
TOMATO	TOMATO
TOP	TOP
TOWEL	TYWEL
TRACK	TRAC
TRACTOR	TRACTOR
TRAIN	TREN
TRAY	TREI
TROUSERS	TROWSUS
TRUCK	TRYC
TUNNEL	TWNEL
TYRE	TEIAR
VAN	FAN
VEST	FEST
VIDEO	FIDEO

WELL	WEL
YARD	IARD
YEA	IA
ZIP	SIP
ZOO	SW

Additional (see text)

A	Y
IN	YN

References

Y Geiriadur Mawr: The Complete Welsh–English English–Welsh Dictionary. Llandysul: Swasg Gomer, 1986.

Y Geiriadur Lliwgar: Welsh Children's Picture Dictionary. Caerdydd: Usborne Publishing Ltd, 1979.

Index